PRAISE FOR WOMAN, CAPTAIN, REBEL

"Meticulously researched and evoc
Rebel provides not only a captivating
but also introduces readers to the in:
Thurídur, a tough and fiercely independent woman who deserves to
be a role model of determination and perseverance for us all."

—Eliza Reid, internationally bestselling
author of *Secrets of the Sprakkar*

"A crime has been committed in 19th century Iceland, and in steps
a mysterious seawoman moonlighting as a detective, dressed in
male clothes. Margaret Willson unravels this legendary casework of
Captain Thurídur, down to the finest detail, with a brilliant portrait
of old Iceland by the sea."

—Egill Bjarnason, author of *How Iceland Changed the World*

"In *Woman, Captain, Rebel*, Margaret Willson delivers the moving
biography of Thurídur Einarsdóttir, an Icelandic sea captain born
more than two hundred years ago into a life so constricted and yet
so vast. Gender nonconforming, a legal gadfly on behalf of the vul-
nerable, an amateur sleuth, a skilled navigator, and a leader of men,
Thurídur was a person of extraordinary accomplishments. How
many such stories have been lost? What a gift that Willson has written this one for us."

—Andrea Pitzer, author of *Icebound*

"A chance encounter on a windswept isle. A weathered plaque in an
ancient community that revealed a secret. Then the door opened up

to the past and the story came tumbling out, saved by the Icelandic storytelling tradition. As the author says, learning about Thurídur, a 19th century fishing captain changed her life. Reading about this remarkable woman's journey will challenge your ideas about history and change yours too."

—Major General Mari K. Eder, author of
The Girls Who Stepped Out of Line

"All credit to Margaret Willson for excavating the story of Thurídur Einarsdóttir in a century which can at long last appreciate this feisty and resilient Icelandic seafarer. The meticulous research is worn so lightly that it reads like a saga."

—Sally Magnusson, broadcaster and author of *The Sealwoman's Gift*

"A remarkable tale of a woman unafraid of taking risks, and an urgent reminder of the generous capacity of the human spirit. By exploring the complexities of community—and its power to both scaffold and destroy—the tragedies of a 19th century Icelandic fishing village land startlingly close to home. A compelling read and a parable of a life well lived despite overwhelming odds, *Woman, Captain, Rebel* is a book we all need now."

—Caroline Van Hemert, Ph.D., award-winning
author of *The Sun is a Compass*

"A beautiful story of one woman's perseverance against tragedy, hardship, and the open seas."

—Katharine Gregorio, author of *The Double Life of Katharine Clark*

"With her deft use of detail, Margaret Willson transports us to Iceland in the early 1800s, a harsh land of flood and famine, of boats crushed against rock by the sea. Here, Thurídur Einarsdóttir, a woman, shrugged off convention and became a fishing captain. *Woman, Captain, Rebel* is an adventure story with a woman at the center of it, a compelling portrait of a life marked by compassion, resourcefulness, and resilience."

—Anne Gardiner Perkins, Ph.D., award-winning author of *Yale Needs Women*

"Willson skillfully tracks and dramatizes the astonishing saga of fishing captain Thurídur Einarsdóttir, a nineteenth-century Icelandic hero. *Woman, Captain, Rebel* draws upon both the author's rich imagination and available historical evidence on Thurídur's life, crafting a remarkable and moving story of a woman of integrity who fought against all odds, rough seas, and a hostile society. Thurídur finally receives the recognition she deserves, and fishing no longer admits the North Atlantic cliché about the absence of women at sea."

—Gísli Pálsson, Professor Emeritus of Anthropology, University of Iceland

"*Woman, Captain, Rebel* is a captivating read! Drawing upon decades of inspiration and years of meticulous research, it will appeal to scholars of Icelandic history, gender, fisheries, and coastal communities. As it's so beautifully written, it will just as easily appeal to a casual reader hoping for a good tale of adventure and an unconventional life lived two centuries ago in rural Iceland."

—Courtney Carothers, Ph.D., professor, College of Fisheries & Ocean Sciences, University of Alaska Fairbanks

"Margaret Willson has produced a superb narrative concerning an extraordinary woman who made her mark on Icelandic history. The book speaks to wider issues of gender and equity through the empowering actions of Captain Thurídur and is a joy to read, leaving one inspired and enlightened."

—Níels Einarsson, Ph.D., Director,
Stefánsson Arctic Institute, Iceland

"Margaret Willson is a master at weaving accounts of Thurídur Einarsdóttir's remarkable life with ethnographic descriptions and keen anthropological insights. This is an extraordinarily rich account of community life and culture, set in the vivid context of Icelandic land and seascape where lives may change at any second."

—Fiona McCormack, Ph.D., fisheries anthropologist,
University of Waikato, Aotearoa/New Zealand

"Only recently have women in authority at sea been treated with respect. That's why Willson's knowledgeable reconstruction of Captain Thurídur Einarsdóttir life is so valuable. You'll be amazed at all the vicissitudes faced by a principled, kindly and anomalous pioneer on the fishing industry's margins. This well-researched book gives a new meaning to the term Icelandic sagas and a deeply unexpected angle to our understanding of women's early maritime past."

—Jo Stanley, Ph.D., maritime historian and author

WOMAN, CAPTAIN, REBEL

The Extraordinary True Story
of a Daring Icelandic
Sea Captain

MARGARET WILLSON

 sourcebooks

Copyright © 2023 by Margaret Willson
Cover and internal design © 2023 by Sourcebooks
Cover design by Ploy Siripant
Cover images © borchee/Getty Images, RedKoala/Shutterstock, Lukasz Szwaj/Shutterstock
Internal images © lublubachka/Getty Images

This publication is designed to provide accurate and authoritative information in regard
to the subject matter covered. It is sold with the understanding that the publisher is not
engaged in rendering legal, accounting, or other professional service. If legal advice
or other expert assistance is required, the services of a competent professional person
should be sought.— *From a Declaration of Principles Jointly Adopted by a Committee
of the American Bar Association and a Committee of Publishers and Associations*

Published by Sourcebooks
P.O. Box 4410, Naperville, Illinois 60567-4410
(630) 961-3900
sourcebooks.com
Library of Congress Cataloging-in-Publication Data

Names: Willson, Margaret, author.
Title: Woman, captain, rebel : the extraordinary true story of a daring
   Icelandic sea captain / Margaret Willson.
Description: Naperville : Sourcebooks, [2023] | Includes bibliographical
   references and index. | Summary: "A daring and magnificent account of
   Iceland's most famous female sea captain who constantly fought for
   women's rights and equality-and who also solved one of the country's
   most notorious robberies. Many people may have heard the old sailing
   superstition that having women onboard a ship was bad luck. Thus, the
   sea remains in popular knowledge a male realm. When we think of examples
   of daring sea captains, swashbuckling pirates, or wise fishermen, many
   men come to mind. Cultural anthropologist Margaret Willson would like to
   introduce a fearless woman into our imagination of the sea: Thurídur
   Einarsdóttir. Captain Thurídur was a controversial woman constantly
   contesting social norms while simultaneously becoming a respected
   captain fighting for dignity and equality for underrepresented
   Icelanders. Both horrifying and magnificent, this story will captivate
   readers from the first page and keep them thinking long after they turn
   the last page"-- Provided by publisher.
Identifiers: LCCN 2022026564 (print) | LCCN 2022026565
   (ebook) | (trade paperback) | (epub) | (adobe pdf)
Subjects: LCSH: Þuríður Einarsdóttir, 1777-1863. | Women--Iceland--Social
   conditions. | Women--Iceland--Biography. | Ship
   captains--Iceland--Biography. | Iceland--History.
Classification: LCC DL373.T49 W57 2023 (print) | LCC DL373.T49 (ebook) |
   DDC 949.12/03092 [B]--dc23/eng/20220622
LC record available at https://lccn.loc.gov/2022026564

LC ebook record available at https://lccn.loc.gov/2022026565

Printed and bound in Canada.
MBP 10 9 8 7 6 5 4 3 2 1

*This book is dedicated to Brynjúlfur Jónsson and
the people of Stokkseyri and Eyrarbakki who have
kept knowledge of Captain Thurídur alive.
In Memory of Siggeir "Geiri" Ingólfsson.*

SOUTHWEST ICELAND
AREAS VISITED BY CAPTAIN THURIDUR

Reykjavik

Álftanes
Hafnarfjördur

Ölfusá River

Grindavík

Thorlákshöfn

EYRARBAKKI
STOKKSEYRI

N
W E
S

Kambur

EYRARBAKKI

Gardaer
Stéttir
Big Lava
Efra-Sel
West Peathouse
East Peathouse
Brattsholt
Tradarholt
Kalastadir
Grimsflös
Gata
STOKKSEYRI
Rocky Brook
Gaulverjabaer
Baugstadir
Loftstadir

NORTH ATLANTIC OCEAN

Tears are shaped like rowing boats, pain and heartache pull the oars.

Jón Kalman Stefánsson, *Summer Light,*
and Then Comes the Night

CONTENTS

✳·»✳«·✳

LIST OF KEY
CHARACTERS

✳·≫✳≪·✳

Ari Jónsson	shopkeeper, son of Gamlason
Bjarni Einarsson	Thurídur's brother
Brynjúlfur Jónsson	son of Margrét Jónsdóttir, writer of the account of Thurídur
Einar Eríksson	Thurídur's father
Erlendur Thorvardarson	Thurídur's second "husband," Thórdís's father
Gísli Thorgilsson	husband of Sesselja Grímsdóttir, leaseholder of Kalastadir farm
Haflidi Kolbeinsson	one of Thurídur's deckhands, brother to "Poet" Jón
Helga Bjarnadóttir	Thurídur's mother
Hjörtur	a rich miser who lived at Kambur farm
Ingibjörg Jónsdóttir	Thurídur's long-time deckhand, friend, and farmhand
Jakob Árnasson	pastor, mediator, doctor, archdeacon, and friend of Thurídur

Johnsen (original name Jón Jónsson)	assistant to County Commissioner Thórdur Sveinbjarnarson
Jón Egilsson	deckhand and farmhand of Thurídur
Jón "Shank" Geirmundsson	farmer and friend of Thurídur, father of Sigga
Jón "Poet" Kolbeinsson	one of Thurídur's deckhands
Jón Ólafsson	Thurídur's first "husband"
Jón "Rich" Thórdarson	deputy for whom Thurídur worked as a deckhand for many years
Margrét Haagensdóttir	Bjarni's wife, Thurídur's sister-in-law
Móri	the ghost who haunts Thurídur's descendants for nine generations
Salgerdur Einarsdóttir	Thurídur's sister
Sesselja Grímsdóttir	deckhand, farmhand to Thurídur, and later wife of Gísli Thorgilsson
Sigurdur Gotsvinsson	deckhand to Jón Rich and Thurídur, son of "Gosi" Jónsson
Sigurdur "Student" Sívertsen	a clerk at the Eyrarbakki store
Thórdís Erlendsdóttir	Thurídur's biological daughter
Thórdur Árnason	pastor and doctor who ran a medical facility inland from Stokkseyri
Thórdur Sveinbjarnarson	Árnes county commissioner in the 1820s who tried the Kambur and other cases
Thorleifur Kolbeinsson	younger brother to Haflidi and "Poet" Jón Kolbeinsson
Thórunn Kristjánsdóttir	Salgerdur's biological daughter and adopted daughter of Thurídur
Thurídur Einarsdóttir	fishing captain and advocate

A NOTE ON ICELANDIC NAMES AND OTHER CONSIDERATIONS

Icelandic has a few letters that are different from those in English. Because these are confusing to non-Icelandic-speaking readers, I have retained Icelandic accent marks but used the Roman alphabet throughout the text. For the Endnotes and References Cited, since people consulting the Icelandic material will by definition be readers of Icelandic, I have retained the correct Icelandic letters.

Icelanders have a naming system that, instead of using a surname, uses a patronymic of the father's first name followed by "son" if a boy and "daughter" (*dóttir*) for a girl. So Jón's sons would be Jónsson and his daughters Jónsdóttir.

To minimize confusion between the many characters who have the same or similar names—half the Icelandic male population seems to have been called Jón—I have used nicknames whenever any source material gives one; when nicknames were not available, I have a few times created one based on aspects of that person, noting this liberty in an endnote. When no easy nickname was available, I have put in identifying phrases to jog the reader's memory.

For community place-names, I have retained the Icelandic name, also providing an English translation when possible. These place-names, as well as those of farms and landscape, are often wonderfully descriptive, so for farms, if it is a very clear descriptive meaning, such as Stóra-Hraun (clearly meaning Big Lava farm), I have used English but included the Icelandic word or phrase the first time it is used. For ones that are more complicated, I have given an English explanation when possible. Some names have obscure meanings, so in those cases I have just kept the original Icelandic.

This book is nonfiction. All of it, including quotes and weather conditions, is taken from accounts by people who were actually there or heard the account from someone else who was. When I have written conversations not in quotes, these are still taken directly, or closely paraphrased, from the original account. Where I have put in people's considerations or attitudes, these are either from what the people said they thought at the time or taken from an overall pattern of their actions. Statements such as "she smiled" and "he looked at her and then away" are narrative liberties taken from the context of the account.

A PREFACE OF DISCOVERY

From infancy I have been taught that throughout history women achieved less than men, contributed less, were less. In the United States, we have still not managed to pass an Equal Rights Amendment stating merely that women are equal to men before the law.

In our unequal world, any ability to have power or influence seems manipulated by the birth we are given. It takes more than strength to see otherwise, to step outside consensus to the role in which we are cast. As we realize this, and year upon year passes, bitterness too often replaces anger, insinuating itself into our deeper consciousness. It eventually eats the soul.

Where, I ask my friends, do we find models that show us different paths, different realities to help us shape who we are?

I worked as a deckhand on fishing boats when I was younger, the lone woman among men. It is an adage that the sea is a realm owned by men, its adventures, bravery and wealth. I was implicitly told that to work in this "male" occupation, I needed to mostly act as a man, submerge those female qualities deemed weak. Women were interlopers; very few worked as deckhands, and there were almost no captains. And these odds were, supposedly, better than in the past, bolstered by improved gender equality norms that, since about the 1970s, allowed more female incursion.

We are told that in previous centuries, except for the rare and early pirate chieftain, there were no female sea captains. None. Zero. Women almost never worked at sea at all, and those who did usually disguised themselves as men. A woman captain was unthinkable. Men ruled the waves.

The single exception, it seems, was the acclaimed Captain Thurídur of Iceland.[1]

I learned of Captain Thurídur through a "chance" trip to Iceland—for those who believe in chance. In the early 2000s, my Icelandic friend and Seattle housemate Dísa was planning a short trip to her native Iceland for an international project related to seabed research. When she invited me to visit her there, I jumped at the opportunity. After all, when else would I get a chance to see Iceland—then not the popular tourist destination it is today.

After I arrived, Dísa generously took me to see the sights of her homeland. About an hour's drive east of Reykjavík, on a coast of pale-yellow grasses that swept flat to a watercolor sky, we arrived at the rural oceanside community of Stokkseyri. I looked around at the scattered houses, the high stone wall between us and the sea.

"Stokkseyri is one of Iceland's oldest communities," Dísa told me. "Its first settler, Hásteinn Atlason, arrived in AD 900, a Norse chieftain like so many other early Icelanders, fleeing persecution in Norway. From his ship, he tossed a stake—a *stokk* in Icelandic—into the sea, deciding that where it came ashore he would stay and set up his farm. That makes the first part of the town's name, *Stokks*. The second half," she continued, "an *eyri*, is a flat piece of land by the water—good for just such a farm as he hoped to build. At what became Stokkseyri."

I looked around and adjusted my perspective. "Have people lived here continuously since that time?"

"Oh yes." Dísa laughed. "I am sure some of the people here are his direct descendants."

I wondered what that must feel like, to live in a place with so much inhabited history and memory imbued in the landscape. "How much has it changed?" I asked.

"Not that much," Dísa replied. "Not the land. Aside from the occasional volcanic ash fall, flood, and earthquake." She laughed again, looking toward the ocean. "They keep having to raise the height of the seawall." She shrugged expressively. "Floods have always been a problem here."

I gazed around the grassy meadows, now noticing how few feet they lay above sea level. The tide was out right now, revealing shoals and tumbled rock fields stretching out into the sea several hundred feet. Presumably they all got covered at high tide—and then the sea would be very close to the wall.

We wandered past a century-old wooden church encircled by a graveyard. Beyond it, as we walked along a street of homes, we stumbled across a rustic stone-and-sod hut surrounded by a low, turf-covered wall.

The hut appeared dilapidated. Memories once important,

now forgotten. A cold wind cut through bright sunlight, snaking between the buttons of our turned-up coat collars. Beside the hut, atop a weathered stone, lay a carved plaque dated 1949, only a few years after the end of World War II.

I opened the hut's unlocked wooden door, hanging loose on its hinges, and bent my head to enter beneath its low crossbeam. Dark, dank, the only light from one tiny hole of a window. It felt like a cave. As I crawled back out into the sunshine, Dísa was bending over the Icelandic inscription on the plaque.

"It's a reconstruction of the nineteenth-century fishing hut of a celebrated fishing captain," she explained.

I looked at the hovel. "People lived here?"

Dísa nodded. "Seasonally. During the fishing seasons. They fished all winter."

I imagined the mounded structure covered with snow, ice everywhere.

Dísa gave me a quiet smile. "Much of our history is not a gentle one," she said. "In the 900s, Iceland set up the earliest democracy in Europe, but during the six hundred years it was later under Danish rule, most of us lived in pretty dire poverty." She looked at the hut before us. "The homes weren't much better than this. For many, the bodies of livestock that shared people's cramped quarters provided the only heat they had."[2] Her gray-blue eyes took on a distant cast. These were her own ancestors she was talking about. "Every winter brought a time to be endured, many cold, snow-covered springs the threat of starvation." She looked away from me toward the distant mountains. "Iceland on the surface appears very similar to other Nordic countries. But it is not. Six hundred years of oppression and poverty do not heal in mere lifetimes. It bleeds through in our literature, music, poetry, our perspectives of life, our relationships to our land." Her gaze now followed an oystercatcher flying above the seawall. "We are survivors, Margaret, harboring all the acquired insight, strength, and scars that word implies."

I remained silent upon hearing this.

Dísa returned to reading the plaque: "Of Captain Thurídur, it says she lived from 1777 to 1863."

I stopped my contemplation of the landscape. "She? The fishing captain was a woman?"

"Yes." Dísa paused, scanning her childhood memory. "My grandmother used to tell me stories about her."

I had some trouble registering this. This female sea captain, about whom I had never heard a whisper, was celebrated enough that this community raised a historical commemoration in her honor almost a hundred years after her death?

That meant this community had let her become a captain—more than let; crews entrusted their lives to her, accepted her as their leader through these uncompromising Arctic waters.

How would a society, or intimate community, react to a woman in this kind of role? How did she even manage it? Generally speaking, societies did not react well to women speaking their minds, attempting leadership roles—to see this, we only have to consider the women accused of witchcraft or declared insane and committed to mental asylums for countering their husbands. Such rejection of female leadership held even more at sea. Physical bravery, daring, these were—are—traits accorded almost exclusively to men.

So how did this woman become a sea captain? How was this possible? Was it even true?

I looked over the pale blue Arctic sea before me that seemingly stretched to infinity. I felt cheated. Why had none of us ever heard of Captain Thurídur?

Hauntings come in various guises—trauma, lost love, remorse—they also come as troubling unanswered questions. When Dísa returned to Seattle after completing her research trip bearing a bound stack of sheets her mother—the first certified female librarian in Iceland— had given her, I knew such a haunting had just stepped over my threshold. The sheets turned out to be photocopied pages of a book from 1945, an edited compilation of a series of newspaper articles published in the Icelandic weekly periodical *Thjódólfur* between 1893 and 1897, written by Brynjúlfur Jónsson. Their subject was Captain Thurídur and an infamous robbery case she had apparently solved. It seems that in addition to being a renowned sea captain, she was also a sleuth.

Dísa and I became instantly captivated. Through long winter evenings, bilingual Dísa translated the pages while I typed the English into my laptop—making a complete hash of the Icelandic names. Pregnant with the child who is now my godson, Dísa's belly grew alongside our excitement. In Captain Thurídur, we had discovered a woman for the ages. Through tempests of oppression, adventure, joy, betrayals, and grief, Captain Thurídur spoke a universal voice, her clear-eyed perception reflecting a reality that women throughout the world have known for centuries, an inspiration to the power of compassion-imbued strength. This was more than a single life; it was a timeless parable within the intimacy of lived experience. Why, we asked, does the world not know of her? Why had movies not been made about her incredible life?

But then, she was a woman. How many remarkable historical women who were not queens do we ever get to know?

This started my quest to find the complete story of Captain Thurídur, this woman who seemed to contradict everything we've been told. What I found—her intelligence and courage, the sheer audacity of her defense of justice regardless of convention or hierarchy—was more remarkable than anything I could have imagined.

HELL RESURRECTED:
A PROLOGUE

1783–1784

The sun fades away, the land sinks into the sea,
the bright stars disappear from the sky
as smoke and fire destroy the world
and the flames reach the sky.[1]

The End of the World, *Völuspá*, from the Icelandic Poetic
Edda, compiled in the thirteenth century

We stand confident in isolated moments of our lives, imagining that
the land we think we know is stable, will stay the same forever—or at
least as far as our imagination runs. How naive we are!

In 1783 Hell came to Iceland. Escaping its underworld confines,
an inferno invaded the realm of the living, spewing its guts, dancing
to a rhythm of the damned.

Hell's arrival started with deceptive innocence. Along much of

Iceland's South Coast, grassy pastureland forms a strip several miles wide, its landward side abruptly giving way to sheer, glacier-encrusted mountainsides. On its shoreward side, a frigid, wild Atlantic Ocean stretches without obstacle to Antarctica.

In late May of that year, after a comparatively mild winter and spring, local residents noticed a strange blue haze creeping stealthily along icy hollows and narrow mountain valleys.[2]

In early June, a week or so after the appearance of the mysterious haze, a series of earthquakes rattled the land. These did not immediately alarm local inhabitants. On this primarily volcanic island, earthquakes were—and are—fairly routine. Strange was that these earthquakes didn't stop. Mountainsides began to slide.

Then things turned alarming.

A rolling "black haze of sand"[3] enveloped the sky. Sudden bursts of flame thousands of feet high erupted from behind the mountains. When local farmers, being curious and sturdy souls, clambered up the cliffs to take a look, they found fissures cracking open the sod where only months before their sheep had grazed.

The nearby Skaftá River, one of the largest in Iceland, was hundreds of feet deep and over four hundred feet wide in places, requiring a boat to cross.[4] First a vast volume of fetid waters mixed with sand rushed down its riverbed. Then the river disappeared. It dried up to nothing. This was seen as a very ominous sign.

The farmers were right. Two days later, molten, flaming lava replaced the water, a raging torrent that quickly filled the deep riverbed to its brim, then spread across the countryside. The flow split, charging down other suddenly dry riverbeds, an ash-dim landscape now punctuated by deadly ribbons of light. Daylight disappeared; ash fell thicker than rain.

In one parish, as lava flowed directly toward a church full of Sunday parishioners, their pastor preached to prepare them for imminent death. Through a seeming miracle still evident in the landscape today, the lava stopped just before it reached them.[5] But Iceland's God was stingy with his miracles; only devastation came in ready supply. The blue haze continued to cover the earth, the sun the red of fire, the moon of blood,[6] strangling all life beneath. People called it the "haze famine."

During the next year summer never came; ash fell from the sky in shiny, blue-black glassy threads like petrified seal's hair[7] that cut, choking people as they tried to breathe.

What winter hay farmers managed to collect was now mixed with sulfur, fluorine, and ash, killing the sheep and cattle that ate it. Sand and worms filled the innards of the sheep, swelling their softening bodies as flesh fell from their bones.[8] The water turned a tepid light blue. Plants burned, withered, and died. The snouts and hooves of animals turned bright yellow and raw.[9] People watched their live stock waste away and die, knowing that had they slaughtered them earlier, these animals might have saved their own lives. Fish perished in a poisoned sea.

No aid came to the Icelanders, not from the ruling Danish king, not from anyone. Refugees streamed west across southern Iceland, their homes destroyed, their loved ones dead, begging for shelter and any morsel of food. They came to households that were themselves desperate. More than ten thousand Icelanders died, 25 percent of their total population. Even by 1800, the already decimated population of Iceland stood at about thirty-six thousand, half of what was reported in the year 1100.[10]

After the eruption had subsided, in the winter of 1784, a teenage boy stumbled alone through Stokkseyri District, a refugee flee- ing the horrors he'd seen in the southeast, where volcanic fires still flamed. In these freezing temperatures, he wore a thin coat and tattered hat. His family dead, he could only walk west, hoping to find shelter, a morsel of food, anything to keep him alive one more day. He'd walked at least a hundred miles, somehow crossing rivers where a sluggish lava flow still advanced amid the dirty snow. Wind blew bitter across these flat, treeless reaches between the mountains and the sea. Through the swirling flurries, he could see perhaps fifty yards.

Then he saw a house. At least he thought it was. In winter, the low, rounded, turf-roofed buildings merged into the surrounding landscape, appearing to an inattentive eye as mere mounds of snow. A rush of relief came over him because he knew, at least for tonight, he was saved. No one would turn away a wandering soul in this weather, especially in this year of death. Even today, it is considered unthinkable to turn anyone away, especially in winter. Indeed, it is illegal.[11]

The boy stumbled to the farmhouse and weakly beat upon the door. When it opened, he begged for shelter and food.

The farm's tenant was seven-year-old Thurídur's father, Einar. He told the boy they had no food. Like everyone else, he and his wife, Helga, Thurídur, and her nine-year-old brother, Bjarni, were on the verge of starvation themselves. And refugees, just like this boy, kept coming without respite, without end, begging, begging.

The boy pleaded for shelter at least. Einar refused again. He knew his actions likely condemned this boy to death.

The boy stood in despairing shock. A curtain of falling snow engulfed him. How far to the next farm? And how would he even find it? He'd already walked so far. He didn't know this countryside. This had been his last chance.

In hopeless revenge, he cursed this family, their hearts as frozen as the land around him. Upon his death, he spat, he would rise as a specter and haunt them all. He wouldn't stop with the living but follow their descendants long past when Einar had rotted in his grave, for nine generations, to a future so distant it was unknown. He would make this family rue many times Einar's lack of human decency; he'd make sure others forever remembered his evil act.

With this, the boy turned away and wandered toward the sea, looking for another farm where he might find someone with a more human heart.

Other farmhouses huddled nearby, but he never saw them. Local people found his body frozen at Skerflód, in a ditch about a mile from Thurídur's father's farm. In a landscape laden with meaning and memories, that ditch still exists today.

Fearing that his specter would rise to unleash his curse upon them, they buried him as deeply as they could in the frozen earth, hoping the grave would keep him securely in the ground.

It did not. He rose as Skerflóds-Móri (*móri* meaning a specific kind of male ghost), one of Iceland's most enduring specters, seen by hundreds of people, the malignant reminder of Einar's heartless deed.

For young Thurídur, an innocent witness but a descendant none theless, Móri lurked, ever present, undead alive, watching for any opportunity to cast on her his destructive shade.[12]

1

DARING TO BE
DIFFERENT

1788–1791

A cold spring morning, bright sun, infinite sky—but most importantly a flat, windless sea.

Thurídur's father, Einar, noted this with satisfaction. A good day to give his eleven-year-old daughter her chance on the boat. With her red-gold hair and bright blue eyes, Thurídur was irrepressible, almost impossible to deny when she wanted something. And what she wanted was to go fishing.[1]

The family had all survived the 1783 eruption and ensuing famine, five years ago now, in part by eating seaweed and beach plants they'd dug from the shore before the sand froze.[2] But it was Einar's rowboat that mostly kept them and the two deckhands he hired alive. Their luck, he knew; those with boats mostly survived, while those without didn't.[3] Once ocean currents cleared the sea of poisoned ash and the fish stopped dying, Einar had immediately set out fishing with his then eleven-year-old son, Bjarni, and a few others. Bjarni had proven to be steady at sea, methodical, even "precocious."[4] He'd made a good deckhand. One day he'd inherit the rowboat, their single precious asset.

Einar turned from his musings and consideration of the weather to inform Thurídur this was her day to try her hand at fishing. She'd be on the boat for up to twelve hours, he sternly reminded her, without food and only sour whey to drink.[5]

Thurídur was so ecstatic that this warning flew past without seeming to make an impact. He'd expected that. She was a special one for sure, clever, already with a mind of her own. Whether that would serve her well or ill, he had no idea.

To go to sea, Thurídur would need some skin sea clothes. In the open wooden rowboats, this sea clothing, usually made from the skin of sheep,[6] was their only protection against icy snow, sleet, and bone-numbing wind. Everyone wore a skin anorak over thick sweaters, a skin sea hat, special skin shoes over thick knit socks, and thick, specially designed knit sea gloves.[7] Without sea clothes, hypothermia killed you in no time.[8] Einar spoke about the clothing with his forty-seven-year-old wife, Helga, ten years his senior.

Helga looked up from caring for their newest child, a two-year-old daughter they'd named Salgerdur.[9] Most babies seemed to die, not making it past their first few years,[10] but Salgerdur was doing all right so far. Thurídur can borrow Bjarni's extra set, Helga told Einrar. The one she usually dried and rubbed with fish oil while Bjarni wore the other set to sea.

Bjarni also had extra skin sea trousers, tied at the waist and ankles over knit underwear. But Thurídur didn't need those—they'd never fit her anyway. She could just wear her usual two black wool skirts like most women and girls.

Einar knew of only a few women who wore trousers at sea—although no one said much if they did.[11] Even he could see that the long wool skirts were miserably cumbersome on a boat. They got wet, very heavy, and never really dried since no one had much heat at home.[12] He and Helga burned dried sheep's dung and seaweed when they had it. The dung burned smoky and the seaweed fast—but at least it burned. Sometimes when they got lucky, they found driftwood along the shore. But none of this would dry a wool skirt.

The skirts were also lethal. It was a given that most people drowned in the freezing water if a boat flipped. But women in their heavy wool skirts didn't stand a chance.

No matter. Lots of women wore skirts to sea. So could Thurídur.

Bjarni's oversized sea anorak hung on Thurídur's petite frame flapping like a cape behind her; the mittens dwarfed her "delicate"[13] child's hands. She didn't care. She was going to sea! She bounded across the rocky, seaweed-covered shore past infant yellow grasses and lacey lichen newly emerged from snow.

Pulled up high on the bank and set in place with blocks, Einar's boat of timber imported from Denmark boasted a rounded bottom, no decking or sails, only simple sitting thwarts placed crossways to its beam.[14] Scattered along the shore lay about twenty similar boats, most in pretty bad shape, being constantly dragged over rocks and left outside with few materials for repairs.[15] Some were just like Einar's, several bigger, hosting six and even eight oars,[16] the bigger ones all belonging to the church or landowners, out of reach for a small tenant crofter like Einar. Still, he did have a boat. That was more than most people.

No one was surprised to see Einar with a child in tow; they expected teenagers, even children to work at sea—Bjarni had started at the same age as Thurídur and at fourteen was already an experienced deckhand. Einar's bringing his daughter was also fairly common; they all knew women and girls working at sea. They had too few people to choose from to be picky; anyone with decent strength was a good candidate.[17]

But even being accustomed to female deckhands, Einar's waiting crew of two or three men surely greeted with some skepticism the news that he was bringing this girl in her outsized clothes to fish with them; sitting down, Thurídur barely reached above the gunnels.

Oh well. He was their skipper, and it was his boat. If he wanted to bring this child with him, that was his choice.

After Einar and his crew dragged the boat to the water's edge, they stopped to recite the Seaman's Prayer: "Almighty merciful and gracious God...I ask you, my Lord, for protection and blessing on this dangerous voyage. Be close to us... Protect our lives and souls, boats, and catch from all dangers..."[18]

No one went to sea without the Seaman's Prayer—they needed all the protection they could get.[19]

Einar and his fellow skippers faced a particularly tricky shore in the Stokkseyri area.[20] Between the land and the fishing grounds lay a filigreed labyrinth of jumbled lava skerries framing narrow channels just big enough for small boats to navigate—a ten-oar was really too big. These skerries sit above sea level at low tide, but as the water rises, they submerge, lurking just beneath the surface of a deceptively tranquil sea. All the local skippers knew these channels, their currents, and tides like the backs of their hands. They had to—a mere bump against razor-sharp lava could shatter a boat in seconds. No matter how close to shore, that almost always meant death.

Beyond the reefs, the seabed drops rapidly to deep, gravel-bottomed pools populated by migrating deeper-water fish such as haddock, halibut, and cod, making for a very short row from shore to rich fishing grounds, perfect for these easily maneuvered rowboats. But where the rising seabed of the open ocean meets the already treacherous skerries, high surf can quickly build in even a fairly mild southwest wind, creating a terrifying gauntlet through which any returning boat must pass.

Einar and his crew—with Thurídur—rowed this skerried traverse until they reached a spot Einar considered had potential. He told them to stop, and letting the boat drift along the current, they put out their handheld, single-hook lines.[21] Thurídur eagerly followed suit, tying a rock weight and hook to the line her father gave her. She baited it with lugworm they'd dug up from the shore[22] and dropped it over the side.

As "soon as her line hit the bottom, a fish bit the hook."[23]

Cod and haddock each bite a hook differently, a cod taking it in a sharp jerk while a haddock tugs it in a series of subtle bumps best felt by holding a taut line between thumb and forefinger. Einar and his entire crew knew this, of course, so they immediately recognized the fish on Thurídur's line as a haddock. Haddocks, having soft mouths, are easily lost if not steadily brought in. They can also be quite large, a full forty-four inches and weighing as much as thirty-seven pounds.

Everyone on the boat paused to watch as, with "no little enthusiasm," Thurídur worked to pull in her first fish. In the contest between girl and fish, Thurídur at first appeared to be winning, then the haddock, clearly as strong as she was. Bjarni's huge gloves engulfed her small hands, making the line almost impossible to grasp.

Then one of Thurídur's gloves fell off. Seeing she could control the line better without the enormous flapping mitt, she shook off the other one and used her bare hands. The silvery, purple-gray haddock gradually grew short of breath as she brought it in. Proudly she tossed it to the bottom of the boat, where it flopped in airless despair.

Quickly she put out her line again, still using her bare hands. And immediately she got another bite. That one went the same way as the first. Repeatedly. Over the hours, Thurídur learned to leverage her frame against the boat's gunnels so she wouldn't exhaust herself bringing in one fish after another.

By the day's end, it had become clear Thurídur was "luckier with the fish than most." Being a skipper who recognized a good deckhand when he saw one, Einar quickly had properly sized sea clothes made for her and hired her for the spring season. As was normal for all young beginners, he paid her half of the share given to full deckhands when the fish catch was divided. But she couldn't work winter season, he told her firmly, until she'd passed her catechism at fourteen. When he was a child, his father had been fined for keeping Einar from his studies,[24] something he was determined wouldn't happen to him.

Einar's deckhands watched this interaction with interest. This girl seemed very lucky at sea. Fine with them if she joined the crew.

Lately, Einar had begun to notice the telltale discolored flat patches on his skin, the painless ulcers on the soles of his feet. Leprosy.[25] Bad on this coast and he'd seen it in others. But he was only thirty-nine.

How'd he get it? They said it ran in families—his parents? Nobody really seemed to know.

There was a hospital inland where lepers were supposed to stay, but what was the point? They couldn't do anything for him anyway. Once he went there, he wouldn't be able to leave. Who'd take care of the farm and fishing? No. Maybe it'd go away.

Leprosy does not usually go away. When Thurídur was four-teen,[26] it killed him.[27]

Beyond dealing with grief and loss, his death left his little family—wife, Helga, seventeen-year-old Bjarni, fourteen-year-old Thurídur, and five-year-old Salgerdur—in an even more precarious position than they'd been before.

Helga, Bjarni, and Thurídur all knew that county (*sýsla*) and district (*hreppur*) authorities would be watching them carefully. Single women were normally considered unable to sustain a family alone, so to avoid having to support them, the district generally separated such families, the mother becoming a contracted farmhand and, unless she could find foster parents for them, the children being auctioned off to the farmer who agreed to take them for the lowest district-provided stipend.

The contracted farmhand system was engineered to control the impoverished population and ensure ready cheap labor for farmers. In this system, almost anyone not a member of the tiny landowning elite[28] or who held a farm leasehold—which required the often-unattainable wealth of at least three cows[29]—had to work for a farmer in a contract they could negotiate only once a year during May Moving Days.

Auctioned-off children officially became paupers with no pro-tection or personal rights, the hosting farmers able to treat them as they saw fit, including feeding them scraps and making them sleep with the dogs. The stipend paid by the district to the hosting farmer became the pauper's debt, which they had to repay before they could marry or gain their rights as an equal citizen. These paupers too often lived humiliated, abused, and beaten, frequently never able to pay off their stipend-derived debts, existing in a miserable poverty that ended only when they died.[30]

With this knowledge, the teenage Thurídur and Bjarni considered their future. No one was going to sustain their family except them. And the only way they had to do this was fishing on the rowboat Bjarni inherited from their father.[31]

He hired a small crew of two or three others, and they set out on the dangerous seas themselves without their knowledgeable skipper father. Others looked at the teens doubtfully; this was unlikely to turn out well.

Much to everyone's surprise, not only was Bjarni reasonably competent, but Thurídur proved consistently a "luckier fisherman than anyone else";[32] it was obvious to boats nearby that she kept pulling in fish even when they caught next to nothing. Starting with just the shorter spring season, the siblings soon also pursued the longer—and harsher—winter. Bjarni quickly raised his sister's beginner's half share to full.[33]

This was only fair, his deckhands agreed; her large fish catches after all increased their own shares. Although Bjarni was their official skipper, Thurídur's presence gave them confidence. Beyond catching lots of fish, she was showing a startling observational ability, able to read weather with almost uncanny accuracy. As Bjarni grew accustomed to letting her direct when and where they should row, the crew agreed that he was lucky to have her—and so were they.

The rest of the community watched this and took note. Although fishing was one of the only areas where women and men legally received the same pay, "it was considered a new thing that a girl not yet twenty was made equal to the men when the catch was divided."[34] They'd made almost no comment at all when Einar had given Bjarni—his son—a full share when he was only fourteen.

The crew watched the brother and sister, so very different, work together in tight companionship. "Calm and reticent"[35] Bjarni was "gentle and methodical," while the gregarious, boisterous Thurídur already "wanted to do big things." They also watched as she grew from a child to a slender young woman, "somewhat thick across the shoulders, medium tall or a little more," her lively face with "character," her blue eyes "bright and quick," her voice "not soft, yet not unpleasant." In her speech and actions, they found her "confident and interested."

The community also found her "peculiar and different,"[36] but then, so were lots of people. Once Einar died, Thurídur had replaced her wool skirts at sea for the far more practical skin sea trousers. Soon after, she started wearing trousers for all outside farm work, donning a skirt only when she worked inside or went to social gatherings. No other women did this, but young Thurídur defiantly wore trousers regardless of what anyone else thought.

People noticed, of course, but no one said much—at least not overtly. Thurídur was taking her own path, but locals in general decided they liked this feisty woman with her "quick-witted" mind. For one so young, they found her already "good at finding solutions, careful and clear-sighted." Seamen began going to her for advice— because she always had a good answer.

One person noticing Thurídur as her sea reputation grew was Jón Thórdarson, a clever and complex man in his own right; by the time he was only twenty-three, he'd already earned the nickname Jón Rich.[37]

Jón Rich's birth in 1770 was not auspicious. He was Gudlaug Jónsdóttir's first child, and for a time it seemed neither mother nor child would survive the ordeal.[38]

Then someone remembered that Dr. Bjarni Pálsson happened to be in the area, the highly respected doctor and naturalist who had set up the leprosy hospital Einar had decided to avoid.[39] To his credit, Dr. Bjarni came when people ran to fetch him. He had also managed to save the lives of both Gudlaug and newborn Jón. But he warned Gudlaug that "if she became pregnant again it was not sure how that would go." Even more, "he was unlikely to be there even though he'd by chance been there now to help her."[40] She and her husband listened; Jón was their only child.

Even as a boy, Jón was unusual. In this subjugated Iceland, personal entrepreneurship was a path few considered—petty thievery from the merchant store seemed a much more accessible way to get extra food. Almost no one born poor—the vast majority—ever made it out of poverty. But Jón was different. At five, he began telling anyone who'd listen that he planned to be rich. He was "little pleased with his parents' poverty,"[41] positive that were he in their situation, he would easily leave it behind. But Jón did more than complain. While still a child he began on his single-minded aim toward wealth.

The Icelandic diet, consisting mostly of fish, mutton, and some cow's milk, had almost no fat. Butter—pure fat and requiring lots of cow's milk to make—was highly prized, and when they had enough milk, people on the farms allowed themselves a pat of it each day. Establishing his lifelong dedication to thrift, Jón decided he didn't need his ration of butter, especially since it had commercial value.

Instead he collected it in one-pound boxes. When a box was full, he went to the Danish-owned merchant house in the nearby community of Eyrarbakki and traded his butter for *brennivín*, a popular Danish imported schnapps that was about the only alcohol Icelanders had to drink. Life was harsh. Brennivín numbed all kinds of pain.

Jón sold his brennivín—at a profit, of course—to his neighbors in very small shots they could marginally afford. Soon he'd sold enough to buy an entire small barrel of brennivín. This he also sold, again in small shots. He also bought tobacco. The tobacco he kept until the merchant house ran out, and then during the fishing season when people had a bit more to trade for it, he sold it by the inch, again at a good profit. Soon he had "two pennies for every one."[42] Jón was now about seven.

In the late 1770s, about the same time Thurídur was born, a flood had destroyed Jón's parents' leased farmhold, and they had moved to another one near the sea. While Jón lived there, he found another money-making opportunity, one he related to others later when he had become a district deputy (*hreppstjóri*), so no one was likely to come after him for his youthful exploit of stealing. He told this story as a moral tale, saying that because of it, he had vowed never to steal again and to treat his own tenants—when he owned his own farm—well enough that they would never want to steal from him.

By Jón's account, he was walking along the beach one evening looking for driftwood. Tenants were allowed pieces of driftwood under two feet, but anything larger they had to hand over to the landowner. On this walk, Jón saw on the beach in front of him a huge "red wood log."[43] This, he decided, he was certainly not going to give to the landlord. But he had to figure out how to collect and then sell it without getting caught. He ran home to grab a shovel, dug a small trench in the sand next to the log, and as the tide rose, the log rolled into it. Then, with Jón's help, the rising tide covered the log in its trench with sand, making it invisible to everyone else.

After this, he went to the beach at various intervals when no one would see him and sawed off two-foot rounds, a size acceptable for him to own. These he carried up to the house and then split into staves, which he sold. By the time he'd sold the entire log, he'd made a decent addition to his butter, brennivín, and tobacco funds. All while he was barely a teen.

Jón and Thurídur. Two young, exceptional, and strong personalities in one small community, one a boy, the other a girl. It could turn out very well—or very badly.

2

WHAT PRICE SURVIVAL?

1797–1799

·»··«·*

Twenty-year-old Thurídur and her handsome fellow deckhand exchanged glances as they rowed on Bjarni's boat to the fishing grounds. Jón Ólafsson, a very different man from the ambitious Jón Rich of the same first name, had been working with Thurídur and Bjarni a few seasons. With well-to-do parents and generally well liked, Jón Ólafsson was considered a "promising" man and a good potential marriage prospect. His only noticeable fault was that he drank a bit too much—but then, so did a lot of men.

As Thurídur and Jón pulled in fish, laughing and teasing each other, it was clear to everyone that they "agreed with each other well."[1] So well that the next year, when Thurídur was twenty-one, Jón Ólafsson asked her to marry him.

Although Thurídur quite liked the idea, the prospect of marriage, particularly as a woman, was one she wanted to consider very carefully.

Marriage was not at all a given in Iceland. To curb the impoverished population while also ensuring a steady cheap labor supply for farmers,[2] the authorities had enacted policies to keep people single, allowing marriage only to landowners and farm-leaseholder heads of household. Since Iceland had many more women than men, this meant only a minority of women ever married.

Jón Ólafsson, with his prosperous parents, had an excellent chance of acquiring the required tenancy, even a good one. This meant that upon finding the oft-elusive leasehold, he could marry and provide his new bride a decent place to live.

Excellent for Jón Ólafsson, but what about Thurídur? As she looked practically at what this future would bring, she saw three possible scenarios.[3] She could refuse the proposal and remain with her brother, contentedly working as they were. The issue here was that when Bjarni eventually took over the leasehold management from their mother—which as the man of the household he would—Thurídur's status would drastically change to her becoming legally his farmhand. As leaseholder, he could also then marry, leaving Thurídur not only legally under her brother's control but his new wife's as well.

As a second possibility, Thurídur could still refuse Jón Ólafsson's proposal but move and become a contracted farmhand for someone else, able to change her locale only once a year during Moving Days. For these positions, farmers often paid just food, clothing, and shelter, where—not a huge shock—female farmhands received less of everything than men. Contracted farmhands had the same status as children, legally unable to leave the property of their "master" without his permission. If they ran away, he or his wife could have them fined, imprisoned, or beaten—as long as they didn't actually maim them.

As a third option, Thurídur could accept Jón Ólafsson's marriage proposal. Compared to the dismal prospects of her other choices, marriage brought her the opportunity to leave her family's tenant farm and start a new life in partnership with Jón Ólafsson on their own leasehold property.

But marriage, particularly for women, also had its downsides. Although free of a future farmer's dictate, it by law placed the woman under the legal control of her husband,[4] the status difference so defined that he was expected to sleep on the outside of the bed with his wife against the wall as a mark of his elevated position.[5]

Thurídur accepted Jón Ólafsson's proposal, but given these realities, she told him she wanted to go about this cautiously. Once he found a leasehold, she'd move in with him, but she didn't want to get officially married until they'd lived together long enough to make sure they got along. In this, she was defending her independence, wanting to be sure of the man she was with before she committed to the kind of power imbalance marriage entailed.

Her demand was considered very odd indeed but one their local society would tolerate—as long as they had a leasehold and could support themselves. Although Danish and Icelandic authorities frowned upon couples' having sex as well as living together outside wedlock, most Icelanders—unable to get the required leasehold for marriage—saw it as their only choice besides celibacy.[6] Europeans, placidly ignorant of these oppressive restrictions, denounced this as Icelandic "immorality," even more so when Icelanders had children in the same condition.[7]

Jón Ólafsson was fine with Thurídur's stipulation. He was just delighted she'd accepted at all. He immediately set about looking for an available leasehold farm, which, they both knew, might take months or even years. Until then they'd live apart as fiancés.

For Thurídur's brother Bjarni, the news of her engagement brought alarm. Although as a son he had the stability of the leasehold inheritance, Thurídur's moving out would leave him to work the farm completely alone, especially since their younger sister Salgerdur showed a distinct lack of interest in any outdoor work. Making matters worse, Thurídur's new fiancé left Bjarni's boat after the engagement, moving to fish out of Thorlákshöfn (Thorlák's Haven, after Iceland's patron saint, Thorlákur), a fishing area to the southwest.

At least, Bjarni could reassure himself, Thurídur still remained at his side fishing.

Unless the ambitious Jón Rich Thórdarson got his way. Which, it seemed, he usually did. At least eventually.

The early fortunes of the young Jón Rich had not ascended on a steady incline despite his best efforts. Any tenuous stability his family had collapsed when his father died, leaving Jón's mother, Gudlaug, in the now familiar gloomy scenario of a single mother whose young son the authorities would likely soon take. Luckily, her uncle Thorvaldur Bergsson, a single man in his early seventies, saved them this fate by accepting responsibility for the both of them. They moved in with him at his West Peathouse (*Móhús*) leasehold farm.

Then when Jón was thirteen came the eruption of 1783, when all hell broke loose.

Unlike Einar, Uncle Thorvaldur did not have a boat, making his livestock his only hope of survival. And at an age when he might wish to have others caring for him, he now had responsibility for his niece and her teenage son. Like everyone else, he fed his animals the hay he'd collected. And like everyone else, the poisoned hay killed them. Now he had nothing to feed himself, his niece, or her son. So, in about 1786, he killed himself.[8]

This left Gudlaug with no relatives and no farm. She managed to get herself a farmhand position where the farmer allowed her to bring Jón, likely because at sixteen he was considered an adult. At this time, Jón also began going to sea.

A mere four years later, in 1790, when Jón was only twenty, he somehow managed to buy himself a six-oared boat. No one understood how he did this, a person born to such poverty managing this kind of cash outlay at all, let alone in a person so young.[9] Regardless, Jón made himself skipper of his boat, at which he proved—as with most things he tried—to be very capable. He and his mother also soon acquired the leasehold of West Peathouse farm—the same one where they'd previously lived with Uncle Thorvaldur.

On December 3, 1793, when Jón was twenty three, he managed the almost unthinkable: he bought a farm—with his mother's help, since her name was on the contract. Not leased—but bought it for the impressive sum of seventy Danish state dollars (*ríkisdalar*). Such transformation just did not happen. Somehow Jón did it. He leased that farm out and collected the rent while he and his mother remained at West Peathouse.[10]

Lacking any credible explanation, a community rumor began circulating that Jón had got himself a pair of the fabled "demon pants" (*skollabrækur*), or "corpse pants."[11]

For these, you made an agreement with someone who was about to die. Once they did, you dug up their body, skinned it from the waist down while making sure not to cut any holes in the skin, and made a pair of pants. These you wore like tights until they grew onto your own skin. You also had to steal some money from the poorest of poor widows and put that money in the pants where a man's scrotum would be. This scrotum would always attract money and never be empty when the wearer looked into it. How else could Jón get so much when everyone else had nothing?

Regardless of mystified rumor, from here on, everyone called Jón Thórdarson Jón Rich. He had, against all odds except gender, already achieved his seemingly unattainable goal.

He'd grown into a broad man, a noticeable figure with a full beard and dark hair that he wore fashionably falling to his shoulders. His reputation as a skipper increased during the 1790s; that he also went to sea "daringly"[12] was not particularly surprising, since he'd been taking risks in his aim to get rich almost since he was born. He caught more fish than most, so prospective deckhands competed to work for him. Even if he was a risky bet, no one had been killed with him so far.

But, for all his excellent deckhands, Jón Rich did not yet have the best, the deckhand everyone wanted, who caught more fish than any other person and was brilliant at reading weather: Thurídur. And, even though Jón Rich was growing used to getting what he wanted through his cleverness, drive, and sheer force of will, he had not gotten Thurídur. Everyone knew she would never leave her brother's side at sea.

Then came the Great Flood of January 9, 1799.

While everyone slept, a southeast midnight wind flew across the vast emptiness of the Atlantic Ocean. By the time it reached Iceland's

South Coast, it carried a storm surge hundreds of feet deep. At the time, some people blamed an underwater volcanic eruption or sea earthquake. Today meteorologists speculate it was the perfect combination of a hurricane wind, strong coastal currents, and a high winter tide. It tore across the land like a tsunami.[13]

Thurídur and Bjarni awoke to the sea's thundering roar. Far too loud. They jumped out of their beds in the family common room and ran into the night. There they saw through the murky dark a frothing, ghostly sea right in front of them. The sea was supposed to be on the near horizon beyond quiet pastureland. Instead it clawed in churning chaos almost to their feet.

Their first concern was their beach horses. Many people let their horses graze on seaweed along the shore, even staying out overnight.[14] Bjarni and Thurídur had left six of theirs on the beach that night, along with some fifty horses of their neighbors. By the time they heard the surf, their six horses—and the other fifty—had been swept out to sea.

"Let's get our other horses up to the farmhouse courtyard!" Thurídur shouted. "There they'll be safe, but not in the stable."[15]

Their Stéttir farmhouse stood on slightly higher land, but they'd stabled their two other horses in a nearby, small turf-and-stone building almost imperceptibly lower than the house. Perhaps the difference wouldn't matter. But perhaps it would. Battling the storm, they immediately rushed to the stable and dragged the terrified horses up to the courtyard.

After securing the two animals, Thurídur and Bjarni watched the flood rise ever higher. Soon it demolished their stable. Had the horses still been inside, they would have drowned. The flood never reached the courtyard.

Around them waters rose, a torrential river born of the sea. It seeped under the doors of farmhouses, ripped through the small, membrane-covered windows, and filled houses with water. Violent surf smashed other farmhouses to pieces, carrying the timber frames far inland and scattering them across the marshes. Winds blasted apart the storage building of a wealthy man named Haagen.

Nearby Eyrarbakki had a levy, built specifically to protect its Danish-owned merchant house. It had worked during two previous floods, but against the Great Flood of 1799, it didn't stand a chance.[16] The raging sea flattened it, galloping greedily ten miles inland, its onslaught stopped only by the cliffs of sheer mountainsides. Winds decimated Eyrarbakki's recently built merchant storehouse. Then the flood swept away everything inside: the wares, beans, and rye.[17]

Several people found shelter at a higher farm, only to become threatened as water rose on all sides, encircling the farm. In a daring rescue, others managed to save everyone.

As surging seas inundated the buildings of Old Lava (*Gamla-Hraun*), the small farm next to Bjarni and Thurídur's Stéttir, its inhabitants prepared to evacuate. But one old invalid man confined to his bed high under the gable of one of the buildings refused to budge. Magnús Snorrason of the neighboring Big Lava (*Stóra-Hraun*) farm offered to take him, but the old man said he'd lived enough. He bade them all good night and "awaited his death."[18]

In the days that followed, the retreating Great Flood revealed miles of devastation, farms reduced to scattered rubble. Houses that did not collapse had their belongings washed out and strewn around the countryside. Most they never recovered, both because the belongings disappeared in the storm and also because people finding them rapidly carted them off.

Of Haagen's property, nothing was found except a shred of his money chest. The farm where Jón Rich had grown up was completely destroyed, with only a part of the home meadow left. Many stables washed away, leaving people with no fuel or winter hay for their animals—with summer still many cold months away. In Stokkseyri District, which included both the communities of Stokkseyri and Eyrarbakki, from its population of about four hundred, the storm destroyed more than forty-two farms and killed at least sixty-three horses and fifty-eight sheep. At least twenty-nine people fled the area, some deciding that settling elsewhere was a better idea.[19]

Yet, with all this devastation and the death of so many animals, not a single person died in Stokkseyri District, not even the old invalid man.[20] In the morning, people searching for him found the entire farm washed away. Except a single gable where the old man still lay in his bed very much alive.

But what people did lose were their boats, left on shore high above any reasonable tide line. In Stokkseyri, of the twenty-four boats on the shore, the Great Flood destroyed twenty.[21] The gentle and well-liked Deputy Jón Einarsson lost his eight-oared boat, others the same.

Of the four boats that somehow made it through, one belonged to...Jón Rich. The accounts do not say why these few boats survived the storm; perhaps these were richer owners who had boathouses few others could afford. Maybe they just got lucky.

Bjarni was not so lucky. His small boat was gone. Size matters little when the loss is your livelihood.

When Jón Rich heard about Bjarni's losing his boat,[22] he wasted little time. The Great Flood had served him well; now he'd get what he wanted.

Since the winter fishing season usually ran from February 2 to May 11,[23] he'd have to move fast to hire Thurídur as his deckhand for that current winter—before someone else snapped her up. He approached her as soon as possible with his proposal.

"I am not man enough to row with you," Thurídur replied to his inquiry.

Having watched Thurídur at sea for ten years now, and used to choosing his crews from eager applicants, Jón Rich did not take this as a serious claim. "Don't you dare to go with me?" he replied with a dig at her courage.

"I lack brawn, not bravery,"[24] Thurídur shot back.

"You have strength to take a fish for me like everyone else," Jón Rich rejoined, now getting frustrated and deciding to press his case. "The harder work others will do. They are willing for the sake of their share." This he knew to be true, since everyone in the area knew Thurídur caught more fish than anyone.

To this Thurídur replied that she had already committed herself for the season to fish for her brother, who would soon be building a new boat. Fishing contracts were taken very seriously, with heavy penalties levied against those who did not honor them,[25] although presumably if the skipper lost their boat, there was likely the option of wiggle room. But that was not Thurídur.

At this point Jón Rich realized he wouldn't get any further. Thurídur would not renege on her brother's contract, regardless of whether he had a boat or not. But Jón Rich hadn't got where he was by letting others best him. Instead, knowing he had the upper hand, he decided to bide his time. "Let's let it go this time around then," he said. "But don't hire yourself to Bjarni again. Row with me next winter."

"I'll let Bjarni decide that," Thurídur replied, still not giving an inch on her loyalty to her brother.[26]

But inside she knew she needed to make a decision. If she didn't leave Bjarni, she wasn't going to fish. If neither she nor her brother fished, how would they sustain their family—or themselves?

3

UNCERTAIN TERRITORY

1799–1802

When Thurídur returned to their Stéttir farm, she found Bjarni sharpening his beloved carpentry axe—over the years he'd become a good carpenter. A gentle man who seldom revealed his feelings, he was also prone to dark moods, withdrawing into depression. Their mother, now fifty-nine, had decided after the Great Flood to give up managing their farm, making Bjarni official leaseholder and head of household, adding to his considerable responsibilities.

Thurídur watched her brother. She had to confront the dilemma Jón Rich's offer had just presented to her. As everyone knew, Thurídur was the kingpin of her brother's small fishing crew. But until her brother succeeded in replacing his boat, the difference between fishing with Jón Rich and not fishing at all was stark. She told Bjarni about Jón Rich's proposal and their conversation.

"I would prefer you stay with me," Bjarni replied quietly. "At least as long as you can." He knew he had nothing to offer.

"Our mother will get a greater catch from my work with Jón than with you," Thurídur said. This was hard. But they both knew it was true.

It defeated Bjarni. "I can hear that you want to go to Jón," he said. "And it is your decision."[1] He turned away and stared at his carpenter's axe.

After this decade of working together so closely, not only would Thurídur soon leave the farm to live with her fiancé, Jón Ólafsson, but between the Great Flood and Jón Rich's unrefusable offer, she wouldn't be on any boat Bjarni might get built. They both knew it was the best for their mother. But that didn't make it any easier.

Thurídur returned to her family's Stéttir farm after her first winter, staying in the seasonal fishing hut and working for Jón Rich. After only one season, people were already calling her Jón Rich's star deckhand, indispensable to his crew. She liked that, working with new people, a larger crew, and pulling in great catches.

But Bjarni—she knew him well, and the moment she saw him she could tell how the cloud of her departure was affecting him. He'd managed to acquire a new four-oared boat to replace the one lost in the Great Flood, and he'd hired himself a new crew. Still it was clear to her, and everyone else, that Bjarni had lost confidence at sea without her by his side; after all, they'd been fishing together since they were children.

Beyond losing his sister beside him at sea, he'd been having to work the farm alone, bringing home the eventuality that Thurídur's fiancé, Jón Ólafsson, would acquire a suitable leasehold farm and she'd leave their farm permanently. As a man, Bjarni had the more secure circumstance of the two of them; he'd inherited their family leasehold and boat. But in being made head of household, he also now had the responsibility of managing everything: their mother's care, their younger sister (uninterested in either farming or fishing), the farm, boat repairs, the fishing. All without Thurídur.

So his news to her was not really a surprise. He told her he'd taken the escape option he'd had since Helga passed to him the leasehold. As the head of household, he could marry—an option not available to Thurídur until Jón Ólafsson found them a farm. Bjarni told Thurídur he'd found a wife to share his work. The only question now was whom he'd chosen.

The new bride turned out to be Margrét Haagensdóttir,[2] daughter of the same Haagen whose wealth had washed away during the Great Flood. Now a poor man, he was already gaining respect for how philosophically he'd accepted his loss. "I'm just as happy having to eat seaweed as I was as a wealthy man,"[3] he told people.

Regardless of Haagen's admirable attitude, his sudden poverty had equally affected his family, who may not have been as sanguine about eating seaweed instead of rye and meat. For the abruptly poor Margrét, Bjarni's proposal offered a small but well-functioning farm that included a new boat with her prospective husband as skipper. Given her now limited choices, it presented her an excellent alternative to seaweed. She quickly accepted, they married, and she moved in.

Almost immediately, neighbors as well as Thurídur realized that this was not a good match. Thurídur watched as a "hard" and "domineering"[4] Margrét overwhelmed gentle and reclusive Bjarni; in no time his influence on the farm receded to a shadow.

Thurídur refused to let this happen to her. She'd worked this farm since childhood, knew exactly how to make it work.

Margrét, in her new role as wife of the farm's official head of household, thought otherwise. Thurídur was a farm dependent, Margrét's underling with no say whatsoever in how Bjarni and his new wife ran the farm. When Margrét told Thurídur to perform a task, she'd better do it when and how Margrét deemed best.

This did not work for Thurídur. Also, Thurídur had special rights as a seawoman. It was accepted practice that when a man returned from sea, the women of the household would kneel at his feet, remove his boots, wet socks, and outer sea clothing, clean them, and then hang the clothes to dry, later returning them to their proper place, ready for the seaman the next time he went out. While the women did this, the seaman went off to bed to take a nap.

Men on the farms usually took naps in the early evening after they'd seen to the livestock. Meanwhile, the women continued to work: cleaning and storing the milk, preparing the dinner and food for the next day, working until they called the men for dinner.[5]

Seawomen enjoyed a status in some ways closer to that of men. Like the seamen, no one expected them to take care of any sea clothing, including their own. They were also entitled to take a nap after they returned from sea, liberated from the attendant female-assigned domestic chores.[6]

Thurídur had now been fishing for thirteen years, commanding increasing respect. She certainly expected her seawoman status. So although Margrét had every right to order Thurídur around on the farm, Thurídur also had the right to demand her sea clothing be taken care of and that she be allowed an after-sea nap while the other women worked.

Not a surprise to anyone, things quickly went from bad to worse, the two women butting heads constantly, neither willing to give an inch to the other.

It took only a few months for Thurídur to face the claustrophobic inevitability of her changed position on the farm. She stared across the pastures of this place she'd called home for as long as she could remember. The meadows, marshes, mountains all looked the same, but it was a space transformed, completely altered by the addition of one new resident. Margrét was a permanent fixture—no doubt on that—and she was not going to change. Thurídur could no longer placidly wait for Jón Ólafsson to find them a leasehold farm.

But what else could she do? She couldn't leave unless she had somewhere to go, some other farm that would take responsibility for her. The only possibility was to get herself a farmhand position on a decent farm run by a reasonable farmer. It'd likely only be for a year until she moved in with Jón Ólafsson; she could cope. She'd worry about the details later. Come May Moving Days, she was leaving. Bjarni had made his choice; he'd now have to live with it.

By the beginning of this new nineteenth century,[7] the ghost Móri had decided to expand his haunting from just Thurídur's family to include the entire community. He'd been around for close to twenty years now, mostly near Thurídur's family's Stéttir farm, and lots of people had seen him. Recently, he'd become a shape-shifter, taking the form of a dog in addition to his usual tattered, rust-colored hat and coat-wearing boy self.

"Móri has many a dance," people began to say. "Mostly on the North Wind."[8]

But now Móri had morphed into multiple Móris. The fault lay squarely with Jón Rich.

Ghosts were an ever-present concern in Iceland. Most people saw the line between the living and the dead as permeable, the presence of ghosts an echo and a moral compass for the mortal world. Many ghosts were thought to be fairly benign, deceased people who hung around perhaps because they'd died in some awful way or they'd done an act for which they needed forgiveness before they could rest in peace. Sometimes people who hoarded money returned to check on it. But some of the most damning and malevolent ghosts arose from people who died because they'd been refused food or shelter in need, especially children. Like Móri.⁹

Jón Rich made the same mistake as Thurídur's father, Einar, had, with much less excuse—or no excuse. In the late 1790s, even with his increasing wealth, he turned away a starving teenage girl who'd come to his West Peathouse farm begging for food and shelter. As a result, she died only a half mile from Móri's death ditch.

Not really a surprise, the girl's troubled soul did not leave this earthly plane, becoming instead a wandering spirit people soon called Peathouse-Skotta (*skotta* being a female ghost) in a public indictment of Jón Rich's shameful selfish behavior. She and Móri quickly found each other, joining forces to bring their accusing wrath to an entire community.

Working together, Móri and Peathouse-Skotta created sudden fogs that led people astray and harassed sheep and even cows until they became witless and ran off cliffs. Peathouse-Skotta haunted Jón Rich without respite. She chewed his special blue socks at the heel to the point that he'd put on new ones in the morning just to have them destroyed by evening. She started on the securing ties of his shoes.

He began wearing very short ties on his shirts, so she couldn't grab them and strangle him.[10]

Then the undead companions graduated from livestock and dangerous harassment. They turned to murder.

Their first victim was a man in Stokkseyri they drove insane. He was later found strangled at the bottom of a well. Then, just before Christmas of 1799, they attacked their next victim, a man named Tómas Björnsson from a farm near Eyrarbakki. Tómas had walked through snow the few miles from Eyrarbakki to Stokkseyri to buy smoked mutton, a traditional food for Christmas festivities. In the twilight gloom of a winter's early afternoon, he left to walk home, crossing the narrow and swift Lava River (*Hraunsá*) between the two communities.[11] He never made it.

People found him the next morning very near where Móri had died, his body ripped apart, bloody, and bruised. This in a country that had no predatory mammals except the small Arctic fox.

Tómas did not stay in the ground either, and soon joined Peathouse-Skotta and Móri. In a ménage à trois of terror, they brought the entire community almost to a standstill. During the day, people ventured out only in groups and after dark not at all. Something had to be done. The blame for Móri lay with Thuridur's father, but he was now dead himself. The current responsibility belonged to Jón Rich.

Increasingly pressured by others and feeling threatened himself, Jón Rich finally decided to do something decisive, at least about Peathouse-Skotta. During the winter after the Great Flood, he wrote a letter to the farmer and deputy "Cloister" (*Klaustur*) Jón Magnússon of Church Farm Cloister (*Kirkjubæjarklaustur*), a farm farther east along Iceland's south coast.[12] Well known for his ability to "see beyond his nose"—an Icelandic phrase meaning able to perceive things others cannot[13]—Cloister Jón had skills that also included the laying of ghosts.

In his letter, a desperate Jón Rich offered Cloister Jón the huge sum of thirty Danish state dollars to get rid of the ghosts. He was rich now. If he had to, he could buy his way out of this.

In response, Cloister Jón came to Stokkseyri, telling Jón Rich he'd do the job only if he received half the sum in advance—having heard about Jón Rich's mounting reputation as close with his money, he wanted to make sure he got at least something for his work.

By all accounts, Cloister Jón did lay both Peathouse-Skotta and Tómas, who were never seen again. When he came to Jón Rich to get the rest of his payment, he reported that he couldn't find Móri anywhere. But since Móri had been Thurídur's father's responsibility and nothing to do with Jón Rich, he should pay up. Jón Rich, seeing an opportunity to save fifteen Danish state dollars, refused. The two men parted on very poor terms.

Soon after Cloister Jón left the scene, people saw Móri at Thorlákshöfn, that fishing area some distance west, running away from a fishing boat where he'd clearly been hiding, still very much in evidence, waiting to give Thurídur and her siblings trouble in any malicious form he could imagine.

While Móri nursed his vengeful intent to ruin Thurídur's life, at the same time a man arrived in the area who would affect her life in a very different way.[14]

At thirty-one, the same age as Jón Rich and seven years older than Thurídur, Pastor Jakob Árnason brought to Stokkseyri a

major controversy, not because of his own qualities but because of
a new hymnal, spawned by a so-called Icelandic Enlightenment.
European Enlightenment ideas had long circulated among Iceland's
elite, but its major influence over Iceland's general population came
spearheaded almost entirely by one very powerful man, Magnús
Stephensen.[15] Of an elite Icelandic family, he'd been horrified by
the post-eruption stench of poverty, starvation, and death he had
encountered in the spring of 1784. He saw its cause not as disaster-
derived devastation or overt inequality but instead as moral and
cultural sloth.

Intolerant of traditional Icelandic religious and secular ideas,
Magnús, who had lived a number of years in Copenhagen, had little
interest in preserving the Icelandic language or literature. Among
the many changes he implemented was a plan to "improve literary
taste" by replacing "irrational" elements in Iceland's traditional writings with those then popular in Europe. These changes, Magnús felt,
would raise common Icelanders from the "morass of intellectual and
spiritual sloth into which they had fallen,"[16] an attitude commonly
held by Europeans and elite Icelanders whose life experience stayed
far from the oppression and near-starvation of the rest of the country.

As part of Magnús's Enlightenment campaign, he published a
new hymnal that all churches were told to adopt, replacing the one
first published in 1594 and by then in its nineteenth reprinting. The
original hymnal, Magnús felt, was too mystical, full of abstract theo-
logical content he was convinced people thoughtlessly sang without
understanding. His new hymnal focused on practical thought, such
as loving thy neighbor and striving for the betterment of one's moral
life.[17] The community in which Thurídur lived had used their previous hymnal for hundreds of years; many felt the connection to their

religious and spiritual selves undermined, their liturgy robbed of its beauty, poetry, and depth.

So Pastor Jakob arrived to the Stokkseyri area as an outsider, burdened with the unenviable task of imposing Magnús's detested hymnal. In addition to being lambasted for its uninspired and mediocre verse, the new hymnal also represented a centralized control seemingly intent on shredding Icelanders' spiritual and literary heritage.

Everyone in Stokkseyri waited for the showdown they couldn't possibly win.

4

COMPROMISES OF HONOR

1801–1803

Jón Rich approved of the new hymnal;[1] many others did not, call-ing it "shameful and disgusting."[2] The church's lead singer, Brandur, a shipwright with four seafaring daughters, expressed his fury about the new hymnal to anyone he could find. A vigorous, tall, broad-shouldered man with intense eyes and a ruddy complexion, Brandur had an infamously quick temper. Once while in his smithy, he threw a flaming-hot sledgehammer at a man who'd annoyed him. The man escaped only by leaping out the door just in time.[3] What Brandur would do when the novice Pastor Jakob tried to force him to lead the new hymnal was anyone's guess, but if someone was going to stand up for them, it was Brandur. They all waited for the New Year's service, when Pastor Jakob was set to introduce the con-troversial hymnal.

A modest stone-and-turf affair,[4] the Stokkseyri church was packed. Generally fishing was not allowed on a Sunday, so all the fishing folk could attend. Everyone settled into the pews, men on one side, women on the other. Even for a normal service, this was *the* event of the week. Many men brought a small flask of brennivín, so they could slip out for a nip if the sermon went too long.[5]

Brandur came in with his wife and seafaring daughters. As lead singer, he would have been given a copy of the new hymnal—which he might have neglected to bring with him, of course. Wearing a skirt for the occasion, Thurídur, still stuck at her brother and his wife's farm, undoubtedly attended along with the rest of their household. Jón Rich, recently married to the well-connected Gudrídur Gísladóttir—considered a good woman well suited to him—made his usual dramatic appearance. People with status like Jón Rich now had had their own special seats near the front.

Jón Rich and Gudrídur wore notably fancy clothes to church, about the only outlay Jón Rich deemed worthy of its cost.[6] He sported a black coat, a red velvet vest with silver buttons, black trousers, and shoes with fancy edging. Instead of the usual sheep-colored socks, Jón Rich's—now remaining unchewed—were blue, both a fashion statement and apparent symbol of wealth. On his dark, shoulder-length hair, he wore a black furry hat with white trim. Gudrídur, grabbing this rare opportunity to splurge, wore three beautiful black wool skirts instead of the usual two, tiered to reveal their contrasting red, blue, and green hems.

The congregation watched their new pastor as he preached. Despite the power he held, he seemed a shy sort of fellow. Could he stand up against Brandur? Soon the pastor cleared his throat and nodded to Brandur to begin a hymn from the new hymnal.

Those who'd been taking their customary Sunday naps woke up. Brandur stood, stolid, his mouth firmly shut, refusing to sing the hymn. His silence was deafening in its defiance of the imposed hymnal and by extension the new pastor who'd brought it.

Pastor Jakob briefly glanced at Brandur. Then with a calm expression, he began singing the new hymn himself. At this point Brandur held up his copy of the old hymnal, which he surely knew by heart anyway, and in his booming voice he began to sing the usual hymn.

For a bit, both men sang at the same time, each a different hymn in a cacophony of discordant song. Brandur sang louder. Finally, not having near the vigorous voice of Brandur, Pastor Jakob gave up. Nobody could hear him anyway. Brandur's single voice filled the small church as he finished the hymn alone.

After the hymn, Pastor Jakob continued the service as if nothing had happened, although likely without another hymn. The moment the service ended, Brandur rose and stalked out.

"Come on, those who wish to keep the faith!" he shouted, his rebellion fueled by success.[7]

Outside, everyone hung around in the snow, waiting to see what would happen. When Pastor Jakob finally emerged, he called together a few men, including Brandur. Everyone else listened as Pastor Jakob tried to convince Brandur to sing the new hymns while Brandur steadfastly refused. Impressively for him, Brandur also managed to control his temper.

Yet, while Brandur fought to keep their hymnal and all it represented, the community also recognized that pastors held almost unassailable power, acting as their moral judge, the right hand of local deputies, and often the only source of education or medical aid.[8] In standing up for them, Brandur was taking a risk; this tussle was about so much more than a song.

Later that evening observant local eyes noted that as Pastor Jakob set off toward home, he made a detour along the way at Brandur's farm, obviously to confront him in private about the hymnal. Speculation ran high that this was a venture from which the gentle-seeming pastor might never emerge alive.

But here Pastor Jakob gave the community an inkling of the man who, by his mere position, would now become one of their leaders. They could already tell he was a shy introvert, but that evening during this first visit to Brandur, he showed both his understanding of his role as a mediator between his mostly powerless parish and a controlling church authority.

Although no word ever leaked of what was said between the two men, it seems likely that Pastor Jakob convinced Brandur that the new hymnal was an edict over which neither of them had influence. Brandur continued to attend the church he'd helped build, but he offered no more open resistance to the hymnal and stopped being lead singer. But even though Pastor Jakob appointed a new lead singer, Brandur never considered himself crushed in this exchange; in fact he boasted for decades how he'd stood up alone against the church and won.[9] Controversy still swarmed around Reykjavík's disliked hymnal. But Pastor Jakob had shown he understood how to effect compromise that left both parties with their honor intact. It was inevitable that the community would lose the fight to keep their hymnal, but they had also gained a compassionate, caring pastor.

Clerical postings in Iceland varied widely. Distributed by the bishop, some positions did not include a farm or attached house, the ministers having to survive entirely on their meager salaries. Other postings included a farmhouse and often quite large church properties that the pastor could farm and even lease out for income. These pastors often became quite wealthy.[10] Pastor Jakob's posting came replete with multiple church properties, including the excellent Gaulverjabaer farm and rectory a few miles east of Stokkseyri (*Gaulverjabaer* meaning "Place of the People from Gaular," the part of Norway from which the first settlers there came).

Educated not only as a pastor, but also as a doctor, Pastor Jakob was a godsend for the Stokkseryi area; since rural Iceland lacked doctors, many parsons filled that role regardless of their medical knowledge.[11] He had even worked in the apothecary of Dr. Bjarni Pálsson—the same celebrated doctor who'd started the leprosy hospital that Einar had avoided and who had, thirty years earlier, saved the lives of baby Jón Rich and his mother. Additionally, Pastor Jakob had recently[12] married the intelligent midwife Elín Eríksdóttir.

But as he settled into his parson's life, which included employing numerous farmhands and servants at Gaulverjabaer and his other church properties, Pastor Jakob realized he had a new problem. A "sweet man,"[13] he treated his employees well, but unfortunately his "peaceful nature was more prominent" than his farm-managing abilities. Some of his employees slacked on the job, inciting the more dedicated workers to complain that they carried an unfair portion of the workload. Pastor Jakob also seemed unable to give anyone a direct order, instead making obscure suggestions that left people confused over what in the world he wanted.[14] Dissatisfaction grew among everyone. Pastor Jakob needed to do something before it all erupted into crisis.

This was not a part of pastoring he'd been prepared for. What could he do? Pass all this along to someone else? Yes! He certainly could; after all, he had plenty to do in his myriad other duties. He'd hire a steward—excellent plan.

The man he chose, Jón Halldórson, immediately improved employee dynamics, and the farms began to function well. Pastor Jakob breathed a sigh of relief. If he was lucky, Steward Jón would stay with him for years (happily for Pastor Jakob, and his workers, he did).[15]

On the gossip mill Pastor Jakob also soon learned that the twenty-five-year-old Thurídur wanted to leave her family farm. He'd already heard about her stellar reputation on land and sea. Could he perhaps invite her to work for him as a contracted farmhand?

Thank our heavenly Lord! Thurídur had an escape.

Working as a farmhand for Pastor Jakob during all but the winter months, when she was fishing for Jón Rich, was about the best offer she could get. She quickly accepted his invitation and on the prescribed May Moving Days of 1802 left her family home for Gaulverjabaer.

In her new position, Thurídur knew her status was no more than a farmhand and that she would work under the direct command of Steward Jón, a person as dominant as herself. He was also an excellent manager, something she recognized immediately. It didn't matter that they were both strong-willed; she respected and liked him. She could tell the feeling was mutual; he made it clear he considered her smart, knowledgeable, a great addition to the farm. Thurídur also liked her fellow farmhands; they found her entertaining, clever with a good memory, knowing "more than others of many things,"[16] a hard worker who enlivened their days. No one seemed concerned that she almost always wore trousers.

In Pastor Jakob, Thurídur found someone to admire, and he soon became her close friend. He felt the same way. Over the months, they recognized in each other a shared intellect and mutual sense of justice rooted in their deep faith in God.

At Gaulverjabaer she'd found acceptance, a peaceful, stable new home. But she knew it wouldn't last. She'd already made a previous commitment.

Only a few months later, north of Reykjavík at Laugarnes, Thurídur's fiancé, Jón Ólafsson, finally found a good leasehold farm, including a building they could improve. In the spring his parents would quit farming and join them. It sounded perfect.

He immediately told Thurídur. Finally! They could move in and start their lives together.

What timing. Why couldn't he have found the farm *before* May Moving Days, when she was desperate to leave her brother's farm? Then she'd never have moved to Gaulverjabaer, a place she now didn't really want to leave. She couldn't break her farmhand contract with Pastor Jakob anyway, so they'd have to wait until the next Moving Days for her to move.

Don't renew the contract, Jón Ólafsson asked. That will leave you free then to move in with me next May. This is what they'd been waiting years for.

But that was before she'd been living happily at Gaulverjabaer. Still, she was engaged, and managing a farm with Jón Ólafsson would provide her more security and self-reliance than being a farmhand, no matter how much she liked living where she was. She wouldn't renew the contract, she promised him. And come May, she'd move to Laugarnes.

But she never found the words to tell Steward Jón and Pastor Jakob.

Come May she still hadn't said anything. Pastor Jakob smilingly invited his new friend to renew her contract, fully expecting her to accept.

I can't, she told him abruptly. I'm moving in with my longtime fiancé. She knew she should have told him earlier, but, well, she hadn't.

Pastor Jakob looked at her in surprise and dismay. "There you will have it worse than here," he blurted out. When he was distraught,[17] he always found it easier to show affection through his actions than words.[18] He quickly controlled himself. Thurídur had her own life to live; someone like her would never stay a farmhand. "Of all my servants, I'll be sad to lose you," he finally said once he'd recovered himself. "But I'll not resent your happiness nor stand in your way. Although you shan't stay with me beyond this year, I'll remember you and you may come to me if you have need."[19]

Thurídur warmly thanked him. She'd never expected that here she'd find such a kindred spirit.

After saying a fond farewell to her newfound friends, she left and moved in with Jón Ólafsson.

Almost from the start, things with Jón Ólafsson did not go well.[20] And after such a long wait. He and Thurídur disagreed on who should direct their various tasks and plans. Jón Ólafsson, always a drinker, got depressed; to keep his bleakness at bay, he drank more. You have to pull back, Thurídur told him not once but many times. I will, I will, Jón Ólafsson promised. Each time he was sincere, but each time he got drunk again. With alcohol, he was losing the battle.

Thurídur "was better endowed with many things than forbearance." Although they'd got along living separately, a union of cohabitation had become a disaster—smart she hadn't married him. It was also not going to get any better; she could see that. So, best to leave before they grew to hate each other. After only fifteen weeks she told Jón Ólafsson she was leaving.

Some people blamed Móri for the breakup—somehow placing Jón Ólafsson's alcohol consumption on Móri's tattered shoulders, citing as "evidence"[21] that although the handsome Jón Ólafsson was perhaps "feckless" and he always imbibed, he never drank as much as during those weeks with Thurídur. Móri wasn't about to let one of Einar's children have a happy union.

Breaking up quickly, Jón Ólafsson and Thurídur didn't hate each other; around the hurt and disappointment, they even remained cordial. Jón Ólafsson knew that Thurídur wouldn't stand for a drunken husband. Why couldn't he control himself?

After Thurídur left, he stayed at Laugarnes for a year, moving the next spring to another farm where he lived for many years while continuing to fish out of Thorlákshöfn. He never married. People said he forever regretted losing Thurídur.

Humbly Thurídur returned to Pastor Jakob, asking if he would take her back as a temporary laborer, a role not really legal but that people sometimes did. Even though it was now late summer, he immediately said yes, inviting her to stay through the next May Moving Days. She was again safely at Gaulverjabaer.

But, this too was not to last. Only a few weeks later, a message arrived from her mother, Helga.

Take me away from here, she begged her eldest daughter. Or come yourself.

Once Helga had given up managing the farm, she'd become dependent on her children for her well-being.[22] This worked fine while Thurídur lived there, but not now.

I never have enough food, she wrote. I'm being neglected.

It was a plight Thurídur had seen too many times. Older people, particularly women, when no longer able to manage their leasehold, passed it along to their children, becoming dependent on them for their continued survival. Some children treated their elderly parents well, but many did not[23]—including, it seemed, Thurídur's brother (who she suspected had little say in this) and her new sister-in-law.

Thurídur walked the slight hill of lovely Gaulverjabaer farm, its meadows the lush green of high summer, hay tall, dancing in the breeze and ready to harvest; in the near distance shimmered a topaz sea.

No! How could she leave here again so soon? Did she have any choice? Unlike her brother and sister-in-law, she had no leasehold farm; as only a farm worker and deckhand, she had no way to sustain their mother herself. Pastor Jakob couldn't take responsibility for Helga. It was too large a commitment; he was barely established himself. Caring for elderly dependents such as Helga meant providing food as well as servants to look after her in a burden of care that would only increase as she grew more infirm. Thurídur sighed deeply. This time she wouldn't make the mistake she'd made last time. She'd go directly and talk with him.

Once Pastor Jakob heard the situation, he sat in silence a moment. "I have no better advice," he finally said, "than for you to stay with me through the haymaking season and I will pay your wages for those weeks. Then you go to your brother's, for I cannot take your mother with you although I would wish to help you as far as I can."[24]

Neither of them even considered the option taken by many, that she just ignore her mother's plea.

So Thurídur worked scything and storing his hay. Then, with a heavy heart and determined resolve, she left. She was—somehow—going to have to get along with Margrét and at the same time protect her mother. It was not a pleasant prospect.

5

DARK SHADOWS
AMID JOY

1803–1806

All too soon, Thurídur stood again in the courtyard of Stéttir, this farm that for so many years she'd called home—also the place she thought she'd left for good. It teemed now with flying resentment; even the arrival of Bjarni and Margrét's infant daughters seemed to bring no joy. She'd been shocked to see their mother suddenly thin and frail beyond her years. Margrét's presence loomed larger than ever, gentle Bjarni abdicating his head-of-household role entirely, withdrawing further into himself, retreating from an external gloom to a solitary internal one.

Then, into this depressing situation arrived a surprising bright spark in the shape of Erlendur Thorvardarson.

At twenty-five, a year younger than Thurídur, strong and handsome Erlendur had a good reputation as "able, reliable, and trustworthy."[1] He also held the leasehold to half of East Peathouse farm, next door to Jón Rich and his wife—and didn't share Jón Ólafsson's conflict with alcohol.

After visiting Thurídur several times, Erlendur made his intentions clear: he wanted to marry her, the sooner the better. Because he held a farm leasehold, he saw no reason to wait.

Erlendur was clearly a good prospect. Making the proposal even better, Thurídur liked him. Marriage would liberate her from her brother and sister-in-law's farm. The only obstacle was the reason she'd come here in the first place—her responsibility to Helga.

But she'd learned since her last relationship; as a successful seawoman, she brought to any union her own separate income. If someone wanted to marry her, she'd negotiate what she wanted.

She told Erlendur she was interested in his proposal, but if she accepted, Helga would accompany her. Thurídur would at the same time contribute to both her mother's care and to the farm generally through her fishing income—as well as her partnership in the farming, of course.

This worked for Erlendur.

Then she told him her other condition: just as before, she wouldn't get married until they'd lived together to confirm they got along. She didn't tell him, but confessed to other friends, that part of her concern was that Móri might interfere with any marriage she tried. Perhaps Móri wouldn't notice if they were just living together without the public formality of marriage.

I prefer to marry immediately, Erlendur told her, but if this is how you want it, I can wait.

So in the spring of 1804, Thurídur and Helga moved in with Erlendur at East Peathouse. The same year, Thurídur became skipper of a four-oared spring season boat while continuing to work winter season as a deckhand for Jón Rich. Although it was less profitable and the season shorter—from about mid-May to late June[2]—Thurídur did well with her spring season crew, increasing the amount she contributed to her new household. Helga slowly regained some of her health. Thurídur and Erlendur found they enjoyed each other's company and worked well together. It seemed that this time she'd found an amicable relationship with a man who accepted her as an equal partner.

But close by, dark shadows lurked. On the other half of East Peathouse farm lived Erlendur's two elder half siblings from his mother's first marriage. They both held reputations very different from his.[3]

The younger of the two, Thórdur Erlendsson, was considered sly, prone to disturbing behavior that erratically erupted into uncontrollable fits of rage. Most people tried to avoid him. The eldest half sibling, Margrét, who acted as the nominal manager of their half of the farm, "had a very bad temperament" and a reputation even worse than Thórdur's. She was also not a good manager, neglecting the upkeep of their home, called Símon's House (*Símonarhús*), to the point it had become a derelict hovel. She consistently manipulated her mentally unstable brother. Both equally volatile, they had constant arguments that often escalated to fistfights, an excuse Margrét used to kick Thórdur out.

Unfortunately for Thórdur, no one else wanted him around either, making it almost impossible for him to get hired or to find anywhere to live except with his abusive sister. In a cycle neighbors saw repeated with tiresome regularity, Margrét would eventually decide she needed Thórdur's labor again and call him back, using him essentially as her unpaid farmhand. Because he had nowhere else to go, he always came.

Not a surprise, the thirty-one-year-old Margrét and Thurídur did not get along; Margrét soon began telling people she opposed the planned marriage, giving her reason as...Móri. Since Móri's curse lay on Thurídur's father's descendants, Margrét claimed the scandal of an incriminating ghost hanging around would "shame" her family's reputation. Not that they needed Móri's help on this score. It was apparently the only excuse she could find to object to her half brother's clearly excellent match to a woman Margrét couldn't control.

Meanwhile, Thórdur developed a lustful fixation on Thurídur. When she rebuffed his overt advances, he decided in his delusion that if Thurídur was free of Erlendur, she would clearly choose him instead. With this in mind, he approached Margrét for help in breaking up the relationship.

It is very unlikely even Margrét thought Thurídur would go for Thórdur—and would theoretically have opposed this, since it would still bring Móri to the family. But Móri wasn't really the issue. Margrét quickly realized she could use Thórdur—as she always did. This time it was to get rid of Thurídur. They just needed to find a reason for Erlendur to turn against her.

The months passed pleasantly between Erlendur and Thurídur, and as the shortening autumn days darkened toward winter, her body gave her joyous news. She was pregnant.[4]

Although this meant immediate precautions such as not walking under hanging laundry (said to cause a newborn's umbilical cord to wrap around its neck[5]), it did not preclude fishing. Thurídur wouldn't have stopped anyway.

Take it easy, a concerned Jón Rich told his star deckhand.

To no avail. Thurídur clambered about the boat, rowed as hard as ever, and pulled in one heavy fish after another while her belly grew and she presumably kept loosening the waist string of her sea trousers. She fished the entire winter season from early February through early May—until she was seven or eight months along.

In continuing to go out so late in her pregnancy, Thurídur wasn't much different from other seawomen.[6] Whether working as contracted seagoing labor for a farmer or with their own families, women were seldom spared from sea work no matter how pregnant they got. And they had close calls, going into labor at sea and barely making it to a mossy bank or rocky beach before the child came. A few women actually gave birth aboard the unsteady and confining rowboats. In one account, the crewmate husband, not having a knife at hand, bit off the umbilical cord with his "worn-out teeth."[7]

Luckier women stayed in bed for a week before the birth while neighboring women brought them food such as bread and butter, the belly flesh of smoked mutton, sausage, and other cooked food. Men having a role in the preparation of this food is never even suggested.[8]

In early summer, Thurídur gave birth to a girl—healthy, thank God. She stared at the tiny infant. Never had she felt such joy.

Among the special items for her child, Thurídur surely had a rocking crib, said to prevent seasickness later.[9] She also carefully considered her new infant's name, particularly important, since people believed children shared traits of their namesake. Knowing this, Thurídur named her daughter Thórdís after Thórdís Markúsdóttir. It was a choice both intentional and controversial.

Born a century before Thurídur to a wealthy, elite Stokkseyri family,[10] Thórdís Markúsdóttir started with large tracts of inherited property, which she quickly increased through buying her siblings' land and other property, soon owning thirty to forty farms and several fishing ships. While still in her early twenties, she became the largest landowner in the area.

The local parish expected Thórdís and another large landowner to build and maintain the local church, which Thórdís did, only stopping when the other landowner refused to contribute. The Church, at this time trying to increase its property holdings, also got into conflict with Thórdís as a landowner—interestingly much more than with the wealthy male landowners—steadily increasing its attempts to undermine her reputation and secure her wealth. Then in 1709, when Thórdís was forty-one, one of the men opposing her presented an envelope containing two little books he and his wife said they'd found near the beach. One of the books was about magic spells; on its flyleaf were written the names of both Thórdís and her sixteen-year-old son. Below their names, just to make sure it was obvious, was written the word Stokkseyri. They quickly accused Thórdís of witchcraft, the case going all the way to the Althingi Parliament.[11]

The magic here is how these little books—even made of the sturdy cotton fiber used for paper at this time—lay somehow readable and untouched by rain, damp, or tide on an Iceland beach to be conveniently found by people opposing Thórdís. Regardless, on this dubious evidence, a court convicted Thórdís of witchcraft. Luckily for her, Iceland's witch-burning era had passed, although not by much, as the last person convicted to burning in Iceland was in 1685.[12]

Thórdís spent much of the rest of her life battling the Church and died about twenty years later. Her death records note that the Church, still trying to get its hands on her land, was just about to expel her.[13] Even so, Thórdís managed to keep her wealth, which for a hundred years passed through her female rather than male descendants, some of whom lived in Stokkseyri District while Thurídur was alive.

This was the woman after whom Thurídur defiantly named her daughter. If fate allowed, Thurídur's first-born daughter would be poised to continue the legacy of this impressive woman, who not only owned land but also her own ships.

Stokkseyri was a busy waterfront during January, with hundreds from all over the country arriving for the winter fishing season, their horses bearing chests of food and other supplies. Soon dozens of boats would line the rocky shore, pulled up side by side, each with crews of between six and thirteen people.[14] A few of the smaller boats belonged to tenant farmers such as Bjarni, but most belonged to landowners and the Church. As fishing was a lucrative addition to farming, farmers and the Church sent their contracted workers as crew during the fishing season, with their catch share going directly to the farmer or the Church. Under this enforced labor system, the farmhands had no choice as to their skipper or even whether they went to sea or not. As a part of this same labor system, leaseholders were also often obliged to fish as part of their leasehold payment agreement to the landowner, who was often also the Church.[15]

Although during the winter fishing season Thurídur now stayed with Erlendur at the East Peathouse farm—since it was right next door to her captain at West Peathouse—the transient fisherfolk stayed along the Stokkseyri shore in the stone-and-turf fishing huts, just as she had done before.

Not palatial living by any stretch,[16] the huts had a low door that opened to a single room just high enough for a person to stand. The sides sloped to about three feet high with a small, membrane-covered window at each end. Wooden- or stone-bench beds lined each side, partitioned every three to four feet to delineate separate sleeping spaces; they were also the only place to sit. The Stokkseyri huts generally had three beds on one side and two on the other and, under each, a stone shelf where people kept their gear, particularly sharp objects like hooks.

Each bed held two people—called bed-buddies (*lagsmaður*),[17] who often slept with one's head alongside the other's feet. Because the beds were too short for the occupants to actually lie down, they often nailed a slanted wooden plank against the partition, sleeping in a half-sitting position. They hung their wet sea clothes from center beams, mittens and hats laid on the partitions. The partitions also held each person's piss pot, covered by a plank. One pointed euphemism for going out to defecate in this Lutheran country that had expelled the Catholics was "going to play chess with the Pope."[18]

Icelanders generally slept in the nude, a blanket above and dirt and straw for padded warmth below. But the fishing huts' turf roofs "leaked like sieves whenever there was any suggestion of rain."[19] When that happened, the fishing people slept in their skin sea clothes on a bare bed, knowing they were going to get wet.

The huts also had no heat or cooking fires, although people who lived in them said they stayed warm from the sheer number of bodies crammed into limited space—"warm" being a relative term. The only ventilation came from tiny holes above each bed in the stacked-stone walls. Mice ran everywhere, scampering over inhabitants' faces as they tried to sleep—luckily for Thurídur and her contemporaries, rats only came to the area on foreign ships much later, about 1885.[20]

Despite these living conditions, various people who actually lived in the huts claimed these were some of the best times of their lives. For the vast majority of Icelanders, rural existence was an isolated one where, except at church, people saw only the few who also lived on the farm. The fishing hut life got them away from that, providing a relative freedom that also gave the farmhands a chance to meet others from near and far.[21] While these living conditions were primitive, the people who lived there claimed they did not make them ill—or at least no more than their farmhouses—where the conditions weren't all that much better.

During bad weather days when they couldn't go to sea, the crews sat around doing small tasks like braiding horse hair into rope. They also made up stories and verses or played games; chess was very popular, along with backgammon, tic-tac-toe, and a card game rather like whist. Weather permitting, they wrestled in outdoor games. They became lifelong friends, united by their comradery, common danger, and luck.

Shortly after Thurídur began working for Jón Rich, he organized it so that during the winter fishing season, she got up first and went out to check the weather.[22] He didn't like to get up early, and now there wasn't any reason for him to do so. If the conditions looked good for fishing, she'd wake him; otherwise, he slept undisturbed. Even if they were going to sea, Thurídur's actions allowed him to get dressed in a leisurely fashion while she gathered the rest of the crew and got everything ready at the boat for his arrival. At the end of each fishing day, he also began having Thurídur oversee dividing the catch, sorting, gutting, and stacking the fish for drying. Meanwhile, he went home to supper.

This suited Jón Rich well, but it also suited Thurídur. She was very fast at processing her own fish share, so while her captain relaxed at home, she made a habit of wandering between the boats chatting with other crews, entertaining them with her pithy, clever comments, sharing thoughts on weather, fish migration, and the latest news.

Each year as she worked for Jón Rich, he grew increasingly dependent on her, the same as had her brother, if not more so. Very soon after joining Jón Rich's crew, she began giving her opinions on fishing, the best time to go out or come in, when she thought Jón Rich was too "persistent at sea in surf and reckless sometimes with overloading his ship."[23] He was a decent captain, but she was certainly not going to let him put all their lives in danger. The rest of the crew quickly noted how "very clear-sighted" she was, understanding "everything that had to do with seamanship."[24] And so accurate, her sense of when to come in was never too soon but just in time before the weather rose. Her skills became so evident that Jón Rich increasingly even had her act as skipper to get them in during bad weather.

Thurídur also observed how Jón Rich handled his crew, often rebuking them in a way they felt was too harsh and unfair. Unable to express their anger, they just turned sullen. When Thurídur saw this happening, she began speaking up on their behalf. She never got angry herself—or at least she didn't act that way; more, she just laid out the problem, showing both sides. She was so good at this that over time, when an issue arose, the crew would go silent, looking at Thurídur and waiting for her to resolve it. She had an excellent way of making Jón Rich reconsider his stance, so effective that, as controlling as he tended to be, Jón Rich very often eventually saw she'd made a good point and agreed with her. Soon even he accepted her as the crew's spokesperson—and gradually the crew's relations with him improved.

In the boat and on land, Thurídur, "gregarious" and "entertaining,"[25] enlivened everyone's working hours. The crew members all went to her for advice, and Jón Rich began to form a tentative friendship with her, telling her personal things he didn't tell others. Their boat also started bringing in larger catches than any other boat on the water. That made Jón Rich very happy. They were all doing well, but as captain and boat owner, he was doing even better.

Thurídur made friends with her crewmates, particularly Jón the Younger Gamalíelsson, whom everyone just called Gamlason. Nine years older than Thurídur and also one of Jón Rich's best deckhands, Gamlason had lively bright eyes; a clever man, he also sometimes stuttered when he got excited.[26] With a leasehold at Loftstadir farm on the sea right beside Gaulverjabaer, he was also Thurídur's in-law, now that one of his half nephews, Kristján Jónsson, had recently married Thurídur's younger sister, Salgerdur, a strong match for her that included an alliance with his well-placed family.[27] Gamlason's small son Ari, about the same age as Thurídur's own Thórdís, sometimes came to the shore to watch them. He was an intelligent boy—she could tell that already—even if he showed little interest in fishing.

As Thurídur wandered from boat to boat, a major concern she heard along the shore related to tensions between the rival Stokkseyri and Eyrarbakki communities. Even though Stokkseyri was doing well with fishing, the real power lay in Eyrarbakki, with its Danish-owned merchant trading house and Danish connections, who all watched any rise among Stokkseyri's fishing folk carefully—and critically.

Much of this chatter centered on the Eyrarbakki merchant store's roundly disliked Danish manager[28] and owner, Niels Lambertsen.[29] The merchant house provided a crucial role in the lives of the Icelanders in Stokkseyri District. On this northern island, almost all goods except fish, milk products, and mutton had to be imported. As Iceland's ruler, Denmark had decided a trade monopoly was a lucrative idea, punishing Icelanders who tried to trade with anyone except Denmark's own merchants by seizing their property, imprisoning them in Denmark, and whipping them (Icelanders traded with others anyway, death by starvation often trumping their fear of getting caught). This meant Danish merchants such as Niels Lambertsen were able to sell Icelanders whatever quality of often inedible goods they wished at inflated exchange rates.[30]

Niels had recently obtained the merchant store from its previous Danish owner—who was also coincidentally now Niels's father-in-law. Marrying the daughter, Kristín "Stína" María Didriksdóttir, had cemented Niels's promotion and eventual store ownership regardless of his diligence or abilities. They lived in an Eyrarbakki building so grand it was simply called The House. Built in 1765 and the only large timber structure of its kind on the entire South Coast, The House was modeled on a comfortable Danish home, with large glass windows, spacious rooms, and European furnishings, completely different from the dark, cramped quarters where almost everyone else lived. Only Danish merchants lived at The House.[31]

Because of the lack of local competition, locals had no choice but to trade their fish with Niels for needed food and supplies. Along the shore and elsewhere, people complained that he was "unreliable," "deceitful," and "lazy,"[32] especially when at the store counter, where he traded usually poor-quality goods at inflated prices. He gave them little in exchange for their fish and sometimes even rejected it.

Beyond complaining, some took advantage of the occasional opportunity to pilfer from Niels, perhaps feeling justified in repaying his cheating with petty thievery—or believing that it could hardly matter to a Dane enjoying undeserved wealth. But it did matter. Any thievery from a merchant, no matter how petty, was a direct affront to authority. In the end, it would affect them all, even Thurídur, who never stole a thing.

6

IN THE PALE DEEP
OF SWANS

1806–1811

Erlendur's half brother Thórdur narrowed his eyes, watching Thurídur working busily in the fields of Erlendur's half of their East Peathouse farm, her slim hips outlined clearly in the trousers she always wore, her red-gold hair gleaming in the sun, her lively face, intense blue eyes.[1]

He'd got nowhere in his efforts to break up Thurídur and Erlendur's relationship. Indeed, now that they had a child, they seemed closer than ever. He watched as the little girl came from the house, her mother giving her a brilliant wide smile. That child should be his with Thurídur, not Erlendur's offspring.

Slowly a smile crept across his face. He had an idea.

He entered the gloom of the dilapidated farmhouse he shared with Margrét. She greeted his smile with an annoyed look.

I have an idea, he told his sister. But I need your help.

Margrét stood ready to cut him off, but he sped on, his face suffused with excitement. She could spread the rumor that Thórdís was not Erlendur's child, he suggested with triumph, but was really his. If people asked him about it, he wouldn't deny this was possible— after all, the child really *should* be his. When Erlendur heard these rumors, he'd of course get furious. Then he'd kick Thurídur out.

Thórdur paused. The rest was obvious: Thurídur would then marry him.

Margrét looked at him, her mind working quickly. It seemed her brother had actually come up with a plan that might work. At least to break them up. Thurídur would never then take up with Thórdur, but that was his problem. She smiled. It would take no more than an insinuation here, a hint there for the gossip mill to start, fueled by anyone who resented Thurídur's independence, disapproved of her wearing trousers, or had some other bone to pick with her; they could now happily pass along this nasty tidbit to others—seemingly backed up by Thórdur himself.

She set to work immediately.

Thurídur walked across fields green in the height of summer, hay growing well. In the distance she saw Erlendur. She'd made a good decision by moving in with him.[2] They'd worked and lived together well for three years now. She'd saved her mother, who grew healthier by the day. And Thórdís, dear, dear Thórdís; regardless of weather, each new day arrived on shafts of a shimmering dawn, the child beside her strong and happy, bringing a light of her own.

Thurídur had truly found home.

Except...Erlendur had started acting very strange lately, stopped talking to her, wasn't caressing Thórdís, withdrew daily more and more. She'd seen those dark moods descend on her brother many times before. But this was something else. Not for the first time, she walked over to Erlendur and asked him what was wrong.

He turned away. It's nothing, he replied. Nothing.

But of course, it was something, the destruction of silence.

A short time later, someone told Thurídur of rumors they'd heard, that her daughter was really the adulterous child of Erlendur's half brother Thórdur. Thurídur looked at them in surprise. Could anyone possibly believe this? Even more disturbing, was this why Erlendur had suddenly become distant?

She immediately returned to the farm and confronted him. Was this what was troubling him? He didn't actually believe this, did he?

"I can't swear to my thoughts on this,"[3] he replied.

Shock slid down Thurídur's spine. How could he possibly think she'd demean him in this way—or herself? Especially with Thórdur. After being together three years, he knew her so little? Her expressive eyes sparked in anger.

"Then you'd better leave me if you have no more faith in me than that," she said. "I'll not have a man who suspects me this way." With that she turned and walked away.

Thurídur was again without a home. With Thórdur's unexpected assist, Margrét had won.

Thurídur raced around the community contacting everyone she knew. She needed a place to live, and fast. Plenty of people would be delighted to take her as their farmhand, but now she had not only her mother with her but also Thórdís.[4] Authorities' taking her daughter was unthinkable.

Thank God for "lucky hauls." Deckhands got to keep extra fish when they caught more than others, and also specific rare catches such as halibut, both of which Thurídur managed often.[5] Knowing this, she approached the farmer at the Rocky Brook (*Grjótlaekur*) croft about halfway between Stokkseyri and Gaulverjabaer, suggesting that if he'd take her as a farmhand accompanied by little Thórdís, she'd not only work for him but also guarantee extra lucky haul fish income. The farmer readily accepted. She had a place to live.

Her concern now turned to sixty-six-year-old Helga. She clearly couldn't return to Bjarni and Margrét, since they'd almost starved her last time. That left Thurídur's younger sister, Salgerdur. Now married to Kristján on their own leasehold, it was time for her to step up. So, Helga moved in with Salgerdur while Thurídur, on top of fishing three seasons a year, worked as a farmhand at Rocky Brook.

If life could be so smooth that this all worked. But after only six months, people started telling Thurídur they were seeing Helga again emaciated. It transpired that Salgerdur and Kristján were just as bad at this as Bjarni and Margrét. Was Thurídur the only one to feel any responsibility to look after their mother? Apparently.

She took a deep breath. She was back at the same dilemma she'd faced when she'd worked for Pastor Jakob, only this time it was worse. This time she couldn't go to their mother; she had to find— and somehow pay—someone else to take her.

Lucky hauls. She was using them to pay Rocky Brook, but she had enough saved to buy a cow. Cows, like fish, were a tradable currency, the value of one cow placed at three ewes or 120 ells of homespun cloth—an ell being about two feet. One hundred ells of cloth was the value placed on a farm that could support one cow.[6]

She approached Jón of Simbakot farm, offering him a cow in exchange for looking after Helga for a year. He happily agreed; for a cow, he could look after her well. Thurídur breathed a sigh of relief. She'd done it. Helga slowly began to get better, but older and her body battered from malnutrition, any recovery now came uncertain and slow.

Thurídur squared her shoulders. With no farm to sustain her, she was still single-handedly supporting both her mother and daughter, entirely through her chances at lucky hauls.

It was all right. She'd managed to keep Thórdís.

Perhaps Erlendur understood he'd betrayed Thurídur; perhaps he did not. Regardless, he wasted little time in finding someone else to wed, getting married within the year to a woman Margrét apparently decided wouldn't bring scandal to their family. He moved from East Peathouse farm, later married again a few times, and had several children, two of them through adulterous affairs—ironic considering why he and Thurídur had separated.[7] He never contributed to his daughter Thórdís's care.[8] Margrét continued to live on her half of the property, where she died in 1836—unmarried and alone. Thórdur disappeared; how or why no one knew. Perhaps he died or perhaps he just left. No one seemed to care.[9]

The next residents of East Peathouse farm were Jón the Elder Gamalíelsson—elder brother of Thurídur's crewmate Gamlason—and his wife, Sigrídur Hannesdóttir.[10] Two brothers could hardly less alike, Jón the Elder being a lazy and abusive drunkard. Sigrídur, an intelligent midwife two years younger than Thurídur and from a well-to-do family, did not put up with this long and kicked him out. Then she sued for divorce—something possible for Icelandic women, unlike the women of many other countries.[11]

When Jón the Elder returned to the farm with some buddies trying to lay claim to it and Sigrídur, she took him to court—and won.[12] A superb farmer who read and wrote well, Sigrídur eventually became very prosperous, owning large herds of livestock and even a fishing boat.[13] People began to say that the Peathouse farms, her East and Jón Rich West, had never looked better.

Next door, Jón Rich had recently increased his influence and potential wealth through becoming one of the two deputies (*hreppstjóra*) of Stokkseyri District alongside genial Deputy Jón Einarsson, the same one who had lost his own eight-oared boat in the 1799 Great Flood.

Although deputies held the lowest rung of the Icelandic administrative hierarchy, they were about the only official role of this kind a regular Icelander could hope to attain. Within their district, they were also very powerful, working as officers of the law, organizing the annual sheep roundup, and administering the district's finances, including collecting taxes and distributing payments for paupers.

Getting the deputy position involved lots of backyard lobbying, something Jón Rich did very well. A big perk of the job was that he no longer had to pay taxes to either the Danish king or a poor tax, meaning Deputy Jón Rich now paid no tax on his expanding property holdings. With his forceful personality, he took increasing control over the district, while the older, well-liked, and congenial Deputy Einarsson gradually took a back seat. Soon Jón Rich, now the area's richest man, also decided most things governing the district.[14] He'd achieved his childhood goal.

Jón Rich's intelligent neighbor Sigrídur quickly took a role helping him with district poor tax administration, and in later years, she wrote them herself.[15] With adjoining farms and sharing so much, the two also became good friends.

Jón Rich and his wife, Gudrídur, had three daughters, all of whom, interestingly enough, he decided to name Sigrídur. When asked about this, he replied hotly that he found Sigrídur such a beautiful name that if he had twenty daughters, he'd name them all Sigrídur.[16] Whether he loved this name so much because of his clever neighbor, or some other private obsession, no one ever said.

Thurídur stared down at five-year-old Thórdís, her heart beating with incomparable fear, far greater than any she felt in even the largest surf. Her beloved daughter lay ill, the cherished face flushed and feverish.[17]

As short winter days deepened quickly to dark, Thurídur tried everything to bring her daughter back to health. Sodden rain became sleet, frozen snow caked the earth, the sky hung heavy with cloud; the only winter voice the ominous raven, that black bird that, when finding a fat sheep helpless on its back, will eat its living eyes out. Few portents of death are more potent than the early morning call of a raven.[18]

In cruel early spring, Thórdís died.

Could such unendurable heartbreak come from any sentient god? What now was the point of Thurídur's life? Death laughed at her, intimate and impersonal, her anguish a raw wilderness. "No grief touched me as hard as this death of my daughter."[19]

God had grabbed a blameless soul too young to have committed sin. The responsibility for her care now lay with Him.

Thurídur held her back straight, but her gaze reflected pain deeper than the sea. Her step never faltered. But the life that had always accompanied her was gone.

Just a few weeks later, in a feeding frenzy intent on despair, came another blow, this one of Thurídur's brother Bjarni.

"When will God not shorten these sorry hours?"[20] he murmured to himself one deceptively bright morning in late May. He clutched his bed's headboard, his life suffocating him with the bleakness of a shroud. No matter how high the sun might rise, it still bled color, breathed darkness. Sometimes light haunts as harshly as the demons of sleep.

Why had he married Margrét, so cold and hard? She clearly couldn't stand him, and he wasn't a man to hold his own in an argument. They fought so much people had begun gossiping. Although they tended to blame Móri for the discord, no one explained how the specter managed it. Sometimes it's convenient to have a scapeghost around.

A few days later, very early as he left to go fishing, Bjarni went over to Margrét where she lay in their bed.

"Don't look for my carpenter's axe," he told her. "I'll take it with me." He had it in his hand.

It seemed an odd tool to take fishing, but Margrét neither asked nor made a move to stop him.

With his three-man crew, Bjarni then rowed alongside the rest of the spring season boats out of the skerry-lined channels to the open fishing grounds. He kept his crew rowing until they were the farthest from shore.

Suddenly a rapid storm blew up, everyone rushing to get inside the channels before the surf rose. But it arrived so fast that those farther out started having trouble getting through the steadily mounting breakers. Even inside the channels, backwash rocked boats dangerously from side to side.

One by one, people managed to reach shore. Thurídur, acting as skipper on her spring fishing boat, made it. In the end, the only one still outside was Bjarni. From the rocky beach, all eyes strained to see the single open rowboat tiny on the frigid, slate-gray sea, rising and then disappearing between hills and valleys of swell. They saw the crew rowing hard, oars beating the swirling water, chop so high it splashed over the gunnels.

Perhaps they would make it. The surf was now far too rough for anyone to launch a rescue boat. Whoever tried would immediately capsize.

Then it happened. One instant Bjarni's boat was there, and the next it flipped, its keel spinning in the backwash. Would anyone emerge from the churning sea?

At first nothing. Then one head popped out. Bjarni. Somehow still holding his beloved carpentry axe. He grabbed the keel and, hoisting himself above the water, hewed it into the hull.

He now had hold of the axe handle, clinging to it as the boat spun in circles, smashing from skerry to skerry. "Help!" he shouted. They could hear the frantic tone of his voice, see his drenched hair over his forehead. "Help!"

There was nothing any of them could do except bear witness.

Then Bjarni let go. No one lasts long in these ice-bitten waters. His head disappeared.

The waves smashed the now empty boat from rock to rock, crushing first its prow and then the gunnels of this new boat he had built only a few years before. After a time, it washed ashore empty on the tide. Deep into its keel, pointed skyward like an immobile arm of Death, stood Bjarni's carpenter's axe.

There is an Icelandic saying that you can postpone your fate but never escape.[21] People said Bjarni must have had a dream, a premonition that told him to bring his axe in case it could save him. He was thirty-five.

Later, a parson arrived, not Pastor Jakob but a Pastor Jón Hjaltalíns. He stood near the sea and blessed its wretched waters, calling the souls of the four drowned men to God. He composed a verse to help them along their way.

> *One ship went down*
> *in Eyrarbakki, men tell me,*
> *four men died there,*
> *pale deep in the land of swans.*[22]

Thuríður looked around her. She couldn't stay here at Rocky Brook any longer, not with the echoes of her child's laughter lurking in each corner. Not after her brother had died. This was still May, the month of Moving Days. She could leave—if she found a place that would take her and her mother.

Although Jón Rich[23] was quickly becoming a more prominent deputy than forty-six-year-old Deputy Einarsson, the latter was a kinder man.[24] He and his much younger second wife farmed the large Baugstadir property, near Rocky Brook but a bit nearer to the sea, better land set beside a narrow, fast-moving river. They had a brood of eight children, three from Deputy Einarsson's previous marriage and five between themselves.[25] Reasonably well off and with such a large household already, perhaps they would take Helga with Thurídur as a contracted farmhand if she also contributed through her lucky hauls.

Certainly, they would, they told her.

They enveloped her into their warm and boisterous household. Their daughter Margrét, at four years old only a bit younger than Thórdís would have been, brought Thurídur a healing glimmer of reflected pleasure. Light didn't return to her silent eyes, but they at least began again to engage with the world.

The other half of the property, a farm called Brattsholt, was leased by a family where Thurídur also found friends.[26] The wife, fifty-seven-year-old Gudrún Einarsdóttir, was the great-granddaughter of the same Thórdís Markúsdóttir after whom Thurídur had named her daughter. In that family, the name Thórdís appeared regularly. They, like Thurídur, understood how important it was. Both families got along well, working their adjoining properties together through their various children and other relatives.

Gudrún's feisty teenage daughter, Ingibjörg, smart and strong in her own right, decided she adored Thurídur, a fondness Thurídur found herself able to return. Despite the fifteen-year age difference, a friendship between them grew, getting stronger as the months slid by. Deputy Einarsson's farm was also only about a half mile from Gaulverjabaer, allowing Thurídur to easily visit Pastor Jakob.

Farms full of kind people. It wasn't her home, but perhaps here she could heal.

In this way, three years passed, Thurídur working on the farm and fishing during the fishing seasons, Helga taken care of, living among friends Thurídur grew to love.

Then came the dark winter of 1811. In the house's dim common room, a sharp-edged melancholy seeped into bones already chill.[27] Deputy Einarsson mired in remorse that time might never heal, a gnawing guilt over his son recently drowned, whom he knew he could have saved. Helga had also grown gravely ill, her wrenching gasps going on and on, seemingly without end. Even the bright spark of seven-year-old Margrét brought little laughter to the turf home encased in snow.

Thurídur sat at her mother's bedside gazing at the face she'd seen over the decades weather and age, now wizened, cheekbones too sharp, lips too thin. First dear Thórdís, then Bjarni, and now, it seemed, Helga was being summoned by greedy Death.

7

NAKED WIND

1811–1812

Thurídur brushed the hair from her mother's bony brow, grateful to Deputy Einarsson and his family, who, despite their own grief, showed nothing but kindness during this time Helga needed constant care.

Helga choked as her body writhed in pain. Please, please, Thurídur begged an unhearing god, take her now; she does not deserve this agony.

Finally, late one evening Thurídur could stand it no longer. I'm heading to Gaulverjabaer, she told Deputy Einarsson and his wife.

They immediately understood. The best way to shorten a person's death agony, to let their spirit slip away in peace, was to lay over them the colored chasuble of a pastor's outer vestments, to cloak them in charity that relieved the burden of worldly sin.[1]

Despite the raging winter storm, Thurídur donned her snow clothes and slipped out the door. She bent her head against naked, uncaring winds, striding through drifts of snow to Pastor Jakob's, banging on his midnight door to wake his household.

When Pastor Jakob learned what she needed, he instantly gave her the chasuble with his blessing. The pain of passing from this earthly plane was often harsh; he prayed his own foster parents, who'd recently come to live with him in their elder years, would have easier final hours.[2]

Thurídur hurried back, carefully protecting her precious cargo.

It arrived too late. While she'd been away, her mother had passed. Perhaps understanding the chasuble was on its way, Helga's spirit decided it was time to let go. Or perhaps, at the darkest edge of night, when the soul is closest to death, the bridge became an easier traverse.

Now Thurídur was alone, all her family most dear dead. She paid for Helga's funeral with her fish shares. Salgerdur, even with a husband and farm, apparently couldn't spare the funds.

Thurídur knew she'd done as much for her mother as she could, more than most, including her sister or brother, God rest his soul. She now had almost no family—but also, for the first time since soon after she'd left home, she had no one dependent on her for their survival. Except herself.

Should she try, as a single woman, to obtain a leasehold farm? Over these three years she'd stayed with Deputy Einarsson and his family, she'd managed to save a large stockpile of dried fish from her lucky hauls, enough for a leasehold farm, at least a small one. Women generally acquired leaseholds only through their husbands or family. It was a risk, but possible.

She'd try it! Certainly she would. This time, she wouldn't be dependent on a man. She'd do it herself.

Gata, a small farm in central Stokkseyri, would be available those coming May Moving Days. Near the church, the shore and Jón Rich's much larger West Peathouse farm, it was in terrible shape, with its dilapidated buildings. But it was a leasehold she was sure she could afford. And small was good; most people worked their farms largely with the labor of unpaid kin, help that Thurídur did not have. Being strong and used to hard work, she was confident she could manage Gata herself.

Or almost. She would need a farmhand. She considered and began to smile, a rare occurrence these days. She'd hire young Ingibjörg. Who could be better?

Ingibjörg had already been pestering her parents to let her go to sea. Like Thurídur. Indeed, she wanted to go *with* Thurídur—on Jón Rich's boat, where Thurídur, taking increasing responsibility for choosing his crew, had already added a number of women.

No, her father told his daughter. You're too young.

She was nineteen, much older than the age when boys regularly started. Eight years older than Thurídur was on her first trip.

It's too dangerous, her father objected. Jón Rich is a reckless skipper.

That didn't stand either. Fishing was dangerous, but this never stopped anyone. Jón Rich's boat was also now much safer because the person really directing it was Thurídur. Everyone knew that.

Finally, Ingibjörg's parents gave in. She could go this coming winter season—with Thurídur. Come May, she'd also become Thurídur's farmhand.

May arrived with its days of unfiltered brightness; otherwise it might as well have been winter, the weather was so bad. Stored hay diminished to nothing as stubborn snows refused to melt, and there was still no grass for the hungry livestock. No one had gone fishing for weeks upon weeks. Each day Thurídur checked the weather, and each day Jón Rich got to sleep in. As winter ended, men who'd arrived from all over for the short spring fishing season found no work. No one would hire deckhands if they couldn't go to sea.

Through the bad weather, Thurídur moved to Gata with Ingibjörg and surveyed the huge amount of work she'd taken on.[3] It had to somehow get finished before Saint John's Day, around June 24, if they were to have any chance of decent summer hay.[4] Without hay, their animals would starve next winter. They had about five weeks.

The task was impossible.

As Thurídur observed the unemployed fishermen currently wandering around Stokkseyri with no work or food, she had an idea.

I need workers, she told the itinerant men. She couldn't pay anything, but she could feed them.

Through starving jobless eyes, her offer came as a godsend; she had plenty of labor.

As Thurídur set the men to work, she watched others around her still with no food, the children the worst—hollow-eyed, cheeks sunken, their bodies translucent. Trying to figure out how she could help, she had another idea.

Although people didn't usually consider plants that grew wild in the meadows as food, many were edible. Thurídur knew this—after all, years ago her family had survived the winter following the eruption in part by eating beach plants.

She gathered a group of listless and hungry children, telling them they were going to play a game. First, they'd dig up the roots of moss campion (*lambagras*) and thrift (*geldingahnappur*)—as much as they could find. Following Thurídur's enthusiasm, the children played along.

They all returned to the farmhouse, where Thurídur lit a fire and told them to throw all the roots into a pot, boiling them into a thick and nourishing stew. Unconventional, but the children gobbled it up. At least she'd provided them one meal.

Even though the weather remained terrible, the ground had begun to gradually thaw, thank heavens, allowing Thurídur, Ingibjörg, and their crew of otherwise unemployed laborers to prepare the hay fields. The men liked Thurídur, working with purpose to get everything done.

And together they did. A huge accomplishment and just in time. Saint John's Day was also the official end of the spring fishing season,[5] meaning Thurídur's laborers now had to return to their own farms or contracted farmhand positions.

Thurídur had met her ambitious goal. But even paying her labor in just food, she'd not only used all her fish savings but was also in debt. By taking sole responsibility for this leasehold, she'd put herself in a precarious position. Everything now had to fall just right.

Jens Haagensson, brother of Bjarni's widow, Margrét, woke up in the middle of the night. The date was February 25, 1812, a Tuesday.[6]

Well, he noted with some excitement. It was snowing lightly, but the sea was calm. Excellent fishing weather.

He scrambled over the snow to the farmhouse of his captain,

"Farmer" Jón Jónsson. Farmer was already awake. He was happy to go out.

They quickly gathered Farmer's crew, which included one young fellow who'd just arrived the previous evening, Ingibjörg's brother Einar, and both the half brother and the brother-in-law of Jón Rich's wife, Gudrídur. In the first glimmers of a late winter's dawn, they dragged the boat over the snow and icy rocks into the water.

Nearby at West Peathouse, Jón Rich had a superb view of the shore. This morning he emerged just in time to see Farmer dragging his boat out before them. He bristled. No way was Farmer getting the chance to outfish him.

Thurídur quickly assembled Jón Rich's ten-person crew, five men and five women, including Ingibjörg, Gamlason, and fourteen-year-old Sesselja Grímsdóttir. Sesselja, who'd been regularly fishing with her father, was already considered an exceptionally strong rower.[7]

They dragged out Jón Rich's boat, said the requisite Seaman's Prayer, and rowed the skerry-lined passage to the open sea. No other boats joined them. Following Farmer's lead, they rowed a bit over a mile east to a reef that lay a short distance out from Deputy Einarsson's farm. There, both boats put out their lines and began to fish.

After only two hours, the weather took a dramatic turn, the wind surging, rapidly whipping the sea into churning froth. Jón Rich, Thurídur, and Gamlason looked around. This was dangerous.

Both boats quickly pulled in their lines and raced toward home. Jón Rich usually took the helm while Thurídur handled the crew and called the weather, and Gamlason directed their course—an almost unbeatable team. But in the short time it took to reach the Stokkseyri skerries, high breakers crashed, blocking the passages to shore. Any attempt to cross this filmy white veil would shatter their boats in seconds.

They decided "the only hope to live was to go to Thorlákshöfn,"[8] an unusual choice because it was so far, with a good wind a four-hour row from Stokkseyri.[9] In this weather, it would take them far longer, through increasingly aggressive seas. But they saw no other option. Thorlákshöfn was the only place on this entire South Coast with anything even resembling a cove; everywhere else was now impenetrable surf.

Jón Rich gave the nod and they changed direction, heading west parallel to shore. Farmer and his crew did the same. They rowed for hours in their small open rowboats, and all managed to reach Thorlákshöfn. Freezing seawater drenched their already sweat-soaked bodies, and huge waves slammed against the cove rocks in sheets of ghostly foam. Of particular danger was a large, barely submerged rock known as Kúla at the cove's mouth; the waves rolling in across the ocean's vast expanse broke over Kúla and often rose to enormous heights.

Thorlákshöfn had two landing places, the North and South Landing, each with a natural stone barrier that allowed boats to moor protected from all but the largest surf. But the reef-riddled cove faced southeast, leaving it completely unprotected in a southeast wind like the one that blew that day.

Of the two approaches, the South Landing was considered safer and preferred, people choosing the North Landing only as a last resort when the South became impassable. At the North Landing approach, two sets of rocks, the landward point called Hellunef, embraced a deep channel about forty feet wide where in conditions such as this, deep, unbroken breakers rolled almost to the landing.

A major danger of the South was Sýsla, a flat, high, clefted rock near the landing that protruded into the cove.[10]

By the time Jón Rich and Farmer's boats reached Thorlákshöfn, both approaches had become impassable—meaning they had no choice but to sit outside on the open ocean, fighting wind and weather while also avoiding the waves around Kúla, waiting until the seas calmed enough to make an attempt remotely feasible.

A deep winter darkness fell.

Gamlason sat on the stern thwart across from Jón Rich, where he both directed and balanced the boat to keep it from flipping when waves or wind hit it broadside.[11] Jón Rich held the helm while Gamlason told him where to steer.

Cresting in peaks, the deepening swell increased in size and pitch. Then the full black body of an arching wave near Kúla crashed flat onto their heads and into the boat. Water rushed in faster than they could bail.

"Saints of our Father," Jón Rich entreated, as if some holy power might save them. Then he turned to his solid and earthly crew. "Bail!" he shouted. "Prove yourselves! Bail!"[12]

It didn't matter, human or deity. Water steadily filled the boat no matter how strong they rowed or how fast they bailed. Sinking seemed inevitable.

8

RECKONINGS

1812–1813

"Gamlason," Thurídur shouted. "Take the helm!"

Jón Rich stared at her, startled; a deckhand did not make orders to their captain's crew. More water washed into the boat. Gamlason looked at him inquiringly. Jón Rich shrugged. Thurídur was usually right on these things. If Gamlason could do better at this than he was, then let him try. They were all going to drown anyway.

"Yes," he said to Gamlason. "Take the helm, my friend." Quickly they exchanged places.

Immediately the boat rode more smoothly over the careening whitecaps. The bailers gained ground, the wash now sending in spray but not actual waves.

Jón Rich decided to attempt the North Landing approach. Farmer, farther out, headed for the South, his boat rising then disappearing in valleys and hills of swell. Suddenly a huge wave smashed over Farmer's boat and washed two men overboard. Teeth clenched, Jón Rich's crew kept rowing.

One end of the Thorlákshöfn cove shore rose to a promontory[1] that provided a clear view of the sea. From its top, a person—or their light for boats unlucky enough to get caught out after dark—was also visible to those in approaching boats. As with the Stokkseyri and Eyrarbakki areas, a system of signals had been established to assist crews coming in through rough weather.[2] While both boats battled the seas around them, they now waited for the signal light, knowing those on shore could see a break in the surf that might allow them to row in. Then they saw it.

Gamlason, directing Jón Rich, who had retaken the helm, shouted for them to go, go! As they entered the narrow channel between Hellunef and the outer rocks, backwash from both sides hit their boat.

Seeing them veer toward Hellunef and utter disaster, Gamlason shouted at Jón Rich. "Stay the hell from Hellunef!"[3]

But the boat still moved inexorably toward the rocky point. Gamlason slammed the thwart beside him and shouted again, stuttering with urgency. "S-S-Stay the hell from Hellunef!"

Across the cove they saw a second wave hit Farmer's boat and wash another man overboard. One of Jón Rich's deckhands stared around in terror. "Will any make it alive?" he asked, too loud, his voice ready to crack.

"Shut all your traps!" Gamlason snapped in a quick anger born of pain. Farmer's boat held people they loved. As if his anguish were anything but futile.[4]

Farmer, still farther out, now tried to catch the break. But his boat was too full of water, or he didn't catch it right. Almost to the landing, his boat smashed into Sýsla and threw three more men into the sea.

Jón Rich's crew "rowed for their lives"[5] into the cove, the teenage Sesselja one of the strongest. Ingibjörg rowed, knowing her brother was on Farmer's boat. Was he among those overboard? The boat shot forward, surging toward shore. Still they all rowed, keeping the balance as the wave shoved them into the cove. "By the grace of God," Thurídur later wrote in her autobiography, they'd "arrived safe."[6]

Behind them Farmer, still alive and in his boat, also brought his boat ashore, not as damaged as one might expect. Of his thirteen-person crew, seven remained. Ingibjörg strained her eyes through the dark, looking for the shape of her brother.

Bodies of the drowned washed ashore almost immediately, one so recently dead that his cheeks still flushed pink in an echo of life. Margrét's brother Jens Haagensson, who had so wanted to go out this particular day, had drowned. Jón Rich's wife lost both her half brother and brother-in-law. The young man who'd arrived the evening before for his first fishing trip of the season died. Among the dead on the beach also lay Ingibjörg's brother.

People from Thorlákshöfn quickly appeared on the beach, offering help and food. The crews, wet, tired, and cold, started the long trudge toward Stokkseyri, by land some fifteen miles. On everyone's mind was the heavy responsibility to the families of the dead. Someone had to go to Pastor Jakob to let him know. It was his place to break the news. And they had to tell him soon before the families heard the tragedy from someone else. Deputy Einarsson also needed to know.

They reached Stokkseyri sometime in the middle of the night.

The further four-mile journey to Pastor Jakob entailed crossing the ice-covered but very swift tidal river just beyond Deputy Einarsson's farm.[7]

Surely Jón Rich should go; he was captain and a deputy besides. But he refused. So did everyone else. In the battle between responsibility, fear of the journey, and exhaustion, fear and exhaustion won. Jón Rich looked to Thurídur.

I'll do it, she said.

Still wearing her now frozen clothes, she set off through the blanched winter night, forcing bone-weary limbs through the snow. She first reached the farm of her friends and former employers Deputy Einarsson and his family. Once she'd broken to them the terrible news, she set off again, this time to Gaulverjabaer.

She knew how easily she could fall through the ice on the river she now had to cross. Incoming tides mixed salty seawater with fresh as the river's level rose and fell twice a day. The result was ice fractured with cracks and fissures. On this unstable surface, she set out alone and in the dark.

As ice groaned around her, she realized she was unlikely to make it. At that precise moment, seeing her mortality loom before her, she had an epiphany. It "occurred to her to thank God that Thórdís had left the world before her."[8] She realized how much greater her fear "to see impending death if she knew she were leaving an orphan behind."

As she safely reached the river's far side, Thurídur felt the grief she'd carried since Thórdís's death ebb like a receding tide. Thórdís had at least never become a motherless pauper; she'd lived her entire short life with a mother who adored and protected her. Thurídur had never failed her child by dying first.

She walked on to Gaulverjabaer to wake Pastor Jakob, who

immediately rode out to tell the families—a duty he dreaded, but unfortunately it was not a part of his role that he could hire someone else to do.

As for Thurídur, she walked through a grim winter's late dawn the four miles back to Gata. In her autobiography, she remarked only, "At that point I was quite tired after two days of work and no sleep."[9]

An emaciated, filthy child lay on the bed, unmoving. When Thurídur touched her lice-bitten head, she stared back vacantly, silent.

It's an invalid imbecile, her sister Salgerdur said of her daughter.[10]

So would she just let the child starve to death?

Salgerdur shrugged. Probably better for everyone, including the child, unable to walk or speak, barely human at all.

Thurídur stared at the child's inert form. Thórunn, a three-year-old girl[11]—although hard to tell her age or gender—was the size of a one-year-old, dirty and covered with rashes.

Thurídur's expression remained calm—her gathering emotion visible only in the intensity of her eyes. Salgerdur considered the child a throwaway, ignored and neglected—just as she'd treated Helga. Thurídur thought of her own dear Thórdís—God bless her—who at this same age was triple the size. She touched the child again, this time with determination. She hadn't been able to save her own daughter, but perhaps she could this one. Since she now held a leasehold, legally she could foster her.[12]

Fostering had been a common practice in Iceland since the country's settlement times. In Thurídur's time, families commonly fostered the children of kin and friends who, for various reasons, couldn't do it themselves. For some, one or both parents had died; others had just become one too many mouths to feed.[13] Most importantly, it gave children an escape from neglect and dreaded pauperhood. As late as 1845, a full quarter of Iceland's households included foster children, many of them staying for years, forming deep and lasting bonds.[14]

Fostering required a leasehold farm to ensure stability, the general idea being that a foster child would work for their keep. But tiny, disabled Thórunn would be of little help to anyone, more likely a dependent as long as she lived—if she survived at all.

Released from the sole responsibility for her mother merely two years ago, Thurídur was considering an even heavier commitment. She'd do it anyway. Her niece's death would not be on her conscience.

I'll take her, Thurídur told her sister, picking up the child. In her arms, she weighed almost nothing.

Salgerdur stared at her, her own eyes darkening.

Thurídur looked at the anger reflected in her sister's eyes. When had this animosity crystalized?[15]

As Thurídur walked across the home field with the child in her arms, the aura of her sister's dislike could have cut ice. Thurídur had Thórunn, but she had also gained an enemy.

Thurídur took the child to Gata, cared for her, cleaned her, and made sure she got fed. She hired a housekeeper to look after the girl and went back to fishing.

On the shore, she tossed jokes with Gamlason, Ingibjörg, and the rest of their crew as they busily prepared to go out.[16] It'd been a good season, excellent weather, with trips out every day—except Sundays.

The only Sundays God took a back seat to fish was when swarms of migrating cod guaranteed a huge catch—surely even God wouldn't condone such a waste. On those Sundays, they fished but appeased God by giving a portion of their catch to the poor.[17] All things in balance.

Jón Rich soon arrived, and together they dragged the boat across the rocks and into the water, joining eight other boats on the open ocean beyond the Stokkseyri skerries, rowing west until they were just east of Eyrarbakki, clearly today's best fishing spot.[18] Thurídur, as usual, surveyed the weather. Good now but unsettled, sure to change.

Sure enough, a sudden strong wind soon sprang up. They pulled up their lines and rushed toward the nearby Eyrarbakki shore before the surf rose. Everyone else did the same.

The skerries at Eyrarbakki lay in a parallel line out from shore,[19] closed at one end but open to the sea at the other, creating a fairly deep but narrow single channel to the rocky beach. Boats coming from the east, as they all were that day, entered this passage through a narrow gap in the skerry line, requiring two tight turns hugged between skerries. Only one boat[20] could enter at a time, the first one to arrive taking precedence while others waited their turn. As the waves got worse, Jón Rich's boat skimmed speedily over the water, one of the first to the channel entry.

Thurídur took note of the tide. Returning through the Eyrarbakki passage on an ebb tide was much more dangerous than on a rising one.[21] She nodded in satisfaction. Luckily, the tide was incoming.

They pulled the boat from the water and paused to watch the other boats arrive. Six made it swiftly to shore, but the two clearly with "weaker"[22] crews lagged behind. Thurídur glanced at her crew-mates. Not good. Surf was mounting fast, now cresting over the outer line of skerries.

The lead boat, which held four people, entered the narrow entrance, veered in the churning backwash, crashed into one of the outside skerries, and became solidly wedged against the rocks. No matter how hard they pushed with their oars, the crew couldn't get it off. Violent surf now smashed the boat back and forth against the sharp lava; they'd break up in no time.

As Thurídur and everyone else watched, the second boat close behind them intentionally veered its own course directly toward the skerry. At great risk to themselves, they would try to save the stranded men.

This was going to be tricky. Any overweight made a dangerous difference on these open boats—especially in rough waters; unbalancing could make a boat easily flip. Still, through buffeting waves, the crewmembers managed to pull two of the stranded men into their boat. They'd now overloaded their boat, its gunnels riding barely above the waterline. Any more weight would sink them, an impossible choice of whom to save, with no time for debate. They left the other two men behind.

As the rescuers rowed to safety, the remaining two clung desperately to the damaged boat as it began to break apart, filling steadily with water. On the rising tide, the waves now crashed over the skerry and would soon submerge it. Then they'd drown.

Thurídur glanced at Gamlason. They'd seen this tragedy too many times before. They all then looked at Jón Rich. Any rescue attempt was his responsibility.

He yelled out to the other skippers. "Aren't you going to give me people so I can get those men?"[23]

The other skippers looked out at a sea increasingly white with froth, the skerry a good twelve hundred treacherous, watery feet from shore. They shook their heads. Neither of the men on the rock was kin to anyone on shore. They wouldn't take the risk.

So no one did.

Jón Rich shrugged and turned to his crew. He'd tried, more than anyone else was willing to do. "It's probably not a good idea to attempt to rescue those men from the skerry," he commented. "I'm not going anywhere."

Thurídur kept her eyes on the two men struggling to stay above the sea's greedy maw. "It will be known to the authorities if you don't make an attempt to get those men," she said very quietly.

Jón Rich's other crew members stopped what they were doing and stared. Gamlason glanced at Ingibjörg.

Jón Rich jumped up and glared at Thurídur. "Then you take my job and be responsible for the ship and crew!" he shouted. Not that he expected her to take his angry invitation seriously.

He should have known better.

Thurídur considered her captain's words. She assessed the risk, the distance, her crewmates. She nodded. She could bring a boat alongside the stranded boat to save the men.

"I'll do it," she said to Jón Rich. "I'll guarantee the safety of the crew." She paused. "But I can't promise the same for your vessel." She looked at her crewmates, Gamlason, Ingibjörg, and the rest. They looked from one to the other. They'd go. If she led them.

Jón Rich gave her an infuriated wave and stormed up the bank.

Thurídur and her crewmates quickly pulled the boat back into the water and set off. With Thurídur at the helm, they rowed rapidly through the spray, sliding alongside the skerry in minutes. Then, balancing Jón Rich's boat, they dragged the two men aboard. Thurídur ordered them to shove off—fast. In an instant they were rowing toward shore again. They'd done it. And they hadn't even damaged their captain's boat.

As Thurídur rested on the rocks beside her jubilant crewmates, she looked around. All this drama and still morning. Her keen eyes scanned the horizon. Well, well, it looked as though this was just a passing squall. No need to waste a good day's fishing. In an hour or so they could go out again. She checked out the other boats. They seemed to be deciding the same.

So, they cleaned fish and chatted until the seas calmed. Then they headed out again.

The following year, the authorities issued an award for bravery in the daring and courageous rescue of the two shipwrecked men. They awarded it to...Jón Rich. Who readily accepted it.[24]

Regardless of official accolades, covert conversation along the waterfront—which Jón Rich did not hear, since he was almost never there—was that his crew had begun to consider Thurídur their leader. They said that if she left his boat, so would they. Talk also spread that, even though a woman, Thurídur would make an excellent captain for the lucrative and dangerous winter season.[25]

9
BETRAYAL IS A
MANY-COLORED CLOAK

1813–1815

Thurídur gazed at the new yellow grass poking through a lacy cover of crystalline snow. A promising spring. Between silver-shadowed hollows, lambs scampered, this year coming numerous and alive. Days overtook night, the sun dancing along distant mountaintops fringed dusky ice-blue.

She'd had Gata four years, and it was a leasehold transformed, from run-down and undesirable to well tended and productive.[1] The last few fishing years had been good. Through going out constantly, she'd managed to repay all her farm debts. Ingibjörg was indispensable by her side, a fantastic farmhand who also continued working beside her as a deckhand for Jón Rich—Ingibjörg with him four years now and Thurídur a full sixteen. Little Thórunn seemed a different child, no longer a wordless, immobile invalid but a growing, chattering girl—it turned out she could talk just fine and was perfectly intelligent. With support, she could now even walk.[2]

In the distance, Thurídur saw a stranger walking toward her. After they'd greeted each other, he told her he was a farmer from farther east. He had a young cow he wished to sell. Did she know anyone who might be interested?

Thurídur looked the farmer up and down. "Well," she said, "you've come to the right person, as I'd like to buy a young cow." She paused. A cow was a large purchase. She'd repaid her debts, but she didn't have that kind of fish stores at hand. "Let me secure the money first."

With that she jogged across the pasture toward Jón Rich's nearby farmhouse to see if he would forward her the funds for the cow. This was something Thurídur had never asked him in the sixteen years she'd worked for him. His reputation for being stingy had only grown. She could see evidence of his parsimony from her adjoining farm. Although well maintained, his West Peathouse farm did not look like the home of a wealthy man; he never hired farmhands, working it instead with his immediate family. Although farmhands were often paid just food and shelter, she knew his attitude was that since his family was staying and eating there anyway, it eliminated any extra outlay at all.[3]

Thurídur also knew that he—infamously in the minds of many— fed his family very little, including his mother. When they scythed and stacked hay in late summer—arduous work done completely by hand up to twenty hours a day—he allowed them one daily bag of seaweed and a bottle of milk.

Thurídur smiled with some irony as she arrived at Jón Rich's home field. His wife and daughters, well aware of the Icelandic proverb that any family with several children has a favorite, knew Jón Rich favored his youngest Sigrídur. So when hunger began to overwhelm them, they sent her to beg for a boiled sheep's head to fill their bellies, knowing she was the only one with any chance of success.

Despite this reputation, Thurídur considered Jón Rich a friend. He asked her advice all the time, and she mostly ran his boat as well as his crew, adding significantly to his wealth. He knew she was good for anything she might borrow; he could see her every day next door. So, once she reached the farmhouse, she told him about the cow and asked if she might borrow money to buy it, repaying him through her fish shares.

Jón Rich considered this. "Don't let the cow get away," he said. "When you get her here, there will be some way the money will come."

Despite his reputation for stinginess, Jón Rich was also reliable. So if he failed to refuse, people generally took his word as a promise. Thurídur certainly did. She returned to the waiting farmer and told him she'd take the cow.

"Good," he said. "I'll come back with her next week."

Duly keeping his own word, the farmer arrived with the young cow a week later just as Thurídur was returning from a day at sea. She greeted him and quickly headed over to Jón Rich.

"You knew," he said when she told him the cow they'd discussed had arrived, "that I promised you nothing."

"That's true," Thurídur replied, pushing away a dawning cold realization. "But usually you have kept better than your word."

"I have often told you before," he said, "that I lend no one money. I'll let no one get used to that."

Only Thurídur's eyes reflected her anger mixed with a growing disdain.[4] Jón Rich knew he'd put her in a humiliating position as unable to deliver on her word. This man she'd advised, worked for loyally for sixteen years, had just betrayed her, even set her up. There was really nothing more to say to him. She was not going to beg.

She walked back to the farmer.

Unfortunately, she told him, she'd been unable to secure the funds she'd promised.

She'd miscalculated.

Her major miscalculation had been thinking she and Jón Rich were friends. She should have known that Jón Rich's only solid friendship was with his money.

The farmer looked at Thurídur, his face flushed in annoyance. He'd brought his cow all this way on her word.

Thurídur gazed back at him. "Don't promise the cow before tomorrow morning," she asked the farmer, knowing he'd immediately start looking for another potential buyer.

He assessed her steady, determined face. "I'll not refuse if a buyer comes forth," he said after some consideration. "For it has not proved well to trust you." Thurídur unflinchingly returned his gaze. They both knew how hard it was to secure the price of a cow. "Yet, I won't offer the cow for sale tonight," he conceded. He'd give her that. He then told her where he would stay at the farm of a friend.

"I thank you for that," Thurídur replied. This time she wouldn't let him down. This time she'd go to a real friend.

That evening Thurídur did the chores as usual, ate supper, and waited until the others had gone to sleep. Then she stealthily stole from her bed, put on her clothes, tiptoed to the door, and crept out, closing the door silently behind her. Across meadows lit by spring's undiminishing light, she walked quickly east toward Gaulverjabaer.

Despite the late hour, she knocked on the door. "I need Pastor Jakob's help," she said when a servant opened it. "Do you think he could see me?"

Since it was Thurídur, they'd wake him and see.

Pastor Jakob dressed immediately and came down.

Thurídur explained what had happened and her dilemma. Would he consider lending her money for a cow? Otherwise she'd lose not only a cow but the goodwill of their eastern neighbor.

Pastor Jakob studied her a long moment. Thurídur deserved better than this. And as it turned out, he'd been exploring a new venture to increase his already healthy wealth, one in which Thurídur's timing could hardly be better. Or at least that's how he presented it to her.

"I'll give you an opportunity for that," he said. "I'll lend you the price of the cow"—he paused, watching her carefully—"if you'll be captain this winter on an eight-oared boat that I intend to have built."

Thurídur sat in silence a moment digesting the implications of what Pastor Jakob had just said. It was a responsibility for which she was long overdue. She'd skippered smaller autumn and spring boats for years, but not winter boats, the ones with honor, where captains got paid one and a half shares instead of the deckhand's usual one.[5] She was almost forty; men much younger and with much less reputation became winter captains all the time. But she was a woman. Pastor Jakob, clear-sighted enough to realize Thurídur was the best captain he could possibly find, had decided he'd trust a woman leading his valuable winter boat—but not just any woman. He'd trust Thurídur.

Her decision didn't take long. "I'll try that," she told Pastor Jakob. In slightly disingenuous modesty, she added, "If men dare row with me." They both knew perfectly well crews would clamor to work with her.

The sole person sure to be displeased with this new arrangement was Jón Rich. He'd not only lose his best deckhand, who made him so much money, he'd have to face Thurídur competing directly with him at sea—on a boat that was bigger than his. What would happen was anyone's guess.

10

COMMANDING
TURBULENCE

1816

After Pastor Jakob lent her the money, Thurídur strode meditatively home through the early morning light—at this time of year, dark made only a fleeting and twilight appearance. She had a lot to consider. Clearly best that Jón Rich not learn of her new role until she had a crew in place; otherwise he'd try to interfere as much as he could. She'd have to step very carefully.

She arrived at Gata just as Ingibjörg was getting up. Thurídur was always an early riser, so no one noticed that she'd even been away. The weather fine for fishing, Jón Rich would be expecting her to wake him as usual so he could be on the water before anyone else. But this morning, she first had other business.

She found the farmer from the east and paid him. Jón Rich had broken his word, but she'd kept hers—thanks to Pastor Jakob. She led the cow back to Gata, then walked over to West Peathouse to wake Jón Rich for fishing.

When he emerged, he looked angrily at the sun already well up in the sky, then even more angrily toward the sea, where he saw boats on the water ahead of him.

"Why have you woken me so late?" he demanded. "Other boats have already gone out. You know I should always be the first!"

"More people than you like to sleep in the morning," Thurídur replied blandly.

Hah, Jón Rich thought. She overslept. It never occurred to him what his actions the previous evening had now set in play.

Jón Rich was pleased. It had ended up being a good fishing day—even with their late start. He'd leave his very capable crew to secure his boat while he returned to West Peathouse. Thurídur could see to dividing, cleaning, and stacking the fish. She always did.

But Thurídur did more than that. She quickly cleaned her fish share; then, as was her usual habit, she sauntered along the shore chatting with other crews.[1] But now she chatted with purpose. Having watched carefully over the years, she'd noted the best deckhands as well as captains. As she ambled in seemingly aimless sociability, she quietly approached those she considered excellent, covertly asking their interest in joining her on a new eight-oared boat next winter season.

Because she always wandered around like this, no one noticed. She asked tall, lanky Bjarni Helgason of Heysholt farm, who immediately accepted. She invited others, including the sixteen-year-old Jón Egilsson, shy and withdrawn, but whom she spotted as a capable hard worker. She invited several women including Ingibjörg—the lone member of Jón Rich's crew she approached—and Ingibjörg's younger friend Sesselja. On her own boat, she would always encourage women.[2]

It seemed that despite any modesty shown to Pastor Jakob, she had absolutely no trouble collecting a good crew of eager deckhands. Those she approached knew well enough to keep their mouths shut—why jeopardize a sterling opportunity? In this close-knit and gossip-laden community—somewhat amazingly—no one else heard even a whisper of her activities.

The final day of the fishing season arrived. Jón Rich prepared for this traditionally celebratory time with pleasure. In a season of excellent weather, he'd done better than anyone—as usual.

He called his crew to his warehouse, now well stocked with dried fish, to offer them the customary shot of congratulatory brennivín.[3] This is when he'd also invite them to renew their contracts for the next winter season—expecting them all to accept. Where else would they do better? He'd keep everyone—except the seventeen-year-old Sigurdur Gottsvinsson. A withdrawn young man, Jón Rich decided he was better off without him—especially with the dubious reputation of Sigurdur's parents, Gosi and Kristín.

Stunningly handsome, tall, and well built, with curly dark locks to his shoulders,[4] Sigurdur was the son of the equally handsome, generous, and popular fifty-three-year-old Gottsvin "Gosi" Jónsson, who captained a boat out of Thorlákshöfn and lived on a farm a bit east and inland from Stokkseyri. In a society where a man's ability to hold his liquor was an admirable trait, Gosi was one of the best. He could also throw up at will, so he never passed out. When he drank, he did often become violent—although even then never toward the weak and wretched. People suspected—were fairly certain—Gosi stole things, lots of things, even sheep, a capital offense. His nickname, Gosi, was short for Gottsvin and also meant knave, a moniker that seemed to suit him. No one turned him in because—well, turning someone in to the Danish authorities was a pretty horrible thing to do, inviting potential torture, imprisonment, and even death.

Everyone overall liked Gosi and, truth be told, was also rather afraid of him. His favorite phrase when he was pleased—"I'm fine, man alive!"—was known by most everyone.[5] Also, his thievery "ethics" of never taking from the poor, his cleverness, and his generosity earned him a certain amount of respect.

In one account, one of his teenage half-share deckhands came to him during the Thorlákshöfn winter fishing season asking for help. He'd stolen a small cask of brennivín, and with the authorities now conducting a hut-to-hut search, he had no idea what to do; if they discovered it, things would go badly for him.

Seeing that the boy was very embarrassed as well as terrified, Gosi took pity on him. "He should not steal who knows not how to conceal," he told him in admonishing verse. "But bring the cask here."[6]

When the boy did, Gosi dunked it into a vat of whale oil. Then he set it beside the door where, now smelling strongly of oil, it stood when the authorities came searching. No one paid any attention, assuming it contained whale oil.

When Gosi finally allowed the boy to take the oil-scented cask, he made him promise never to steal again—and it was said he never did. The same, however, could not be said for the clever Gosi.

He and his wife, Kristín, had several children, all handsome and smart. Many locals blamed much of Gosi's bad behavior on Kristín, but Thurídur retorted to this that people were just prejudiced because no one knew which of the farmhands on Kristín's parents' farm had been her real father.[7] But then, Thurídur often took a contrary position on these kinds of things.

Still, their son, Sigurdur, Jón Rich decided, he was better off without.

With a broad grin, he called his crew into his warehouse—except Sigurdur, whom he told to stand outside. Then he handed around the celebratory shots of brennivín, passing a shot to Sigurdur through the doorway.

"I hope such good of you all," he said, raising a toast to them, "that you will remain with me for the next season. Except for Sigurdur. I don't want to carry him in my boat."[8]

Thurídur—presumably after tossing back her shot—glared at Jón Rich. Everyone looked at her. She was the one who called out injustice on their behalf. "You don't want to carry Sigurdur, the best fisherman?" she yelled.

"No," Jón Rich replied. "He loses every other fish that touches him." He paused. "But what say the rest of you?" He waited confidently for a response. Universal affirmation would now promptly follow.

His crew glanced at Thurídur, letting her speak first. Previous years, she'd always replied quickly in the affirmative, with the rest following her lead.

But this year she said nothing, just stared out the door where Sigurdur now sat, his deep-blue eyes clouded, his shoulders reflecting his anger and dismay. Jón Rich's boat with Thurídur was the best opportunity in the region.

The silence stretched. No one said a word, all staring at Thurídur as she said nothing at all. Finally, she turned to Jón Rich, her face calm but her intense eyes shooting their telltale sparks.

"Because you did not lend me the price of the cow," she said, "it has now come to this that I must leave you." She then explained how Pastor Jakob had loaned her the money in exchange for her becoming winter captain of his new eight-oared boat. Jón Rich's boat was only a six-oar.

The whole space paused in stunned silence—except perhaps the chokes of various crewmates on their brennivín. After a long moment, one of them slowly got to his feet.

"I'll go with you, Thurídur," he said.

"Me too," said another.

One by one, crew members echoed them. "I'll go," they each said. "Since Thurídur is going."

Jón Rich stared at them all, his mouth agape. Finally, he recovered his voice. "This is the worst trick you could have played on me!" he shouted at Thurídur.

Thurídur looked at his inflamed face and laughed. He'd done it to himself.

As she walked away, other crew members caught up to her, offering again to join her crew.

Thurídur paused and smiled at them. These were her friends, a tight team—being at sea together did that. "I have no wish to hire crew members away from Jón Rich," she said gently but firmly. "That I will not do. I have hired all my crew already to make sure I take no one from him." Except Ingibjörg. But Ingibjörg wouldn't have stayed without Thurídur anyway.

Thurídur briskly walked back to Gata. Captain Thurídur. Finally.

Jón Rich was so angry he could spit. The winter fishing season was now well underway; his boat now fishing without Thurídur, and she going out with her new crew had resulted in her now catching as much as he was, if not more.

He slogged through the snowdrifts toward his farmhouse, past East Peathouse, where his friend Sigrídur Hannesdóttir lived—the one with the same beautiful name as all his daughters.

He paused. Perhaps Sigrídur could help him....[9]

He stopped by her farm and told her his woes with Thurídur, how she'd betrayed him, undermining his standing with his crew. How he had to encounter her now, out there each day on the sea, humiliating him.

Sigrídur was sympathetic. Why is not clear—perhaps she disapproved of Thurídur's wearing trousers, or perhaps she just believed her friend Jón Rich's side of the story without question. Regardless, she and Jón Rich devised a plan together for his vengeance; in a time-honored tradition, they would do it through verse.

Before and right after Iceland came under Danish rule in the 1300s, the country produced a body of remarkable literature called the Icelandic sagas. About the political and physical fights, love trysts, power plays, and betrayals among various people and families during the country's four hundred previous years of independence, many of these sagas, peppered with verse, were passed down both orally and through written word, generation after generation for hundreds of years. They brought vibrancy and validity to the retention of Icelanders' language and[10] helped keep their sense of a spiritual self alive through centuries of physical, social, and economic oppression.

Icelandic society as a whole placed a huge emphasis on verse; some farmers memorized thousands of poems and dozens of sagas.[11] Composing verse was a national pastime, applauding, commenting on, or mocking everything; Icelanders created verse about the weather (always the weather), fishing captains, their neighbors, scandals, tragedy, faith, and love.[12] Being a good poet, a *skáld*, was— besides being a winter fishing captain—one of the most respected abilities an Icelander could have. Everyone who could played with verse, even the poorest of poor farmhand.

Verses were also used as powerful weapons to curse or to publicly shame or humiliate one's enemies. And this is exactly what Sigrídur and Jón Rich decided to do: produce verse meant to mortify, the kind called the same word (*niðkveðlingar*) that in olden days meant a curse of placing a horse's head on a stake to exact revenge.[13]

Together they devised malicious verses viciously mocking not only Thurídur but her entire crew. To make sure he had plenty, Jón Rich got others to write additional ones—for which he must have paid something. He'd show Thurídur what humiliation felt like. Her crew would quit, and she'd have to stop being a captain.

A week later. Dense gray clouds hung close above people's heads, a flat sea, but bitter cold. To those nearby watching Captain Thurídur and her crew busily pull in their catch, it was obvious she was doing well.

Suddenly they all heard a shout from Jón Rich's boat.

"Bjarni, Bjarni Helgason!" someone shouted in verse. "Like a long, skinny shoelace, he's a knitting needle case!" A knitting needle case was not only embarrassingly skinny but used by women, a demeaning insult.[14] Then came another verse:

> *Jón Egilsson, that impotent tool,*
> *just adds weight where he sits.*

Eyjólfur Jónsson, quarrelsome fool,
all know he's not long on wits![15]

Across the calm sea, laughter reverberated. It was clear to everyone that young Jón Egilsson was hopelessly besotted with Captain
Thurídur. This was unexpected entertainment.

Then "Kristófer, Kristófer, Cranky Kristófer!" naming another
crew member.

Insulting nicknames flew, citing every one of Thurídur's crew,
all in shouted verse. The laughter increased. "Famine, Ruin, Spider
Dust, Coward, Boring!" Cackling mirth echoed from all sides as
people stopped their fishing to listen and quickly memorize these
witty insulting verses they could then let fly far and wide, repeated
incessantly for the pleasure of most everyone—except those who
were the butt of this verse-crafted harassment.

A second boat joined Jón Rich's, also shouting in verse across
the water, "Sulky, Stupid, Scribe!" A man sitting inside, a scribbling
scribe, was a weakling who couldn't do anything useful, by definition
a lousy fisherman.

All around, roars of laughter rolled from boat to boat. Then yet
another verse got shouted out.

"Thurídur Sheep Stub!" Meaning Captain Thurídur, small and
insignificant, led her crew by the stub of her tiny—and dirty—
sheep's tail. Only the most incompetent crew would let themselves
be led that way.

What in the Devil's name was this? It took little speculation. Jón
Rich's vengeance.

In humiliated fury, Thurídur's crew pulled in their lines. This
is unendurable, they told her. If you can't stop them, we'll leave.

Verses like this would spread and be repeated by everyone, for weeks, months—even years.

Thurídur, her eyes bright with anger, observed and considered. These verses insulted not only her crew but herself as captain for having chosen such deficient deckhands. They were being shouted from several boats. How did everyone learn them? Then she saw sheets of paper. Someone had actually written down the verses. This took planning, especially since not that many could write, let alone afford paper—except Jón Rich. A good idea to distribute them around, but foolhardy, since a paper version provided undeniable traceable evidence.

Once on shore, Thurídur got someone she trusted, very possibly Ingibjörg, to obtain the copied sheets. These in hand, she walked through a winter's darkening afternoon twilight the few miles to Gaulverjabaer to visit her new employer, Pastor Jakob. Any insult to her was now an insult to him. It also threatened his new, lucrative income.

She told him the events, then showed him the written verses.

Pastor Jakob read them in silence. Talking with grieving widows may not have been his forte, but this he could handle.

He immediately gathered those involved at Jón Rich's farmhouse for one of his signature mediation meetings lasting late into the night. People said everyone there left in peace—or at least they stayed silent afterward. As usual, no one revealed the details. But the papers got burned, the insulting versing stopped, supposedly—or at least publicly—forgotten.[16]

Deputy Jón Rich had not managed to exact revenge on Thurídur. Not yet, anyway.

11

INTIMATE BLACKMAIL

1819

Thurídur checked out the weather. Life wasn't bad. She was sharing the sea with some excellent winter captains, including her friend Gamlason, who'd become a winter captain a few years ago—to no complaints from Jón Rich despite Gamlason also having been one of his best deckhands who now competed with him directly at sea.

Come spring season, Thurídur would also be skippering a six-oared spring boat owned by "Student" Sigurdur Sívertsen, the main clerk at the Eyrarbakki merchant store, an Icelander using a Danish spelling for his last name.[1] She laughed softly. Everyone quite liked Student, who got his nickname because, unlike most Icelanders not headed for the Church, he'd managed to get a formal education in Reykjavík and even completed secondary school.

In his midtwenties, Student was a small, modest man with delicately pretty features; most people considered him—unlike the shop's Danish owner, Niels—reliable and reasonably honest. Thurídur was glad he'd managed to buy a boat and was pleased to be skippering for him. About ten years ago, he'd gone through a very bad patch.

At the time, rumors had flown that while the detested Niels was cavorting in Copenhagen, where he, like the other Danish merchants, spent his winters, his wife, Stína, whom he left behind supposedly to keep an eye out for the rampant nighttime stealing, was "on overfriendly terms"[2] with not just Student but his second clerk as well, also an Icelander.

Then Niels got sick in Copenhagen, not expected to live.[3] When Stína then got pregnant with no Niels in sight for months, things got messy. Pregnancy outside marriage was one thing, but cuckolding a Danish merchant was a different matter, unlikely to turn out well for any Icelander involved.

Using desperate subterfuge, the three hired a married woman to be the pretend mother, only to be found out when a farmer in the know, after getting annoyed with Student over a sales negotiation, blasted out his covert knowledge for anyone in the shop to overhear. Gossip now swiftly exploded. Stína had apparently told the second clerk that if Niels died, she'd marry him—giving a strong indication of the child's actual father.

Student's immediate claim of paternity fell on dubious ears. He was too modest. Despite the gossip, few really believed he'd have an affair with his Danish employer's wife. Also, the person Stína wanted to marry was the other clerk, not him—and since two people who'd committed adultery were never afterward permitted to wed, any marriage between Stína and the child's father was now impossible regardless of what happened to Niels. Most decided Student was just exceptionally loyal to his friends.

Unfortunately, word of these events soon reached the desk of one of Iceland's two vice governors, who immediately summoned Pastor Jakob to discuss the matter—not at all good. Very concerned for the parishioners he'd now been shepherding for several years, Pastor Jakob stopped by Deputy Jón Rich's to ask his advice on how best to approach this.

Ah, Jón Rich told him, he had just the thing. Instead of giving Pastor Jakob legal advice, he pulled out what he called his "lucky" flask of brennivín. Pastor Jakob glanced at him. This was an odd response. Jón Rich wasn't a drinker. Also, the offering seemed an uncharacteristic act of generosity on Jón Rich's part.

"Take this with you," Jón Rich said. "It's never failed me when I've had it with me."[4]

Pastor Jakob took the flask with him. Whether he ever offered a drink to the vice governor is not recorded, but since Stína was fined sixteen and a half Danish state dollars and the "father"—aka Student—eighty-one shillings, hefty fines but far less than the penalty most expected, perhaps a drink or two softened the vice governor's judgment.[5] The timing also likely helped, as in 1809 when this case came up, a Danish man turned English decided with the help of a few others to liberate Iceland from Danish rule.[6] The scheme proved short-lived, but it meant the vice governor had bigger concerns on his plate than adultery in some rural community—luckily for Stína and self-effacing Student.

Pastor Jakob and Elín decided they'd add the infant to their growing brood of foster children. Niels did not die—unfortunately, in many people's opinion—but Stína and the second clerk decamped to some other part of Iceland. Student stayed at the store, where he hired as his assistant clerk young Ari Jónsson,[7] Gamlason's clever son, who'd early shown more interest in shopkeeping than fishing.

Student was teaching him the merchant trade—at which he already showed quite the aptitude. Even though Gamlason, and by extension Ari, had a well-connected family, Student was offering Ari an incredible chance to change his life.

Overall, Student had managed to come out of the whole debacle as gracious and smelling fragrant as wild thyme. All the more reason to make skippering for the man a good idea for Thurídur.

For winter Thurídur had a great group of deckhands—or most of them. Her stalwart crew of Sesselja, Jón Egilsson, and Ingibjörg, who'd recently had a child she'd named Thórdís with Sesselja's brother Jón Grímsson, remained with her. More recently, she'd hired three Kolbeinsson brothers.[8]

Thurídur smiled with affection. The two older boys, strong workers, were already becoming her friends. The youngest not so much; he was rather weak, an odd one. She took him mostly to help out. Not that the others were perfect of course.

The eldest brother, Haflidi Kolbeinsson, handsome, smart, and artistic, had at twenty-three already got himself into a bit of trouble. Medium tall with blue eyes, dark brown hair, and a beard,[9] he'd worked as a teenage farmhand at the Big Lava farm for the same wealthy Magnús who during the Great Flood had tried unsuccessfully to convince the stubborn old man to leave his bed. When Magnús had died, his daughter Ingunn, who had inherited the farm, continued to employ Haflidi as a farmhand.[10] When Ingunn suggested marriage, the nineteen-year-old Haflidi was not at all opposed, especially since she now had so much property.

Then Ingunn's young adult daughter got pregnant—by Haflidi.

Furious, Ingunn kicked him out and invited another man, Kristófer, to farm her large property. Since then, Haflidi had taken various jobs and written poetry about his troubles.

He'd made a mistake, but he clearly hadn't meant to hurt anyone; he just liked the daughter—who was, after all, his own age—better than the mother. He worked well at sea, and Thurídur liked him.

The second brother, equally handsome eighteen-year-old Jón Kolbeinsson, a bit shorter than his older brother, also had dark brown hair and a beard, but his eyes were smaller and brown.[11] A good poet like their father, he was "diplomatic,"[12] well liked, and philosophic, with a deep intellect Thurídur appreciated. A nearby farmer, "Woodsmith" (*rennismíður*) Jón, who'd imported a lathe from Denmark—then very rare in Iceland—had taken the teenage "Poet" Jón under his wing and taught him to make spinning wheels, something Poet Jón now did quite profitably on Sundays, working still as a farmhand during the week. When Woodsmith Jón's attractive daughter and Poet Jón[13] got engaged, it seemed the young man's life was looking as rosy as one could hope.

The youngest brother was Thorleifur Kolbeinsson. "Small,"[14] slow to mature, and weak due to bouts of ill health, most locals considered him "miserable-looking," with none of the strength or charms of his older brothers, unlikely to "come to much." He did have one interesting trait: second sight, just like their poet father.

At a very young age Thorleifur had begun telling people his dreams he considered prophetic, if a bit self-serving. At about nine years old, he dreamed he was wearing Jón Rich's red waistcoat, which he was sure foretold he would someday be a wealthy deputy. His father pointed out that this was ridiculous, since Thorleifur was never going to be a deputy or rich.[15]

As a young teen, Thorleifur told people that in another dream he'd found a very good gold ring on the ring finger of his left hand given to him by a man named Jón Woodsmith. No one with that name lived nearby, but when a Jón Woodsmith moved in about a year later, Thorleifur decided the dream meant he was going to marry the man's daughter. Given his "ill-dressed" poverty and small stature, people dismissed Thorleifur's interpretation, noting he was not a desirable match for anyone. After his more attractive older brother Poet Jón got engaged to the daughter, even Thorleifur admitted his interpretation was very unlikely, deciding it instead "heralded his brother's betrothal."[16]

Oh well, Thurídur considered. Even if Thorleifur wasn't such a great deckhand, the rest of them were. She could afford to be generous.

Overall, winter season weather had been dreadful, terrible conditions with winds often blowing from the southeast across the open ocean. But today looked perhaps "not completely hopeless to row," so Thurídur's crew sat grumpily around her Gata fishing hut, listening to blasts of sleet, trying to avoid water dripping through the roof, playing games to pass the time.[17] Along the shore at other fishing huts, crews were doing the same, sitting around waiting, hoping for a weather change.

Thurídur now often rowed out and landed through a channel called Mouse Passage (*Músarsund*) just east of Stokkseyri.[18] A straight, narrow channel to the sea, it provided quick access to fishing grounds particularly to the east; it required dragging one's boat over a skerry reef that cut into the shore, but meant she got to the fishing grounds very fast. On the return, she waited for high tide to drag the now heavy, fish-laden boat back over the reef, making it almost float across.

In the hut, Thurídur cocked her head and listened. Then she slowly stood. Everyone else looked up as she quickly pulled on her sea clothes and slipped out the door.

The short day's light lent a dull gleam to the snow, the heavy, sleet-laden sky seeming a mere few feet above her head. She waded swiftly through sloppy wet drifts along the deserted shore to a point where she could see Mouse Passage and the ocean beyond.

Was that a swarm of small capelin, krill, and sand eel (*silferð*)[19] she saw making a froth along the water's surface?

Yes, it was, masses of them—indicating lots of larger fish swimming behind trying to gobble them up. If she got out there soon, they'd have a field day. She narrowed her eyes, sharp and awake, "melting" the weather, as it was called, meaning being able to see through it. Then she strode back through the sleet to her fishing hut, where she quickly roused her crew to action. They were heading out. Now.

Her crew pulled on their sea clothes and grabbed their tackle. Through sheets of sleet, they dragged the boat over the skerry reef into Mouse Passage and set off. As they rapidly rowed through the channel and put out their lines, the sleet stopped; they'd hit a break. Amid masses of fish, they filled the boat in no time.

Meanwhile at other fishing huts, captains, hearing the break in the sleet and emerging to take a look, were very surprised to see a boat already at the fishing grounds. Jón Rich's annoyance can only be imagined.

Some other boats dashed out, trying to catch the break that was sure to be short. The first of them passed Thurídur returning to shore with a full load. More than full. They'd caught so much they were dragging extra fish behind them.

Unload fast, Thurídur commanded her crew. With the weather still holding, they could maybe make another trip.

They did.

But the window of calm was closing fast. After a short time, Thurídur told them to stop, that it was time to head in. Quickly they pulled in their lines, set the oars, and headed for Mouse Passage, surfing into the channel.

By the time they landed—with more than double the catch of anyone else—the sea had again become impassable. As they processed their quantities of fish, Thurídur's crew looked at each other and smiled. Indeed, they were lucky to work for her. With her keenly observant eyes and startling weather-reading ability, their Captain Thurídur had seen what no one else had: both the coming weather break and the swarms of small surface fish. As immortalized in verse,

> Thurídur sees a sudden shift of the sea
> her answer flies forth, "Men to oars!"
> then onto water so fast you can see
> a slash in the strand their keel scores.[20]

Thurídur sighed, her chest a mixture of happiness and loss. Ingibjörg was leaving, the dear friend who'd helped her build up Gata over these last eight years and who'd been beside her at sea for sixteen seasons, first as a fellow deckhand on Jón Rich's boat, then on her own crew for winter and spring.

Ingibjörg and the affianced father of her child, Jón Grímsson, were finally getting married. They could do it because her fiancé's mother, who'd managed their large Tradarholt farm since her husband died several years before, had decided to pass it along to him, making him head of household—and able to marry.[21] Ingibjörg would move during May Moving Days with a wedding planned for November. An excellent match, Thurídur admitted. Ingibjörg now had her own farm to look after—and she was pregnant again. As an added benefit, the two seemed deeply in love.

Still Thurídur felt the loss of her friend beside her. Perhaps this was how her brother felt when she'd left to live with Jón Ólafsson so many years before, or Pastor Jakob when she'd left there. Experience and age bring insights. Even with a serving woman looking after ten-year-old Thórunn,[22] she could hardly manage and work Gata alone.

Just in time, a welcome farmhand applicant appeared in the form of her twenty-year-old deckhand Jón Egilsson.[23] Although a bit quiet, Jón Egilsson was strong, an excellent worker. And she knew him; after all, he'd been her deckhand for four years. He'd make a more than acceptable farmhand. His timing was perfect.

Working beside him was not like working with Ingibjörg, but overall it was not bad either. Thank God he'd shown up. Doing this work alone, even on a small farm like Gata, was impossible. The hardest labor—scything, stacking, and storing hay—needed someone as strong as she was. And she liked Jón Egilsson. Things could be much worse. Life seemed almost rosy.

Until Jón Egilsson proposed.

What was he thinking? Everyone knew he adored Thurídur, but really? Jón Egilsson was barely an adult, she an experienced forty-three-year-old. The twenty-three-year age difference wasn't that big a deal; many men married much older women, often widows who owned or held the leasehold of a farm—look at Haflidi and Ingunn, an older woman he would have married, if he hadn't gotten her daughter pregnant. Such matches helped both parties, the woman getting assistance on the farm and the man escaping being someone's farmhand for the rest of his life.[24] For Jón Egilsson it was a step upward with a woman he'd admired for years.

But for Thurídur, no way. She wasn't a widow, and she'd got this farm by herself, without a man. More to the point, after Erlendur she had promised herself that she'd never get ensnared in such a relationship again. She'd leased Gata alone and spent the last eight years improving it. If she married Jón Egilsson—not that she intended to—he would, as a man, then hold the leasehold. By law, it would be his.[25] So no. Absolutely not. The idea was absurd.

Jón Egilsson may have been quiet, but he was stubborn—and determined. He didn't give up. In late summer, just as haying was at its peak, when any farmer most needed help and long after May when one could contract new farmhands, Jón Egilsson tried his new gambit: if Thurídur didn't agree to marry him, he'd leave—immediately, regardless of any fine or punishment for breaking his farmhand contract.

If a game of chess, this was his check. She could marry him or he'd leave. Alone she'd have to scythe all the hay, stack it, store it, milk the cow, slaughter animals for winter eating, stable the rest—in addition to skippering an autumn fishing boat. Physically impossible. If she didn't get the hay cut and stored, there wouldn't be enough food for her animals. Without winter food they'd starve. Without animals, she and Thórunn wouldn't have food either. It was blackmail of the most intimate kind.

12

CHOICES OF CONSEQUENCE

1820–1822

For his blackmail-laced persuasion, Jón Egilsson chose the very best time to do it.

Thurídur considered her options. Although legally Jón Egilsson would be head of household if they married, the situation was very different from when she'd lived with Jón Ólafsson or Erlendur, then in her early twenties. Now she was experienced, a respected fishing captain with standing, used to being in charge. She also genuinely liked Jón Egilsson. He was not a mean person—he just wanted her in a way she didn't want him. She could not do the farm work without him. She had no one else.

After these calculations, Thurídur gave in. Or so it seemed. On October 31, 1820, she and Jón Egilsson got married, rather ironically a month before Ingibjörg, even though she had been engaged much longer.

But Thurídur had her own tricks up her sleeve. She had agreed to marriage—but when the time came, she did not agree to sex. She could be blackmailed into one, but not the other. And by the time they married, the haying was finished, Jón Egilsson on her boat for winter season with a contract that if broken carried heavy legal penalties.[1] Winter fishing season ended in May, when she could hire herself a new farmhand. He could then move; she'd even help him find a new place.

Sorry, Jón. Checkmate.

In no time, everyone had learned about Thurídur and Jón Egilsson's intimate activities—or lack thereof. Poor Jón Egilsson. He seems not to have considered this aspect of his notion of blackmail marriage. People composed verses, too juicy a subject to ignore, leaving Jón Egilsson to endure snarky snickering behind cupped hands, becoming a tense and humiliating winter season for him, working every day as Thurídur's deckhand with all the other crew knowing exactly what was—or more precisely not—happening.[2] Silly young fool.

Now Jón Egilsson's manipulation of contracts turned back to bite him—he had the same problem as anyone else when they wanted to leave either a marriage or farm contract; they had to find another farm to take them. But Thurídur was as motivated to help him leave as he was.

Finally, in May, Bjarni's widow, Margrét, and her new husband, Gudmundur Jónsson (this new marriage seeming to go much better than her previous one with Bjarni), came through with a farmhand placement. Thank God. Jón Egilsson could leave and work for them.[3] A good solution for all.

Jón Egilsson and Thurídur managed to part on civil, even friendly terms, the same as she had done years before with Jón Ólafsson. But to replace him, she decided to hire a woman—safer that way— the thirty-year-old Sigrídur Kristófersdóttir, daughter of the same Kristófer who'd taken on Ingunn's Big Lava farm once she'd kicked Haflidi out.[4] She took over Jón Egilsson's place on the boat too. What a relief.

Overall the farming was going well. People remarked how well-maintained, prosperous, and pretty Gata was, how hard Thurídur worked, wearing her usual trousers. For social gatherings, she generally wore a skirt—over her trousers—but now added a man's tail-coat and fashionable male short top hat set above her curly red-gold hair, cut shoulder-length also in the fashionable male style.

During the spring farming, she decided to hire young Snorri Geirmundsson as a temporary laborer.[5] Timid and weak from poor health, poor Snorri had had a hard time finding a farmhand position and place to live once his parents died. Pastor Jakob, who'd been recently elevated to the powerful role of archdeacon,[6] somewhat uncharitably characterized Snorri as "subservient and simple."[7]

That assessment, Thurídur had to admit, was basically correct. Extremely frustrating, but hardly Snorri's fault if he was a bit short of smarts in his saddlebags. He was a decent person, and as a farmer she could afford to give him work, food, and shelter.

"Now snap it, Snorri!" she shouted at him in the fields. She liked the phrase, pithy, to the point. Really, he moved slower than half-dried mud. She tried to keep from smiling as she shouted again, very serious.

"Now snap it, Snorri!"

It must have been a slow news week, because others who heard Thurídur took up the saying until it became generally used, only adding to Thurídur's reputation as clever, her words "chiseled by a strong mind."[8]

Snorri's elder brother, twenty-seven-year-old[9] Jón "Shank" Geirmundsson, a very different man from his little brother, was to find his life intertwined with and even dependent on Thurídur's in some unexpected ways.

Shank had earned his nickname, and his farm had been dubbed Shank Empire, because he slaughtered horses in the autumn, smoked the meat, and sold it to poor people during the spring when they had little else to eat.[10] He paid for the horses by giving the seller the horse's hide, making his profit off the meat, which was always bony—anyone selling their horse for slaughter always starved it first, "walking it to its hide."[11] No reason to waste valuable feed.

Although this business made Shank some money, it was not deemed very honorable, since horse eating was considered deplorable.[12] Still, Shank Jón was enterprising, particularly for a man who'd never learned to write.[13] He also ran a little store selling goods he bought on credit—or perhaps stole—from the Eyrarbakki merchant house; although a "repute of theft lay upon him," most locals considered this more his father's bad influence than Shank Jón himself.

Dark hair lay thin across Shank's scalp above a high, broad forehead, his eyes blue, his face thin and pale with a long, narrow nose. Of "good intellect," he was kind if rather selfish, and "ordinarily even-tempered" although prone to dark moods and jealousy. At twenty-five, he'd married the "good-looking," intelligent twenty-three-year-old Halla,[14] "considered to know her own mind" and from a family with "a reputation for honesty." They had two children, the eldest nicknamed Sigga, whom Shank Jón loved dearly. He claimed he was never sure of the father of the younger child, even though people said the child looked like him.

Only two years into the marriage, Halla became concerned because Shank Jón was often gone at night; she had no idea where. When she confronted him, feeling "nothing good was in the wind," he gave her vague answers and continued on. As their marriage deteriorated, Halla began visiting the Eyrarbakki merchant store to talk over her problems with her friend and confidant Student Sívertsen. Although people considered this an innocent friendship, Shank Jón felt otherwise.

In the spring of 1820, a servant woman at a nearby farm gave birth to a daughter whose father she claimed to be Shank Jón. He denied it—Halla would never forgive him, and even though they weren't getting along, he wanted to keep her as his wife.

But in August, the new mother subpoenaed him. Although he still denied paternity, it now seemed pretty obvious where he'd been spending at least some of his nights. Halla left, seeking refuge with Student, who, having both the income and interest to support her, invited her to make the move permanent. She agreed, telling Shank Jón she wanted an official separation.

Shank Jón fell into depression, begging Halla to return—recognizing now how much he loved her once he'd lost her. She refused, and after the required formal mediation—where he finally admitted paternity—they legally separated at the end of August. Shank Jón's depression slid into despair.

Fire! Fire!

Racing to the scene, people saw smoke, then flames darting from

Shank Jón's Empire. Was Shank Jón still inside? Rushing to rescue him, they quickly discovered he'd barricaded the door on the inside with stones.

Shank, Shank, what have you done? This was suicide. If they couldn't burst the door open, he'd burn alive.

To no avail, the neighbors frantically pushed the door. Finally, a local farmer, his legs as large as those of an ox, known to have the strength of two sturdy men, strode up, took a running leap, and slammed himself against the door. It cracked. He slammed it again, and smoke poured out the crack. Others ran up and together they shoved in the door. Brave souls scrambled into the burning house, emerging a few minutes later dragging an almost suffocated Shank Jón. They'd saved him. But he lay a long time recovering.

Naturally people composed various verses about the event:

Hateful rages storm hard around town
the Devil speeds on,
Shank Empire burned down,
imprisoned inside, its Lord Jón.[15]

Shank Jón didn't try to kill himself again. Instead he poured himself into his businesses. The serving woman with their child moved south, where she married a kind man who accepted the girl as his own.[16] When Halla remained with Student, clearly preferring his company, no one showed much concern; she could do much worse than Student as her second husband. Shank Jón left the district; it was hard to bear such humiliation, as well as seeing Halla happily ensconced in the home of another man. But he wasn't gone for good.

Thurídur gazed around her Gata farm. She'd been here ten years, both the farming and fishing going well. Time was moving by; she was already forty-five.

It was time, she decided, for her to formally adopt ten-year-old Thórunn.[17] She was a captain now and had a farm leasehold, security that promised steady prosperity. All on her own. Thórunn would never become fully able-bodied; that was clear, even though her health had steadily improved. She needed someone to guard over her welfare for life.

Salgerdur and Kristján now had five living children besides Thórunn. They'd also just taken on a new leasehold farm at Efra-Sel—where Móri had decided to follow them, embarking on his promise to curse the family for nine generations. Salgerdur was really his best choice, since Bjarni was dead and Thurídur had no progeny for him to harass into the next generation, let alone nine.

Passersby now often saw Móri blatantly hanging around Efra-Sel, still wearing his peat-colored coat and tattered hat. Not what you might think of as a ghost, they said, but looking solid, real, almost like a living boy—except he wasn't. Not a presence anyone wanted around.[18] He still harassed people, his new specialty being to sit on the single-plank bridge that crossed the turbulent narrow Lava River between Stokkseyri and Eyrarbakki, the very same place he'd reportedly murdered Tómas two decades ago, intimidating those who wanted to cross—and providing a convenient excuse when they arrived late to either community.[19]

So Salgerdur had enough on her hands without having to care for a disabled child. Thurídur could certainly adopt her. It didn't stop Salgerdur from disliking her sister, a moot point really. Thórunn needed someone. That someone was Thurídur.

Next door, Jón Rich's reputation for stinginess continued to grow, now at the level of standard story fare[20]—seemingly the wealthier he became, the worse it got. In charge of the district's funds for the poor, he tended to just not distribute the money. When asked about this, he said, "Those who have cured shark and seaweed never need to go hungry."[21] In that, he of course had his own sparsely fed household as an example.

Beyond seldom spending money on anything—except farms—Jón Rich never let others see his cash. One evening at his West Peathouse farm while he was out, the rest of the household was discussing the weather the previous New Year's Eve[22]—days around that time were an important weather indicator for the coming year's fishing season.[23] Some argued the weather had been good, while others were positive it'd been terrible. Finally, Jón Rich's wife, Gudrídur, had had enough.

"The weather was bad on New Year's Eve," she stated definitively, "because Jón was counting money."[24]

That settled it. Jón Rich would *never* count his money in front of any visitor, and everyone got visitors New Year's Eve. Meaning the weather must have been literally impassable. No one had much to say after this. She was right.

For Jón Rich, it seemed his wealth had less and less purpose except for its accumulation. He sometimes made coffins as a side venture—not that he needed the money. For poor people, he apparently skimped on the wood, at least once using only six planks set so far apart you could see between them. Of course, many poor got buried without a coffin at all, so presumably even this was some improvement. Still.

The county commissioner (*sýslumaður*)[25] tried pushing Jón Rich about this by suggesting he buy a good stone for his own grave.

That's unlikely, Jón Rich replied. A gravestone costs money.

You could just steal one, the county commissioner retorted, immediately immortalizing the conversation in verse:

He was aggressive in life,
of his works that's said,
and that he's lying there dead
beneath a stolen gravestone.[26]

Thurídur had just been presented a very seductive opportunity. If she took it, it could change the course of her life.

Kristófer, the father of Thurídur's new deckhand, could not get along with Ingunn, a problem, since he was farming her Big Lava property. He found Ingunn too hot-tempered.[27] From Ingunn's perspective, he'd been there seven years and the place was a wreck, the farmhouse falling apart, outbuildings dilapidated; he clearly wasn't working on it at all. And he was as cold as ice.

So in the spring of 1822, Kristófer decided to move. This left Ingunn looking for someone else, someone she liked and whom she could trust to take good care of the property. She knew Thurídur both through Haflidi and through Kristófer's daughter, Thurídur's new deckhand Sigrídur. Thurídur was the perfect choice.

She approached Thurídur with her proposal. Big Lava was a large property; the person leasing it would have standing, the possibility of increased prosperity. Quite the opportunity, as well as a compliment on her assessment of Thurídur's ability to take on this large property.

Thurídur looked the place over. It had clear potential, but after years of neglect, it was as bad as Gata had been, only much bigger. The land was also not as good, wetter, and, true to its name, full of heaps of lava. An ambitious project, but it could be an excellent farm. She knew the area well, as Big Lava was very near her childhood home of Stéttir—where Bjarni's widow, Margrét, and Gudmundur still lived with Jón Egilsson as their farmhand.[28]

Thurídur considered. She loved Gata...but...it was small; she'd done as much for it as one could by now. The bigger the farm, the more stability, right? She didn't have kin to support her into her old age, but a farm could; eventually she would pass its management on to someone she trusted, stay there even after she'd stopped fishing. It'd give her a new project.

She'd go for it. Why not? An opportunity. It just needed organization and effort—and she had that.

So, never "short of daring,"[29] she left pretty little Gata for Big Lava. Sigrídur Kristófersdóttir continued to work for her at sea, but she hired her longtime deckhand Sesselja Grímsdóttir as her new farmhand.

This, she was confident, would bring her exciting new success.

She was making one of the biggest mistakes of her life.

13

THE BITTER BITE
OF REGRET

1825–1826

Thurídur could have left her new leasehold in disrepair—that's what
most people did, including Kristófer. But Thurídur was a doer. She'd
make Big Lava even better than Gata. Using her savings, she immediately rebuilt the farmhouse and began her venture of transforming
the property.[1]

But this was not Gata. The land was full of stones and needed
drainage ditches. The work required lots of laborers, and she had
to pay all of them this time—when she could even find them. Most
people ran farms with their families; having to pay non-kin made an
enormous difference in capital outlay.[2]

Her savings evaporated in no time. But, she told herself, she'd
done this before. When the fishing started, she'd refill her coffers.
Then she'd be fine.

The vagaries of nature can be as capricious as thickening mist;
during the terrible fishing year of 1822, even Thurídur made almost

nothing. Her reliance on temperamental weather failed, leaving her not only broke but now lumbered with a farm leasehold, still unable to support herself and Thórunn, let alone become prosperous.

In early spring, she had to face a harsh reality. She could no longer maintain the leasehold rent or now keep it up to even a minimum level; she'd left herself destitute. After only a year, she had no choice but to give it up.

Now Thurídur needed someplace to live. Not a leasehold, since she no longer had the resources required for that, not a farmhand under some farmer's dictate. What else could she do?

She could work alongside someone who needed help managing their leasehold. Ingunn had the perfect idea—she did feel some responsibility, since she'd talked Thurídur into this mess to begin with...and Thurídur had left her a much-improved farm. Jón Bjarnason, the brother of the man who'd fathered Ingunn's own daughter, lived almost next door at Grímsfjós farm. Getting old and tired, he could certainly use this kind of help.

Yes, he liked the idea! Thurídur and Thórunn could join him, working his leasehold together with her farmhand Sesselja.

Thurídur breathed a sigh of relief. She'd made a mistake, but this wasn't a bad outcome at all. She got along fine with Jón Bjarnason, she was still independent and still able to sustain Thórunn. Perhaps in time Jón Bjarnason would pass on his leasehold to her. Things could certainly be worse.

Meanwhile Ingunn, recognizing the large, improved Big Lava might work best being run by family, decided that Haflidi might make a decent match for her daughter despite the unfortunate way he'd begun—he was, after all, the father of her granddaughter.[3] Haflidi quickly accepted her invitation, came back, married her daughter, and, against all probability, the three got along just fine. Necessity can be a great mediator.

Thurídur looked across the meadows to nearby Stéttir farm. Was that Shank Jón Geirmundsson? Why yes, it was. He'd come back. Surprising and not surprising really; this was his home regardless of humiliation. Adultery was pretty common, and desperate people tried suicide far too often—just not so dramatically.

It turned out that Shank Jón had taken over half the Stéttir lease-hold, sharing it with Margrét and Gudmundur. Jón Egilsson was still a farmhand with them—that had worked out well.[4] Shank had kept custody of Sigga, now a young girl about Thórunn's age. He had also quickly found himself a new wife named Kristín—that must help the sting of seeing Halla now married to Student when Shank went to the merchant store.[5] All resolved, it seemed.

Except... An observant Thurídur noted all was not well at the new Shank Jón household. Kristín clearly resented her stepdaughter from Shank's previous marriage, especially since Shank Jón so obviously adored the girl. An echo of his lost Halla?

Over the weeks, in an all too common dynamic of a new wife—or husband—rejecting stepchildren, Thurídur saw Kristín's animosity only intensify.[6] Poor Sigga, the innocent who bore the brunt of all this.

Thurídur's gaze turned pensive. She liked being around children. Thórunn still lived with her, but with children, Thurídur felt the more she had around the better. She remembered Deputy Einarsson's daughter Margrét, of whom she'd become so fond, now no longer a child but grown to a young woman who'd become an adult friend. And poor Deputy Einarsson, Thurídur thought, recently retired and gone totally blind; such a kind man. He'd lived a good life, but she didn't expect he had much longer. He was lucky he had his much younger wife caring for him.

Her thoughts returned to the girl next door. She might just head over to Shank Jón's to visit little Sigga. She could even take some kind of gift or treat; children always loved treats. Cow bones, some shells, or sheep bones? These were often used as toys at the time to represent farm animals.[7] She would think of something.

Treats!

Sigga was ecstatic with her gifts—and with Thurídur.

I can come anytime, Thurídur told a pleased Shank Jón. It was clear how her visit brought light to the face of his dear Sigga.

This was a good idea, Thurídur thought as she returned to Grímsfjós. She could give Sigga some relief from her home life once in a while and enjoyment for herself too. Shank Jón wasn't a bad person at all, she decided. Archdeacon Jakob deemed his behavior "varied" although quick to adjust when reprimanded.[8] Perhaps he'd learned from his mistakes with Halla.

After a few months, Shank Jón came to visit Thurídur. He was going away for a few days on business, he told her. Could she look after Sigga while he was gone? They both knew the child wouldn't fare well alone with Kristín.

Of course, Thurídur replied. She'd be delighted. The farming with Jón Bjarnason had just gotten better. She'd lost Big Lava and Gata, true, but Thórunn was doing well. This life was more than manageable—especially with the added benefit of periodic visits with Shank Jón's daughter next door.

Thurídur stood outside the farmhouse, lost for a moment in remembrance of her pleasant years living with Deputy Einarsson and his lively large family. He'd just passed away, a loss to their community even if he'd been old and ready for God. It had been a bit startling that a mere four months after his death, his widow had already remarried. Well, he had been much older than his wife, who'd been taking care of him for several years now—sometimes grief arrived during the months and even years while a beloved person slipped away in life, their physical death an unspoken relief. A widow has to look after herself. Hopefully she'd find stability in her new relationship.[9]

Thurídur's thoughts turned to a troubling new concern. An Ólafur Jónsson had recently begun slandering and threatening her through his speech and writings.[10] As Ólafur lived right next to her sister Salgerdur, it was no great mystery where his opinions might come from.

Thurídur considered; she could sue this Ólafur, following the example of others who sued for all kinds of things. Three years ago Shank Jón had sued a man who'd hit him on the head.[11] Jón Rich's neighbor Sigrídur had taken her lout of an ex-husband to court to secure her right to keep her farm.[12] Even Salgerdur's husband, Kristján, had sued some woman over a disagreement.[13] Thurídur could demand her rights as much as anyone else.

So she did.

Archdeacon Jakob, in a role becoming a major part of his duties, would mediate the case with a district deputy. She could expect a fair assessment with him. Thurídur shook her head. Archdeacon Jakob, now in his midfifties, was getting older—as was she, of course. But how he'd grown in power and wealth! Not unexpectedly really, for an intelligent, caring minister, whose benefice had included the income from huge church properties as part of his posting to begin with.

Thurídur went to mediation court and laid out her complaint. Confronted with her suit, Ólafur remained unrepentant. Sure, he'd done that. So? He'd pay his three-Danish-state-dollar fine at the end of the winter fishing season, once he had the money.

Still, he'd been made to admit and pay for his harassment. Thurídur had discovered the power of going to court.

Thurídur and Jón Bjarnason looked at each other. How could life be so cruel? Of all things to happen...the farm's landowner and heirs had, after years, suddenly decided they wanted the farm for them-selves.[14] She and Jón Bjarnason had taken excellent care of it—which was likely why owners now wanted it. Regardless, Thurídur and Jón Bjarnason were merely tenants; they had to leave.

Thurídur sat rigidly straight on the low bench outside the stone-and-turf farmhouse. Jón Bjarnason had been old and tired when she'd come two years ago. What would he do now? And what about her? She now had nothing, landless with no assets for a leasehold. Her mistake of leaving the stability of Gata loomed like a dark cloud. How precarious our lives, how quick those choices that impact us forever. She realized that this single decision, like some malignant specter joining Móri, would haunt her the rest of her life.

Her farmhand Sesselja would be all right; she was leaving anyway, getting married to twenty-five-year-old Gísli Thorgilsson. Thurídur remembered Gísli's father—one of the deckhands drowned on

Farmer Jón's boat in Thorlákshöfn in 1812.[15] Gísli was only a boy then. His mother had single-handedly managed their leasehold farm Kalastadir just at the north edge of Stokkseyri for years. But now she was getting remarried herself and moving, leaving Gísli as leaseholder—meaning he and Sesselja could marry.[16]

Thurídur shook her head. Gísli, already a fishing skipper, had a mixed reputation. His fine singing voice made him lead singer at the church, but although he was lucky at sea, his risk-taking rivaled that of Jón Rich in his younger days. He was also known for his imperious temper and for getting into confrontations.[17] Hopefully their marriage would turn out all right.

This made Sesselja no longer Thurídur's responsibility. Her major concern was Thórunn. What was she going to do about Thórunn?

Luckily, Thórunn had become relatively healthy, able to do most farm chores. And now that she was a teenager who could work as a farmhand, Thurídur could look for a position where she'd be treated well and taken care of. After a quick search, she found a farm inland from Stokkseyri. She'd visit and make sure things went all right, but it looked good.[18]

Now she had to figure out what to do for herself, in a predicament that echoed what she'd faced when looking after her mother. The humiliation of becoming a farmhand and living under some farmer's thumb was unbearable. With May Moving Days approaching fast, she was running out of time. Why had she ever left Gata?

Finally, Salgerdur's husband, Kristján, told her she could farm a section of their leasehold—in exchange for rent.[19] It was the best she could do for now.

At least it meant she was still independent. She'd start looking for something else immediately. It'd only be for a year—of that she was determined.

After living near her "husband" Jón Egilsson for five years, Thurídur and he agreed it was time for an official separation. Neither of them had any interest in blaming the other for their inept marriage, and under a recently enacted law, they could enter their reason for separation as being of "different characters," a Danish and Icelandic version of a no-fault separation—rather amazingly possible there, unlike in most European countries.[20]

Regardless of how long they'd actually lived apart, they first had to go through the motions of a mediation with Archdeacon Jakob—who knew the process was only for legal show.[21]

After he formally failed to persuade them to reconcile, they returned the next day for the official proceedings of separating "bed and table," a legal separation, although not a final divorce.

Archdeacon Jakob again presided. In the separation, Thurídur took responsibility for any debts and their mutual court fees. The man usually did this, but Jón Egilsson and she both agreed that it made sense, since Thurídur was a captain with more resources than Jón Egilsson, a mere farmhand.

After the three requisite years, they would be able to get legally divorced and leave this entire embarrassment behind. Finally.

The very next day, Archdeacon Jakob and Thurídur met for another mediation. One of Thurídur's deckhands, Gísli Ólafson, had left her crew without explanation before the end of his contract.[22]

What was he thinking? Breaking a fishing contract was serious. According to the Danish law of 1758, crew members could not leave their position before the end of the fishing season unless they had a very important reason—and the captain had to give permission. The penalty carried heavy fines or even being whipped.[23] To keep her standing as a captain, Thurídur had to take him to court; everyone would know that. Why had he done it—on one of the best boats in the area?

Deckhand Gísli gave a contradictory defense, saying both that he didn't understand he was under contract to Thurídur and at the same time that he thought their contract was over. But even though Gísli gave no credible reason for leaving, Archdeacon Jakob chose to fine him only one Danish state dollar, which Gísli agreed to pay as one sheep, a surprisingly lenient fine considering that Ólafur had paid three times this much the previous year for slandering Thurídur. Equally intriguing, Thurídur—not known for rolling over in the face of conflict—was agreeable, making no protest at all. Nor did she or Archdeacon Jakob press Deckhand Gísli for a better explanation.

All this suggests an unstated understanding, a silent consideration that both Thurídur and Archdeacon Jakob agreed to leave unrecorded, going through the formality of the mediation for the sake of propriety and law but at the same time acting with compassion toward a troubled deckhand.

Regardless of why Deckhand Gísli left, it meant Thurídur needed another deckhand—two, actually, since she was also losing Sesselja to marriage. Hiring got busy during May Moving Days.

For the coming 1826 winter season, she decided to hire Sigurdur, the son of the clever and reputedly light-fingered Gosi, the same young man Jón Rich had rejected ten years before. But that was a long time ago, and Jón Rich, in his midfifties, no longer worked at sea, instead focusing his attention solely on being a deputy and buying more farms, while he had another captain run his boat. Thurídur also hired Sigurdur's teenage stepson as a half share.[24]

Sigurdur had grown up handsomer than ever, astonishingly strong, but to those who knew him, it seemed he did not always have a complete understanding of his actions.[25] Now in his midtwenties, he often ran into trouble. A few years before, he'd worked at a farm that backed up against high, columnar basalt cliffs where ravens nested.

Icelanders considered that ravens could talk, each year having a congress to decide where to go that year. The farmer for whom Sigurdur worked felt he had a relationship with the local ravens and had them fed every day. In return, the ravens always nested in the cliffs and never attacked his sheep as they did on other farms, even if a sheep was helpless, flipped on its back. Instead, they set up an alarm, telling the farmer that his sheep was in trouble.

In late May, the day after the farmer and some other men had claimed no man alive could climb the vertical cliffs to the ravens' aerie, Sigurdur walked up to the farmer and tossed some raven chicks at his feet as undeniable proof he'd actually climbed the unscalable cliffs.

Furious, the farmer immediately fired him, clearly not what Sigurdur expected.

This had left Sigurdur adrift, searching for another farm placement. This he'd recently found by becoming the third husband of the fifty-seven-year-old Vilborg Jónsdóttir and taking over management of her farm. Later, in the odd kinds of complications familiar to blended families, Vilborg's grandson by her first husband married Sigurdur's sister.[26]

Sigurdur was, Thurídur later said, "the most powerful, strongest" man she ever hired.[27] But as deckhands, both he and his stepson were disasters. She managed to let the boy go soon after he started,[28] but Sigurdur, on a proper contract, she was stuck with for the season—contracts went both ways.

Unlike any other crew member during Thurídur's years of captaining, Sigurdur openly disrespected Thurídur and refused to take orders from her, unthinkable for a deckhand toward their captain. Overtly charming and charismatic, Sigurdur also became chummy with Thurídur's friends and best deckhands, Poet Jón and Haflidi Kolbeinsson, drawing them aside and talking to them in whispers. Soon the two brothers began to change their attitudes, becoming people Thurídur hardly recognized, these intelligent, sensitive men who'd worked with her and been her friends for years.

The next May, like Jón Rich before her, she declined to rehire Sigurdur. But, even though complicated and destructive, he was also hard to hate. Thurídur said she actually liked him, even if he "had a touch of evil."[29]

Haflidi also told her he was leaving, but in his case, it was because he'd been offered the position of skipper for the next winter season, a great opportunity. Now that he was married with a child, he had a larger household to think about. His brother Poet Jón stayed. Although Poet Jón was no longer disrespectful with Sigurdur gone, the easy comradery he and Thurídur had shared before seemed lost. A sad change. Thurídur very much liked Poet Jón Kolbeinsson.

This was a time she might have done better to consider Jón Rich's experience and follow his lead.

14

STRANGE HAPPENINGS

1825–1827

May Moving Days meant Thurídur could escape her sister and Kristján's farm. They'd exacted a heavy toll to let her stay there; she'd only lost rather than gained. But whatever the circumstances,[1] she was leaving.

Many larger farms near the seashore had small cottages (*tómthús*) without attached farms that the farmers rented out to itinerant fishing folk or laborers (*húsfólk*) in exchange for fish or other goods—an exception to the farmhand stranglehold that very few managed, since it required an independent stable income.[2] Being a fishing captain, Thurídur had this to offer.

It was a big status change, moving from the minority who managed to obtain some kind of leasehold to the landless majority meant that, in the eyes of many, she'd joined a class of lesser persons;[3] still, it was better than being a farmhand. Ingibjörg's brother-in-law, who farmed part of the extensive Tradarholt property where Ingibjörg and her husband also lived, agreed to rent to Thurídur. She was among friends—but also renting a humble cottage from the extended family of the woman who'd once been her own farmhand.

Thurídur used the Tradarholt cottage as a backup, mostly staying at the fishing hut she still had at her beloved Gata, which she never should have left. Staying at Gata, though, she had to endure Jón Rich next door, taking pleasure in her comeuppance. Even if she was commonly recognized as one of the region's best fishing captains, something he no longer did, she'd certainly lost on the farming—something at which he clearly excelled, at least at buying them. He didn't hide his delight.

Overhearing her tell a group of people how great her fishing season had been, he turned to her. "I want to give you some advice," he said in a voice loud enough for all to hear, happily digging his heel into her face. "That you start farming again so you can lose that fish. That would be solid advice."[4]

The larger Árnes County, of which Stokkseyri District was a part, was going through its own upheaval. The Danish merchant Niels had finally died,[5] not greatly lamented by most in the community. Except that his son Lambert, who inherited everything and took over the store management, proved to be an even worse merchant than his father, something no one had thought possible.[6] Single-handedly, he was destroying one of the largest merchant houses in the country.[7] Even the new Árnes county commissioner (CC) Thórdur Sveinbjarnarson called him intemperate, lazy, and selfish. Poor Student and his assistant Ari had to put up with this.

Early summer left Student and Ari almost overwhelmed, the

shop as busy as the shore during the fishing season.[8] At the end of June and into July, farmers from all over brought fish, wool, and other products to exchange for iron, cloth, corn, and timber. They stayed with friends and family in Eyrarbakki or set up tent camps near the store, hiring young boys to look after their horses, which they left on the upper moorlands. The wait for service could be three days even with Student and Ari working from six in the morning until nine in the evening, while Lambert did almost nothing.

Then there was the growing influence of CC Thórdur Sveinbjarnarson. As with all county commissioners, CC Thórdur was from Iceland's elite, inherently entitled to power and quite different from the "common folk," both in his opportunities and his perception of himself.[9] Born in 1786, he'd been homeschooled by a bishop, then gone to university in Copenhagen, where he studied philosophy and law, graduating with first class honors in 1820. He returned to Iceland, where he worked in the income office until 1822, when he received this desirable county commissioner's position, an excellent springboard for his hefty ambitions.[10]

From the start, he and Deputy Jón Rich did not get along,[11] both with dominant personalities. Even though he was now the richest man in south Iceland, Jón Rich, originally from a poor farming family, stood lower in both the administrative and social hierarchy. No matter how wealthy he got, he had neither the education nor the standing to ever become a county commissioner.

In CC Thórdur's opinion, this self-made man did not properly respect his own authority. Expecting obedience from his deputies, he admitted bluntly that he did not like Jón Rich. Jón Rich was not humble enough, didn't acknowledge that the concept of humility could be applied to him; Jón Rich wanted to be in complete control, with a tendency to look at things only one way: his way. Instead of, presumably, CC Thórdur's. For example, the district tax and poor relief information was all kept in a fancy, imported, red beaver-skin account book. When CC Thórdur, who signed off on the book entries, told Jón Rich to amend it, Jón refused.

"I do not delete nor add to this book," Jón Rich said, annoyed at being told what to do. "I will give it back to the county commissioner as is."[12]

Two men, both ambitious and accustomed to having control, were at loggerheads, while those whose lives they affected watched.

A wealthy man named Hjörtur lived at the inland Kambur (Cock's Comb) farm, set atop a hill beside a distinctive rock outcropping—the cock's comb—amid a collection of other, smaller farms. Not at all well liked,[13] the miserly Hjörtur had years before married a wealthy widow. Since he'd inherited her money when she died, everyone assumed that's how he got rich. He never remarried or had children—too cheap for that—although he always had a housekeeper.

Everyone knew Hjörtur had a large chest of money hidden somewhere. His cantankerous blind neighbor noted that Hjörtur lay on his hoard like a serpent on its gold. "It would be a good deed to take it before Hjörtur dies," he was heard to say. "Otherwise he'll walk from the grave to be with it."[14]

Beginning that autumn, it seemed that something unpleasant was in the air. No one knew exactly what it was, although at least one person had a suspicion.

Soon after the new year of 1827, neighbors noticed Sigrídur Hannesdóttir, Jón Rich's next-door friend, going to the nearby farm of another wealthy farmer, this man also a friend of hers.[15] They shut themselves up alone for a long time, talking about what, no one knew—a very odd thing to do. Even stranger, this farmer, known as being very tight with his money, gave Sigríður lots of presents when she left.

The next morning, the wealthy farmer immediately started making a new door lock, handle, and hinges. Then he built an entire new door, a very strong one reinforced with iron. Once he'd replaced the old door, he dug a hole inside the doorway and placed in it a large stone. Every evening after he'd shut and locked the door for the night, he placed the stone in front of it, making it impossible for anyone to enter or leave. He forbade anyone to move it until he himself had unlocked and opened the door each morning.

He also told everyone in his household not to tell anyone what he was doing. Unlike Archdeacon Jakob, with his late-night mediations, they did not keep their mouths shut, and soon the entire area knew what he'd done—although not why, or what secret information Sigríður had passed along to him. She'd clearly heard something and had warned him, but she wasn't telling anyone else. The locals didn't like this; it smacked of something rotten…somewhere.

Friday evening, February 8, 1827, the wind blew bitter cold, a tempest, the night ink black.[16] The people at Kambur lay asleep: wealthy Hjörtur, Hjörtur's housekeeper, a serving woman named Gróa, and Andrés, a five-year-old boy.

They awoke to the sound of someone breaking the lock to the door and smashing it open. Before the sleepers knew it, four masked intruders had seized them as they lay naked in their beds. Two men grabbed Hjörtur, tied his hands behind his back with rope, and then his legs. They next grasped the housekeeper, tied her up the same way, although not very tightly, and threw her facedown onto the floor. They laid Hjörtur on top of the housekeeper, piled hay and straw mattresses over them, and shoved heavy things—a chest and box—along the sides so the two couldn't lift the mattresses off themselves.

At the same time, another intruder tied up Gróa the same way, although not treating her too roughly in the process. "Are you men or devils?" she managed to ask.

"We are from above," one of them replied. "And we have been sent to get Hjörtur's money. Tell us where it is."

Gróa stammered that she didn't know.

"Tell us where it is," the man repeated. "Then I suppose we won't kill you."

She immediately told him that the money was buried in the dirt floor beneath the lambs at the other end of the room. "Now let me go," she said.

He did not. Instead he wrapped a bedsheet around her head, removed everything from one of the beds, and laid her on it. Then he took young Andrés, who didn't see anything because he'd been sleeping with his nightcap over his face, tied his hands but not his feet, and placed him on the bed beside Gróa.

The captives heard the intruders light lamps and search the house, smashing things as they went. Although the men didn't speak much to each other, when they did they used names of people in the neighborhood.

One of them sat beside the covered-up Hjörtur, threatening that if he didn't reveal where he'd hidden his money, he'd torture and kill him.

Hjörtur was so frightened he went catatonic and couldn't utter a word.

The other robbers intervened, telling the man beside Hjörtur that they should certainly not torture and kill Hjörtur regardless of whether he said anything or not.

After finding whatever they were going to find, the intruders turned to leave. "It's best to now set the farmhouse on fire," one of the men said.

The others demurred, saying they'd done enough.

For some time, the captives lay in fear, doing nothing, listening to the silence. When he was sure the intruders were gone, Hjörtur rolled out from under the mattresses toward a bed where he always kept a knife. This he managed to get before scrambling over to Andrés, who lay uncovered on the bed. Using the knife, Hjörtur managed with his bound hands to cut the rope from around Andrés's hands. He then asked Andrés to do the same with the rope on his own legs and to wrap a bed blanket around his naked shoulders. Once the boy did this, Hjörtur rushed out the door, his hands still bound, leaving everyone else still tied up.

Hjörtur ran through the storm to the farm next-door. Although almost nude and barefoot in the freezing and pitch-black winter night, he was too upset to notice. He yelled to the people inside, demanding they come out and immediately search for the robbers. They could not have got far! he shouted.

The farmer sent two of his laborers running out, wearing almost nothing themselves. They didn't dare go all the way to Kambur wearing so little, but Hjörtur was so insistent, they did run to wake up another closer farmer who had the sense to get dressed before he came out. He also gave the two laborers some clothes to wear so they could all go to Kambur. Hjörtur, now noticing he was freezing, stayed behind complaining that the chase after the robbers was proceeding very slowly.

Meanwhile, Andrés had untied the women's legs, and, wrapped only in blankets, they also exited—leaving poor Andrés behind. The women walked to yet a third croft nearby where the people took them in and cared for them in their state of fear and shock.

At Kambur, little Andrés remained unmoving as the lamp burned down and sputtered out. Not knowing what would happen next, he lay in the dark, alone and forgotten.

By the time the farmer and two laborers arrived, the fire had also gone out, so they couldn't even light a lamp. Andrés was by now so scared that he stayed silent, so they assumed the place was deserted and left again to bring back a light.

When they returned to search, they presumably finally discovered poor Andrés. They also found several items the robbers had left behind: a tattered woolen hat, a cloth rag, a piece of a flask, some tangled rope, and, by the door, a brand-new iron rod. Outside in the home meadow they found a hand-sewn shoe. They then returned to the Kambur farmhouse, deeming it unadvisable to chase after the robbers in the winter dark.

Hjörtur had also returned, dressed, and was now searching the farmhouse to see what remained of his money stores. "The little money I had is gone," he lamented. "It's now less than it should be. That is to be expected, as it was surely their errand to get it."

The farmer went to the women, telling them Hjörtur was now safe at Kambur, and then went home himself. But the laborers stayed with Hjörtur, who didn't want to leave but was also too frightened to stay behind alone—although this is exactly what he'd done to all the others, including the child who'd freed him. Andrés later said that this time in the dark terrified him more than when the intruders had come.

While the laborers stayed taking care of Hjörtur, he never offered them anything to eat or drink. Instead he complained. Why was no one pursuing the robbers?

The laborers listened to the raging storm, a black night not only dangerously cold but now inhabited by bandits who could easily kill them. Neither of them was about to risk those odds.

15

MALICE IS A
MANY-HEADED HYDRA

1827

In the low light of Saturday's midmorning winter dawn, one of the farmers who'd helped at Kambur rode over to CC Thórdur's farm in the interior part of Árnes County to report the robbery.[1]

This was the biggest crime CC Thórdur or anyone else in the area had ever seen. Not, CC Thórdur considered, that it was completely surprising. Fishing communities like Stokkseyri were problematic; he and other authorities all knew that.

When the fishing went well, those in these communities lived in disorder and wastefulness, knowing nothing of thrift.[2] When it didn't go well, they slid toward starvation, wandering around the countryside in uncontrolled vagabondage. They never thought to take on new occupations, just got used to idleness. This went on generation after generation. This was why authorities had to keep the common people in farm servitude. Otherwise they'd go rushing to the sea doing whatever they wanted.

CC Thórdur had his servant saddle his horse. Such a big crime was going to be known everywhere. Clearing out wrongdoers was his responsibility, a large one. It was also his huge opportunity.

He called on his good friend and "right-hand man," the wealthy law secretary Jón Jónsson—or Johnsen, as he called himself, using a distinctly un-Icelandic spelling and pronunciation of his name. Also of the elite class and seven years older than CC Thórdur, Johnsen had also gone to Copenhagen to study law but had only got second class honors. That kept his ascendancy to a lesser tier than CC Thórdur's—and made him a perfect loyal and uncompetitive assistant. The county commissioner told Johnsen the reported events and told him to accompany him to see what they might discover.[3]

They first rode over to interview the women at Kambur, then Hjörtur for an account of the preceding night. The serving woman, Gróa, comparatively together during the terrifying experience, reported that the man who had tied her up wore fishermen's skin clothes, as did the others, and that they all smelled of seaweed smoke. From this, the county commissioner came to the unstartling conclusion that the men had recently come from the seaside.

The two men rode on to Stokkseyri, that suspicious fishing community, and spent the night there. The next morning, Sunday, they positioned themselves outside the Stokkseyri church just as people were leaving. Who knew what they might observe among the unsuspecting congregation who had not yet heard news of the robbery?

As Archdeacon Jakob finished his service and his parishioners exited the church, they saw the county commissioner and his sidekick,

Johnsen, standing like shadowy specters on each side of the door. The two didn't greet or return pleasantries from anyone. Instead they glared, looking serious.

For the community, this boded only ill. Shank Jón, who everyone knew engaged in some rather marginal activities, looked very startled to see the men, but then, who wasn't? Sigurdur, emerging with his wife, Vilborg, and his stepson, looked disgusted. He had no love for such officials; he was, after all, Gosi's son. And everyone knew his intense dislike of Iceland's repressive authorities.

CC Thórdur and Johnsen stared at everyone to no avail. None of the parishioners gave anything away. And certainly no one came over to admit they'd committed a big robbery the previous night. The men returned to where they were staying in Stokkseyri no more enlightened, trying to decide their next move.

That evening Johnsen rode to Eyrarbakki to look for suspicious activities. Meanwhile, CC Thórdur rode over to visit Jón Rich. Even though he didn't much like the man, Jón was a district deputy and supposed to be involved when a crime was committed. Jón Rich also knew the locals, while CC Thórdur did not.

Jón Rich invited him in—he really had to, out of Icelandic hospitality and also, whether he liked it or not, CC Thórdur was his boss. As he heard the robbery details, a cold shiver slid down Jón Rich's spine. That could have easily been him. He now understood why Sigrídur had warned their wealthy neighbor, who'd then blockaded his door—she must have heard something the rest of them had not. Jón was even richer than Hjörtur, and lots of people knew that he kept a chest of money hidden. Probably it was just luck that the robbers chose Hjörtur instead of him—although he would have given the intruders a better fight for his money than that measly coward Hjörtur.

The county commissioner told Jón Rich that he wanted this crime solved and fast. He wanted names. Who did Jón Rich think could have done this? The culprits were certainly still in the district. Jón Rich must know who they were. This vile crime clearly grew from the "corrupt spirit of the times."[4] First the French Revolution only a quarter century ago, and then the Napoleonic Wars, had incited among the uneducated common people a lack of respect for law and government rule. They now demanded a "self-taken justice infected by ideas of freedom and equality." Such attitudes sprang from a serious looseness with regard to religion. This current "age of so-called faith in reason and realism had swept away support of moral and religious equilibrium."

Such talk made Jón Rich uncomfortable. These were his neighbors and relatives CC Thórdur was talking about. Also, even though Jón Rich loved to read, he had no formal education—the same as just about everyone else he knew. Only the elite got that privilege. And disparaging the "new" ideas of religion was a criticism by association of their now well-liked and respected Archdeacon Jakob, a moral man if ever Jón Rich knew one.

On the other hand, he would have been furious had someone robbed him, a very different thing from the small-scale stealing that he knew perfectly well many in the community did—as he'd done himself as a child.

I intend to initiate an investigation immediately, CC Thórdur informed him. He wouldn't give up until he got the robbers—best if it happened in a first examination. The men were here. Jón

Rich must know them. Name names, he demanded. Give me likely suspects.

Jón Rich replied that he knew of no one he considered likely.

CC Thórdur scoffed. He knew no one? He was a district deputy and he had no idea?

Suddenly as in a flash, Jón Rich saw a way out. Inwardly a slow smile grew behind his outwardly serious face. "I'll give you some advice that will serve you better than to press me," he said after a very long pause. "Call in Captain Thurídur to interview. She is so sharp-sighted and observant that I know of no one who is her equal. If she's unable to give you any clues, then I am afraid the guilty will not be found in the parish." If she named names, everyone would hate her; if she couldn't, then she was a failure. An opportunity just fell in his lap.

CC Thórdur stood. Thurídur was this trouser-wearing female fishing captain he'd heard about. It was clearly also all he was going to get from Jón Rich; demanding more was a waste of his time. At least he had a lead. He'd send a servant over to Thurídur the minute he got back.

As Jón Rich walked CC Thórdur to the door, he worked to keep his inward smile from creeping to his face. That had gone well. He'd managed to roll trouble off his own shoulders and right onto those of Thurídur.

At Gata, Thurídur peered through the midafternoon February gloom to see a man walking swiftly along the track in her direction. She'd changed her Sunday skirt for everyday working clothes and was now busily tarring her boat. It was usual practice for any responsible captain, to tar the outside of boats after each season and the inside before the season started, keeping them as watertight as possible.[5]

She recognized the approaching man as CC Thórdur's servant. What did he want with her?

Upon arrival, the messenger told her that the county commissioner wanted to see her immediately. "Come with me," he stated, with little greeting or preamble.

Thurídur straightened and gave him a steady gaze. She wore men's clothing covered in tar, not proper attire to visit a county commissioner. "I will change and then come," she replied.

"No," the messenger said imperiously, full of the importance of his duty—and knowing the instructions he'd been given. "You must come at once."

Thurídur slowly put down her tools, brushing ineffectually at her tar-spattered jacket and trousers. He gave her no choice; she would go as she was.

She arrived at the very nice house where the county commissioner was staying, entered the parlor, and greeted him. CC Thórdur greeted her in return, motioning to the messenger and others hovering around to leave.

Glancing down at her tar-spattered jacket and trousers, Thurídur told him that she'd been working when his messenger rushed her to come without giving her a chance to change. "Yet, I should not have come before you dressed in this way," she apologized.

"The same goes for me as others," CC Thórdur replied. "I have heard before now that your everyday wear is men's clothing. But for that you need a license."

In reality no record of such a license seems to exist—a number of women during the 1700s and 1800s wore trousers while working at sea—although not on land.[6] Still, none of them were required to obtain any license. In medieval times, from the *Laxdaelasaga*, a woman, or man, could be divorced for cross-dressing,[7] and in the 1200s a set of laws stated that a man or woman cross-dressing was punishable by exile—but this set of laws was abolished in 1281.[8] Nowhere is there evidence of this supposedly required license.

Not that this made any difference. As county commissioner, Thórdur could say whatever he liked. He expected Thurídur to be as reluctant as Jón Rich, if not more, to help him find guilty neighbors or relatives. He'd clearly considered this and laid out his trap before Thurídur arrived.

"This license I will obtain for you," he now said, "if you will give me a hint as to who robbed the Kambur farm."

His blackmail made the attempts by Jón Egilsson look like innocent child's play. Effectively the county commissioner gave Thurídur no choice. She'd help him, or he'd prosecute her for wearing trousers.

"Who was robbed and where?" Thurídur asked.

He outlined the facts he knew of the robbery, including the items found at the scene: the tattered hat, the iron rod, and the dropped shoe.

"May I see the shoe?" Thurídur asked noncommittally. No one liked Hjörtur, stingy and mean to his staff. Had it been someone else, they would have all felt more sympathy.

CC Thórdur pulled the shoe out of a bag and gave it to her. Thurídur turned it over in her hands, examining it carefully.

"The woman who made this shoe is highly skilled," she said after some consideration. "It's been worked in a special way which I have seen only at three farms."

"And where is that?" CC Thórdur asked eagerly. This was unexpected; was she going to give him a name now?

With an impassive look, Thurídur told him that the first of these farms was his own.

CC Thórdur flushed, unsure whether to be complimented at the skill of a woman at his farm, probably his wife, or to be insulted at the idea that someone in his household could have been associated with such a crime. Was Thurídur being clever, mocking him, or making some kind of point? He settled on a defensive middle ground. "True," he agreed as if he knew such sewing details himself. "But do you suppose that my men have been on such business?"

"I do not suppose so," Thurídur replied evenly. "The second is from Gaulverjabaer." She paused. "But I am sure the robbers are not from there." She then stood in silence. The county commissioner gave her a steely glare.

"Name the third," he said.

Thurídur continued to gaze at the shoe. "The farm is Stéttir," she said finally. "Kristín, the second wife of Jón Geirmundsson, who was my neighbor for some time, is a skilled worker, and at her place I have seen shoes made the same as this one."

CC Thórdur failed to suppress a smile. "Then I would say you are pointing me to Jón Geirmundsson," he said. He paused, his eyes alight. Jón Rich may not be the greatest deputy, but he'd given him good advice. "But who do you suppose the others were?"

"That gets more difficult," Thurídur said quietly. She laid aside the shoe and met the county commissioner's stare with an unflinching one of her own. "Regardless of the evidence of this shoe," she said, "it is certain that Jón Geirmundsson, if he was involved, will not have been the leader of this foray." CC Thórdur looked at her critically. "He lacks the initiative," Thurídur continued, ignoring his stare. "Nor has he the villainy, unless he has been incited to it." An image of Shank Jón Geirmundsson and his daughter Sigga came into her head. This evidence her clever and observant eyes had discerned disturbed her greatly.

"Who is most likely to do that?" the county commissioner demanded, sitting forward in his chair. Thurídur was doing better than he could have hoped.

"I know of no one more likely than Sigurdur Gottsvinsson," she said finally. "He fears nothing and shrinks from nothing if it comes to that, and he wants to get rich. He has rowed with me one season, and I know him well. Many able boys have rowed with me, but none to match him in strength and ability. Yet, I would not have him again." She paused. "Nonetheless, there is good in him."

"I like these suggestions the more," CC Thórdur replied, rubbing his hands together in delight. "As these two had occurred to me before."

The names had *not* occurred to him, or he would have said something before and not been so frantic for leads. But he'd happily take credit whenever he could. Thurídur, in private, was solving his case for him, which he could later claim was his own clever reasoning. "But," he pushed, "name some more that you consider likely."

"I cannot as things are," Thurídur said calmly. "Except for those two, no one seems likely to me." She paused, holding his eyes with her own. "Nor do I definitely state anything about those two. I am rather suggesting that it could be worthwhile learning whether they were at home the night the robbery occurred."

"Both they and others will be interrogated," CC Thórdur affirmed, the hunter onto his trail.

"Then interrogate me also," Thurídur said. "There must be no suspicion that we spoke of this privately, for if it comes to Sigurdur's ears I would not put it past him to kill me."

"It will not be rumored from me," CC Thórdur replied.

Perhaps he could keep his mouth shut and be cautious in how he spoke so he didn't implicate Thurídur. But she could hardly count on it. He'd got his answers. She left knowing that any tranquility in her life had just evaporated.

16

A RISING SCENT
OF MURDER

1827

Johnsen returned from Eyrarbakki after finding nothing unusual in his ride around the community—it is not clear what he expected to see amid the fishing huts and shoreside farms. As promised, CC Thórdur began immediately setting up his interrogations.[1]

Using Thurídur's findings, he first called in Sigurdur's wife, Vilborg, and their two serving women, asking them about his movements Friday. Vilborg arrived cheerful, clearly not suspecting her husband of any crime, all of them agreeing he'd gone to Eyrarbakki Friday and returned the next day.

Next, CC Thórdur and Johnsen questioned Shank Jón Geirmundsson's wife, Kristín, and their two serving women, who told them Shank Jón had also not been home that night; he'd told them he was going out looking for driftwood. When he returned, he'd left his wet clothes in the entryway, so they had no idea if he'd been missing a shoe. Kristín reported that the skin they used for shoes was dyed, but the serving women said it wasn't, so that proved inconclusive.

CC Thórdur then had Shank Jón send over iron bars he'd made that winter along with the hammer he used: these he had examined by two blacksmiths, who noted that "he must have a larger hammer to work this iron." So he sent for Shank Jón again, who this time sent over a sledgehammer. The blacksmiths determined that the hammer marks looked similar to those on the rod found at Kambur, but this was also inconclusive.

CC Thórdur did interrogate Thurídur as promised, who reported vaguely that some people told her they might have seen movement on the marshes. He tried to get friends of Sigurdur's to implicate him, asking if they'd visited Shank Jón and if Sigurdur had not told them he was thinking to rob Kambur farm. One said he didn't remember, the other that the two had visited, but that was to be expected since they were friends.

CC Thórdur then called in Ari Jónsson, Gamlason's son and Student's assistant clerk at the merchant store. Interestingly, he did not call in Student—or Lambert. It may be that Ari was the one attending the store Friday so was the most likely to know who was there. Regardless, Ari reported that Sigurdur had hung around the shop all day drunk, with no apparent reason for being there—but then, plenty of men did that. The merchant shops encouraged men to drink shots of brennivín there, almost like a bar, a good money spinner for them.[2]

Having discovered nothing from anyone else, CC Thórdur called in Shank Jón. He arrived downcast, unable to stop himself from weeping.

"Ah, that is no double guilt biting you,"[3] the county commissioner said.

"No," Shank Jón replied, "it's because I've become weak-minded from all I've been through."

The county commissioner placed the shoe on Shank Jón's foot—where it fit perfectly. "Why did you send us a useless small hammer with the rods?" he asked.

"I did that in haste," Shank Jón replied.

Was he really looking for driftwood that night?

Yes.

Did he find any?

"No," Shank Jón said. "But nonetheless I went to look for some wood for myself, however it looks."

Would he swear on his salvation he had not been at Kambur that night?

"Yes," Shank Jón said. "In the Lord's name."

CC Thórdur called in Sigurdur Gottsvinsson.

Yes, he'd been around the store all day drunk, Sigurdur told him. Then he'd taken a brown horse from the beach to ride home. When the horse stumbled in the river, Sigurdur had got soaking wet, so he'd gone into a cowshed to wring out his clothing. All this took so long, he'd arrived home only in the morning. He'd seen no one and he'd never been to Kambur. The man who had the cowshed reported he'd seen no disturbance in there.

During the week, CC Thórdur interrogated others. When questioned, Thurídur's deckhand Poet Jón Kolbeinsson reported that he'd also gone hunting for driftwood that night, as it would have been useless to go earlier—presumably because of high tides—where Poet Jón said he'd met a neighbor who confirmed this. Neither of them had seen anyone else, although it seemed that had Shank Jón actually been on the shore the two men would have seen him.

Although it sounded suspicious, none of it proved anything. CC Thórdur grew increasingly frustrated.

The next day, February 15, Thurídur decided to visit Shank Jón Geirmundsson to see how he was doing. She found him in his smithy doing little, his eyes red from tears.

"Why are you so downcast?" she asked him.[4]

Shank Jón stared at his hammer. "I'm afraid of being taken," he mumbled.

Thurídur looked at her friend. "If you are innocent," she said, "then you need not worry. But if you are guilty, there is no better advice than to admit it right away."

"What pains me the most," Shank Jón said, tears now spilling down his cheeks, "is if I am taken to know that my poor Sigga is crying at home." His voice broke. "Look in on her if that happens."

"I'll do that as best I can," Thurídur assured him. "But that will hardly happen if you are innocent."

"I'll be suspected," he said, "because Sigurdur has been here so often this winter to visit me on the farm. They also say that the iron rod found at Kambur is similar to my rods."

Thurídur saw one of Shank Jón's rods leaning next to the anvil and picked it up. Then she glanced at the anvil itself, noticing that it had a small chisel mark so near the center that any iron beaten on it would likely bear its echo. She checked his rods and there she saw, indistinct and faint but clear enough, the reproduction of the chisel mark, confirming her theory.

"The only thing I can advise you," she said as she turned to leave, "is if you are not innocent, to confess as that will improve your case."

"Do you think I am guilty?" Shank Jón asked her, his eyes again filling with tears.

"Lost is the man who must guess," she replied.

As Thurídur walked back to Gata through the early dusk of a snowy February afternoon, she passed the farmhouse where the county commissioners had been holding interrogations all day. It looked as though everyone had gone except CC Thórdur himself, who was now standing at the doorway. When he saw Thurídur, he called her over.

"Have you learned anything?" he asked.[5]

"Little enough," Thurídur said noncommittally. "But what have you learned?" she asked, quickly turning the conversation toward him.

"My suspicion of Sigurdur and Jón Geirmundsson has strengthened," he said. "I'm close to arresting them." He stared at Thurídur meaningfully. "But I'd like to have stronger evidence first."

He had no more evidence than she'd already given him. And he was planning to arrest Shank Jón Geirmundsson on suspicion alone, just as Shank Jón was afraid he would. Thurídur chose her words carefully. "As far as Jón goes," she decided to say, "I expect the iron rod will remove all doubt. Jón's anvil has a chisel mark, and if there is no sign of it on the iron rod, then it was not made on Jón's anvil."

CC Thórdur looked at her, startled. "I've already had blacksmiths inspect the rod," he said.

Thurídur shrugged and walked over to where the rod lay on a table. She picked it up and slowly turned it in her hands. There on the rod she saw plainly what she had so hoped not to find—the mark of Shank Jón Geirmundsson's anvil.

Oh, Jón, who and what induced you to do this? She showed the mark to the county commissioner. "Your blacksmiths didn't look too closely," she said.

CC Thórdur's face flushed in quick anger. "Something like this is easily overlooked," he retorted. Then he curbed his annoyance. "But it looks like proof to me." This was exactly what he needed. He and Thurídur were again talking in private. He could take credit for discovering this important clue.

"For my part," Thurídur said, "I now have no doubt." She paused. "But let your blacksmiths inspect the rod again and the anvil." Let him take the credit. She certainly did not want the burden of having provided this proof on her shoulders.

"That you need not tell me," CC Thórdur said, becoming annoyed again.

Thurídur turned to go. She'd had enough. But CC Thórdur stopped her, his face suffused with eagerness. "But what do you say of Sigurdur?" he asked.

Was Thurídur supposed to solve his entire case? That was his job, not hers.

"According to Deputy Jón Rich, you've said you've seen the tattered hat found at Kambur," he continued.

Jón Rich was certainly not doing her any favors reporting this.

"That is too much to say," Thurídur cautioned the county commissioner. "I never asserted that." She paused as CC Thórdur continued to stare at her. "But I almost did," she admitted finally. "For the tattered hat left at the scene of the robbery is very similar to a hat that Sigurdur's teenaged stepson was going to wear last winter when he was a half-share deckhand with me. I refused to let him wear it because I considered it useless and unsafe to use fishing." Her blue eyes flashed. "That and only that I could testify in court."

"That will be next," CC Thórdur said, giving her the glimmer of a smile. He blocked her exit. "But what do you imagine for the other two robbers for whom I have no suspects?"

"I have learned nothing of them either," she replied to him evenly. He was pressing her to incriminate her neighbors—without the protection his position accorded him.

She stepped around him and walked the darkening track toward Gata.

March unleashed blizzards from the north, covering the entire shore with ice and accompanied by freezing winds that halted all movement, including fishing and CC Thórdur's investigations. It did not halt people's speculation and endless conversation; rumors exploded. A striped blue mitten had been found in the meadow at Kambur that CC Thórdur, who'd returned to his inland residence, ordered kept in an obvious place to see if anyone recognized it. So far, no one had.[6]

On one of these days when the weather did not permit fishing, Sigurdur's father, Gosi, now sixty-five and separated from his wife, went to visit a friend. He'd given up his captainship and management of his farm, although he still fished as a deckhand. He'd taken lodgings and hired himself out as a laborer to avoid, as happened to so many, becoming a pauper in his old age. He sat in his friend's smithy looking distressed.

"You're looking down in the dumps today, old fellow," his friend said. "Would you like a plug of tobacco for your mouth?" Everyone knew Gosi loved chewing tobacco, something he'd now have a hard time affording.

Gosi readily accepted the offer. He'd had a strange dream, he told his friend. "I thought that I walked out of my fishing hut, looked over the bay, and saw it was entirely under ice," he said. "Then I saw four men riding hard along the ice from east at Eyrarbakki, headed out to the fishing camp. My son Sigurdur was the leader, and he rode a white horse. They dismounted at my hut, and Sigurdur's horse was covered in a sweat sheen of ice. It shook itself and sprayed me with drops of blood."

What was this dream? the friend asked himself. Did Gosi think it meant his son was the leader of the Kambur robbery?

A few days later, when the weather had cleared enough to travel, Sigurdur came down to Stokkseyri to check if it might allow for fishing. Nothing doing. Still too much ice.

While there, he ran into Thurídur, and as with everyone, they spoke of the robbery. Did Thurídur not suspect Shank Jón Geirmundsson? Sigurdur asked. Or perhaps Jón Sturlaugsson, a man as handsome as Sigurdur himself and with even more ambition for wealth?

"Not Jón Sturlaugsson," Thurídur replied. "But no guessing. The innocent can free themselves with an oath."[7]

Such an oath before God was considered to establish truth. A false oath jeopardized one's eternal life—unless one doubted the church doctrine, which[8] Thurídur did not. Sigurdur did. "An oath is like the other sayings of men," he said. "The guilty can swear too."

Thurídur glanced at him. "Then something may be concluded from probability."

Sigurdur clenched his fists. "I know you want to get me suspected," he burst out. He stood over her, much bigger and famously strong. "You've said I owned the hat that was found at Kambur. I've heard that reported about you. My wife wouldn't believe you would have told such a lie." His eyes glinted, his face enraged. "But you will take the consequences."

Thurídur stood her ground. So CC Thórdur—or Jón Rich— had blabbed. That meant everyone knew. Exactly what she'd feared. Suddenly Sigurdur turned away and stormed off, not touching her but without any semblance of a goodbye either.

Thurídur watched him go. He hadn't physically attacked her, but his threat made his intentions clear. She no longer felt safe. What was her best recourse? Jón Rich certainly wouldn't protect her. The only person who could, should—and hopefully would—was the county commissioner.

But her request for protection had to come from an official source. And that was District Deputy Jón Rich; this was his duty. Straightening herself, she walked next door to request he write a letter to the county commissioner. She considered Sigurdur quite capable of murder.

17

DO ANGELS STEAL?

1827

Deputy Jón Rich dutifully wrote the letter Thurídur requested. He also informed CC Thórdur that the blacksmiths had rechecked the rods and found the chisel mark. He sent the letter with one of the drivers who handled the horses for the itinerant fishing people who'd flocked to the Stokkseyri area the minute the weather cleared.

A few days later dawned to a deceptively bright sky that belied the intense cold of a hard frost and biting wind that blew the snow into drifts. Midway through the day, CC Thórdur showed up, Johnsen as usual at his side, accompanied by more men. They rode to West Peathouse, collected Deputy Jón Rich, and rode to Shank Jón Geirmundsson's,[1] where they arrested him, placed him in irons, and took him to Haflidi and Ingunn's Big Lava farm to hold until they could move him to Johnsen's place for safe keeping.

Iceland did not have a formalized prison system at this time, so during trials, the accused were generally held at the households of respectable farmers, often in the barn.² Shank Jón was left constantly in irons, allowed visits by no one except Johnsen and the woman who served him food, who was forbidden to speak with him unless absolutely necessary. But Shank Jón expressed no interest in eating or speaking with anyone anyway. Despondency descended on him with the darkness of a cave, his eyes constantly spilling tears.

After CC Thórdur, Johnsen, and their men had arrested and nominally housed Shank Jón, they rode on to Sigurdur's farm. By now evening had fallen, deepening the cold. Sigurdur had just removed his snow clothes after returning to the house from seeing to the livestock. When he heard the knock at the door, he ran outside, gloveless, bareheaded, and in his underwear.

"You are arrested in the name of the law," CC Thórdur told the scantily dressed man.

"I am not the first of those innocently taken prisoner," Sigurdur replied.

Then, not bothering to put on any more clothes and without asking permission, he jumped onto a loose horse, remaining there as they took him to a nearby farm where they decided to keep him for the time being for fear he'd freeze to death if they rode further— although Sigurdur showed no signs of even being cold.

Once they arrived, CC Thórdur had Sigurdur put in leg irons but left his hands free. During the week he stayed at this farm, Sigurdur showed no signs of being downcast, was easy to be with, and unlike Shank Jón, was allowed to be around others. One evening as he and the farmer sat together, Sigurdur pulled out a bitter-looking knife and showed it to him.

"I could have run the county commissioner through with this while he was putting me in irons had I wanted," he said.

Of this comment, the farmer kept his mouth shut.

After a week, Sigurdur was moved to CC Thórdur's own farm, still kept in irons and confined during the nights but allowed around others during the days. There he so convinced CC Thórdur's wife of his innocence that she asked her husband to show him mercy, which it seems he did, allowing Sigurdur much better conditions than poor Shank Jón.

Thurídur worked busily at her Gata sea hut, fishing again at full force. She looked up to see Haflidi approaching.

"Do you need any more crew?" he asked.

"I could add one," she replied cautiously. "But I can do without. Do you have a man to offer?"[3]

He said that he did.

"Is he capable?" she asked.

"You know him," Haflidi said, "for it's me."

Thurídur looked at him. "Now you're lying to me and that's not your habit," she admonished him.

"No," he replied, "I've resigned the captainship, and another has taken over in my place."

Thurídur's skepticism turned to surprise. "That I never would have thought." Who would leave a highly sought captainship? "Why did you do that?"

"I don't know that I might not be taken," Haflidi said with a half smile. "Who knows how many may be taken before all this ends?"

This was clearly a joke. He must have other reasons for his strange decision. Some disagreement on the boat, Thurídur decided. Something he wished not to discuss. That was fine. It was his business.

"I'll take you on for that reason," she said. "Someone else will be arrested before you."

Now she again had both brothers working for her. They were good men. Without Sigurdur, their relationship was sure to recover its old warmth.

Some days later, Thurídur and her crew were sitting around the fishing hut talking—about the robbery of course. What else did anyone talk about?[4] It had almost superseded the weather as the central conversation topic. Various crew members speculated on the clues, the iron rods, the shoe, the blue-striped mitten. Everyone had their theories.

Poet Jón Kolbeinsson asked her if he could have some time off to get some butter, as he'd run out.

Yes of course, Thurídur told him, if you go on a day when we can't go out rowing.

So the next Sunday he went up to Kambur, which sold butter, and bought a quart from Hjörtur.

Sometime after that, people at Kambur noticed that the blue-striped mitten was gone. Even though Jón Kolbeinsson was a well-liked and respected poet, suspicion immediately flew to him since he was not from the farm and he'd come by recently. Someone repeated this rumor to Thurídur.

She shook her head. "Things have gone so far," she noted in cold jest, "that the gossips are implicating even the angels, no matter how unlikely."[5]

Sigga threw herself on the bed and burst into tears. Kristín sighed in exasperation. Since they'd arrested Shank Jón, the girl wouldn't stop crying. Kristín turned to one of the farmhands and told her to get Thurídur—again. It seemed the child loved her above anyone except Shank Jón himself. If anyone could get her to stop crying, it was Thurídur.[6]

Once she arrived, Thurídur consoled Sigga until the girl calmed and fell asleep. As Thurídur brushed the child's hair away from her now peaceful face, she made herself a promise. She'd continue coming as long as Sigga needed her.

Leaving the distraught household, she was walking pensively across the meadows back toward Gata when a man appeared, approaching along the track from Eyrarbakki. Her deckhand Poet Jón Kolbeinsson. He greeted her and they walked on together companionably, talking of the robbery. Poet Jón asked if she thought it would be solved.[7]

I suppose so, she said. "Those who come under suspicion will be ordered to clear themselves with an oath if they can." She gave him a half smile. "That will give the guilty pause."

"Those fellows care nothing for oaths," he replied.

Thurídur looked at him in some surprise. "Do you suppose," she said, "that anyone is indifferent whether he swears a true oath or a false one?"

"I don't say that," Poet Jón said quickly. He glanced toward the sea. "But I know many with enough sense to realize that an oath is a saying of men like much else we are taught."

Thurídur considered this. "Even so," she said, "it's a terrible thing to take God to witness when one is lying."

Poet Jón shook his head. "Yet they say God himself sent a lying spirit to delude Ahab. He was also pleased to do other things in those days that he dislikes now.[8] From this, some become weak in their faith. And when faith is gone, men think of nothing but to get along in this world as best they can."

Thurídur's eyes darkened in concern. "Yet the conscience always exists within people and shows them the way to distinguish good from evil."

"Yes," he replied slowly. "It shows them what convention calls good and evil at the time, but some do not let that hinder them."

"I hope you are not without faith," Thurídur now said, her concern rising to distress. This was the man's soul he was talking about. "I hope—and I have never understood you to say that before."

Poet Jón glanced at her and then away. "No one is without faith," he said. "Everyone believes in something, but no one believes everything. And no one can control what he believes. As far as my faith is concerned, you need not worry; it will equal yours."

"That can neither be measured nor weighed," Thurídur replied. She looked at him intently. What was Jón telling her? "You yourself have the most at risk," she said, watching for his reaction.

Withdrawing into himself, the young man didn't reply.

Thurídur felt herself grow quietly cold. He feels he's spoken too freely and revealed too much of his own thinking, she realized. He's a deep thinker; these are surely his own opinions. A sudden suspicion stabbed her with the burn of ice. His internal conflict over the power of an oath—could this mean her thoughtful friend had somehow been involved with the robbery? As she looked at his pleasant features, she now saw fear. He knows I've seen this, she thought. He's afraid because he thinks I have the ear of the county commissioner.

Thurídur looked up from the tackle she was repairing to see Poet Jón hovering, watching her from the shadows behind her fishing hut. This was getting disconcerting—he was following her all the time now. She pretended she hadn't noticed and casually continued working, but now she made sure she never had her back toward him.

Why was he doing this? Such a good man, but however unlikely, it seemed he must be guilty of something. An innocent man did not act this way. As Poet Jón watched Thurídur, she covertly began watching him.

To see how he might react, she started slipping in vague comments while chatting among their fellow crew, suggesting he might have worse aspects they'd never seen. Poet Jón acted as though he didn't hear, but she could tell he did. She saw his soft brown eyes grow increasingly hooded, revealing more than he thought they did. She saw an increasing terror. But of what?

He began to follow her even more closely, making it almost impossible for her to talk with anyone without him hearing her. First Sigurdur. And now this man whom she'd considered a colleague and a friend for years was stalking her, appearing at every turn as if he'd been lying in wait. His looming shadow seemed omnipresent. Never had she considered violence from thoughtful and poetic Jón Kolbeinsson, but he was showing a side she'd never seen, a very unpleasant side. As she watched the mounting panic in the young man's face, she became convinced it was only a matter of time before he attacked her.

In the second half of March, CC Thórdur decided to appoint Johnsen as official prosecutor of the case, while he appointed his wealthy neighbor Stefán Pálsson, who'd recently become a district deputy, as defense council for the accused. He didn't really think much of this neighbor.[9] For one thing, he was sure Stefán had overcharged him for his board and lodging during a year he'd stayed with him. Stefán tried his best at his duties, CC Thórdur conceded, "but there is some weakness in his temperament that causes me to think he is not one of the good deputies."[10] Regardless, he'd do for the defense—perhaps reflecting the lack of importance he placed on that role.

Starting March 22, CC Thórdur interrogated various local residents over a three-day period. Some said they remembered little of potentially incriminating conversations; the farmer who'd held Sigurdur for a time said he was a good neighbor although terrible when he got angry—and now reported their conversation about the knife. A servant at Sigurdur's house gave her opinion that Vilborg only married him out of fear and that there was no love between them—although Vilborg herself said nothing of this kind and there seems no other evidence of this. Servants at Shank Jón Geirmundsson's said his wife, Kristín, was positive he was innocent, but she'd made him shoes of undyed leather a few days before the robbery. The blue-striped mittens seemed to have been loaned to several people before they might—or might not—have got to Poet Jón. Haflidi's mother-in-law, Ingunn, thought Poet Jón's mittens were blue striped, but Haflidi's wife said no, his were white.

CC Thórdur questioned both Poet Jón and Haflidi, who said they'd also gone looking for driftwood the night of the robbery, returning to Haflidi's late and sleeping there. When Thurídur was questioned, she related her conversations with Shank Jón

Geirmundsson and Poet Jón, including the one about the oaths. Poet Jón was then asked to explain this, as doubt in the divine power of oaths was considered a dangerous opinion.[11]

He said he remembered little of the conversation but tried to explain his meaning as best he could.

After the hearings, Thurídur told CC Thórdur and Johnsen that she was in fear of her life from Poet Jón Kolbeinsson. Either arrest him or give her protection.

CC Thórdur balked. He claimed he now suspected Poet Jón but was still in doubt. Would Thurídur give him her assurance that Poet Jón was guilty?

She would.

"But if nothing is proved against him," CC Thórdur said, shifting the onus away from himself, "then this responsibility may rest heavily upon you."

"Jón may go free for all I care," Thurídur replied, as usual stating her mind whoever her audience, "if you guarantee my safety from him. It must be the duty of the authorities to protect the innocent against evildoers, and it can hardly be a heavy responsibility if it's demanded that they do their duty."

CC Thórdur calmed his reaction of affront. He needed this woman. "Will you then testify in court that Jón is seeking your life?"

"He has never made an attempt against me," Thurídur replied. "But your protection will be too late if it is to wait for that."

Johnsen looked from CC Thórdur to Thurídur, their vital local resource. If anything happened to her, it would not look good for them. In his new role as prosecutor, he decided to speak up. He urged CC Thórdur to arrest Jón Kolbeinsson and protect Thurídur.

Well, CC Thórdur said, working whatever advantage he had, what did Thurídur think of Poet Jón's brother Haflidi? Before she could speak, he gave his own opinion that either both or neither brother was guilty. As he liked Haflidi so much, he deemed it very unlikely he could be guilty.

"I do not suspect Haflidi of anything other than complicity with his brother," Thurídur replied. "But it wouldn't surprise me if Haflidi were loyal to his brother in hiding his secret, even an ugly one, for he is a man who'd never reveal a confidence even of strangers if he knew they'd put their trust in him."

Following this conversation and at Johnsen's urging, CC Thórdur and his men arrested Jón Kolbeinsson and put him in leg irons. They left him with a local farmer where people liked him, saying he appeared cheerful—although the farmer's daughter, who often stood beside the shackled prisoner as he ground grain for them, said when he thought she couldn't see him, his face became drenched in sadness, almost in tears.

During the next weeks as the days grew long and spring slowly emerged, CC Thórdur and Johnsen spoke often with the prisoners, who seemed disinclined to confess anything. It all looked unpromising. The investigators had no idea where to go next.

The first day of summer arrived, about April 20, usually a day of celebration. In the morning Prosecutor Johnsen, going as usual to check on his prisoner Shank Jón Geirmundsson, found him in such anguish he could hardly speak. What's the matter? Johnsen asked him.

I've had a terrible dream, Shank Jón replied.

"Tell me the dream," Johnsen said carefully. "I know better than many how to interpret dreams." Rather disingenuous since Johnsen would quickly use anything Shank Jón said against him, but Shank Jón replied.

"I dreamed," he said, "that Páll Haflidason"—a local man of dubious repute—"cut open my belly. Then the Devil himself came and took out all my innards."

Johnsen worked to keep a smile from his face. Just the break they'd been looking for. "An easy dream to interpret," he said confidently. "Yet there are two possibilities. Either the Devil will take your soul, or else he'll take away the strength he's hitherto given to you to deny the truth." A clearly manipulative, or certainly very convenient, interpretation, but Shank Jón took it to heart.

"It is best now," he said dully, "not to deny it any longer."

Then he incoherently admitted to the robbery, naming Sigurdur and the Kolbeinsson brothers as accomplices, first claiming they'd frightened him into participating.

Here Johnsen stopped him. A confession! Yes! He immediately called a court hearing to make anything Shank Jón said legal evidence. But Shank Jón was so distraught and confused that Prosecutor Johnsen called a halt until CC Thórdur arrived the next day.

Shank Jón lay in despair, unable to eat.

18

HOW DOES ONE
KNOW GOD?

1827

At court the next day, Shank Jón was so confused, disturbed, and mind-sick to be almost incomprehensible. Still he described the robbery. His portion of the loot he'd buried in the hay crib, asking Haflidi to take it were he to die.

As he still refused to eat, Johnsen's wife, a kind woman who'd grown fond of Shank Jón, was sure he now meant to starve himself to death.

Johnsen scoffed and brushed her off. Don't try to persuade him, he told her. But he did go to visit Shank Jón himself and asked him if he wanted to see anyone.

Shank responded listlessly. Those closest to him must now be pained by seeing him, he said. There was no one he needed to speak with except Captain Thurídur.[1]

Johnsen and CC Thórdur immediately rode off toward Stokkseyri in high jubilation, spending the night at a farmhouse along the way where they passed the evening in great spirits. The next morning as they were leaving, Johnsen quietly told the mistress of the house that Shank Jón Geirmundsson had confessed, and they were on their way to arrest Haflidi. He then invited her to feel the saddlebag where he'd packed the irons.

Saturday. The sky above Stokkseyri stretched an infinite crystalline blue, the sea a flat teal with shadows etched in indigo, black lava shimmered between sun and ice. These were days when Heaven visited Earth, when the act of fishing verged on euphoria.

Since it barely got dark this time of year, everyone had made their first run in the early hours and by noon was already returning with a second load. As Captain Thurídur and her crew rowed into the passage, one of her deckhands pointed toward shore. There they saw two men wearing formal dark coats waiting at the landing like ravens at a feast. Haflidi turned blood red and then deathly white. Thurídur looked at him, sadness clouding her usually clear eyes. Everyone knew what these dark figures meant.

As they landed, CC Thórdur walked over to Haflidi and ordered him to remove his skin sea clothes. These clothes gave the wearer sanctuary from anyone laying hands on them regardless of their crime.[2]

For a moment, Haflidi stalled, but it was hopeless. Slowly he took off his sea clothes, he knew likely for the last time.

Seeing what was happening, Thurídur walked over. "As this man's captain," she said staring straight at CC Thórdur, "I demand he be given an opportunity to take some nourishment before he goes." Her crew would be treated with dignity while she was around.

The county commissioner looked at her, then permitted milk to be brought, although Haflidi drank little.

Meanwhile, Johnsen drew Thurídur aside. "Jón Geirmundsson has confessed," he told her. "Now he intends to starve himself to death. Nonetheless, he wants to see you first. Go up there and get him to eat."

Thurídur took a deep breath. So this was where Haflidi's arrest had come from. But if Shank Jón had confessed, perhaps Johnsen would treat him better now. That was the best they could hope for. "I'll try to go up there tonight," she said, "since we won't row tomorrow." The next day was Sunday.³ She'd already been up working since at least two in the morning.

Turning to her remaining crew, she told them to shove off. They were going out for a third run before they quit for the day. As they left, they watched Johnsen and CC Thórdur take Haflidi away.

They led him to where they thought he'd buried the money beneath an outdoor hay crib, everything still frozen and covered with ice, and gave him a wrecking bar, ordering him to dig.

Johnsen stood over him brandishing a whip while Haflidi broke the ice. His hands turned bloody, but still they made him chop frozen earth as the hole grew deeper and deeper. Finally, when even Johnsen and CC Thórdur had to concede the ground hid no treasure, they put Haflidi in irons and took him to a farm for temporary safekeeping.

After their third run, Thurídur worked with her crew to clean and process the fish. Then she took a horse and headed to Johnsen's to see Shank Jón Geirmundsson, riding through a late-night twilight and arriving just after early dawn. People there immediately took her in to see Shank Jón.

"I am finished now," he said when he saw her. "Remember what I asked you—look after my Sigga."

"Are you finished?" Thurídur responded, squatting on the ground beside him, her face both gentle and stern. "Are you going to starve yourself to death? Do you think your Sigga will be consoled by that? She longs for nothing else but to see you."

Shank Jón covered his face in his hands. "It'll only cause us anguish to see each other," he said. "I have no appetite for this. I should just die; that's for the best."

Thurídur placed her hand on his shoulder. "For Sigga's sake," she said softly, "you have to try to get something down. If she gets to see you, she'll feel everything is well." She paused. "But if you starve yourself, she'll never have a happy day."

Tears streamed down Shank Jón's cheeks. He shook his head, unable to speak.

Thurídur rose and requested Johnsen's wife bring her some milk, known from saga times as a rescue for starvation.[4] She offered it to Shank Jón. "If you drink this," she said, "I'll take care of Sigga as though she were my own. But if you don't..." She set her jaw. She needed a tone she was positive Shank Jón would believe. "I will have nothing to do with her."

It worked. The thought was more than Shank Jón could bear. He drank the milk.

Thurídur had food brought to him, waiting until they were alone again before she spoke. The futures of his wife and daughter were still to some extent dependent on him, she pointed out. "Johnsen may well take them in if you are compliant to him."

"I expect nothing good from him." Shank Jón's voice lay bitter in the gloomy barn.

Thurídur shook her head. She'd been observing Johnsen closely. "You don't know him right," she said. "As hard as he is when he's against, he is equally loyal and reliable when he's on your side. Both he and the county commissioner were beginning to get worried about the Kambur case, and they were relieved when you confessed. If from now on you are as steady in the truth as you fought it before, then Johnsen, if I know him right"—and she was pretty positive she did—"will be as good to you as he has formerly been harsh. Then I'm sure he'll be to your wife as a brother and like a father to your Sigga. That will make a big difference to them. But for that to happen, you must live and help reveal the whole truth. Won't it be worthwhile for you to do that?"

"Yes," Shank Jón replied, both defeated and relieved at the same time. "If they benefit from it, I will live, whatever my judgment here on earth."

"You should stand strong and stable in the truth," Thurídur counseled him. "Then you have a hope of mercy both here and in the afterlife."

Through April of 1827, under interrogations by the prosecution, more details of the robbery and its planning emerged.[5] Stefán Pálsson, the man supposedly defending the Kambur robbers, gets little mention. All four robbers steadfastly absolved their wives, sisters, and farmhands of responsibility, taking any and all blame upon themselves.

Sigurdur was the clear leader. He'd discussed the idea often with Shank Jón Geirmundsson, arguing that it was of course a sin to steal from the poor but not from the miserly rich. Especially the wealthy farmers who took a stipend for keeping paupers they then starved and otherwise abused until they often died or became disabled. Also, he contended, petty thievery was unmanly. Embarking on a daring venture where one stole only once to become rich was like a Viking expedition of their noble ancestors.

Once Shank Jón agreed to the robbery plan, they considered several rich and miserly farmers—including Jón Rich. To this, Shank Jón said no because he liked Jón Rich too much. Finally, they decided on Hjörtur and Kambur farm. But they needed a third man.

Poet Jón Kolbeinsson at first rebuffed Sigurdur's invitation to join them, saying this was a crime, something he didn't wish to do.

"Even if it were a crime, which I doubt," Sigurdur replied, "many a man of God now in Heaven had formerly been a criminal but had later repented and been forgiven."[6]

Poet Jón, who tended to doubt in matters of religion, replied that he didn't dare count on that.

One has to either let go of religion and the commandments entirely, Sigurdur countered, or keep everything one has learned. He continued his persuasion. Rather than to wallow in a life of small sins in the hope of eventual grace, he said, was it not better to commit one notable crime and repent for it afterward?

This argument, encouraged by copious amounts of brennivín, won Poet Jón over. He was young, strong, and brave. He could do this. He later told Haflidi about the conversation.

"If you go, I will go, and we will share the same fate,"[7] his brother immediately responded—confirming Thurídur's opinion of how he would react. Taking ill-gotten wealth from a miser suited him fine.

Sigurdur took a knife to the robbery. "This will protect us if need be," he told the others.

He was also the one who suggested burning the farmhouse to destroy the evidence, the others refusing to entertain the idea. Shank Jón Geirmundsson and Poet Jón later sneaked back, concerned because they'd forgotten to remove the chests that secured the mattresses. Relieved that all was quiet, and sure the occupants had all untied themselves, they crept away again.

After Sigurdur heard that Shank Jón had begun weeping in the courtroom,[8] he went to Poet Jón.

Shank Jón will without a doubt confess and expose us all, he said. The only solution was to kill him first. "And if you do that, you can have his share."

Despite taunts from Sigurdur, Poet Jón flatly refused. So Sigurdur next went to his brother. Once Haflidi realized Sigurdur was serious, he not only refused but immediately warned Shank Jón, urging him to run away on the mail ship and leave the country before Sigurdur killed him. But, on the evidence of the iron rods and shoe, CC Thórdur had him arrested before he had time to do it.

Throughout their testimony, the heavy specter of giving a false oath[9] hung in the air like a descending anvil, particularly for the Kolbeinsson brothers. Wrestling with the teachings that making a false oath before God damned one's soul to eternal Hell, versus stating mere words before an indifferent court, sent them into spasms of convoluted religious reasoning. If they perjured themselves, that was one thing, but they could not risk sending their sister and Haflidi's wife to Hell. So they asked them to say nothing in court of what they might have seen—of their returning to the farm the next morning and the sister noticing a strange and heavy sack in the barn—telling them this was "to avoid suspicion following innocent men." But if the court required them to give an oath, they should say Christ had forbidden oaths and that they would obey God over men.

But when the women were interrogated, they told everything they had seen anyway.

In his testimony, Poet Jón said that his discussion with Thurídur about oaths had made him reconsider his beliefs and the relationship of his soul to the afterlife and God; because of this he decided he'd try to avoid being forced to swear an oath at all costs. When he heard about the mitten, he took it precisely so he'd then be suspected and not allowed to take an oath. His plan worked—with a heavy cost. He explained that when he realized Thurídur had begun to suspect him after their talk, he began following her to prove by his actions that he was innocent. Sadly, this backfired in the worst way. Instead of making her convinced of his innocence, it made her afraid of him and convinced her of his guilt. Through his fear, he had both undermined their friendship and betrayed himself.

Once the robbers confessed where they'd hidden the money, Johnsen and CC Thórdur, witnessed by Archdeacon Jakob, Lambert, and Student, had it dug up and returned to Hjörtur[10]—who reacted not with pleasure and thanks but anger because, in a bag so heavy he couldn't lift it, his 1,025 Danish state-dollar hoard was missing 65. CC Thórdur hefted the bag onto his own shoulder, taunting Hjörtur for being weak. Since Hjörtur had also been too cheap to bring a horse, he had to then temporarily leave part of the recovered hoard with the snickering county commissioner.

CC Thórdur allowed[11] an improvement to the four robbers' treatment. Johnsen particularly treated Shank Jón Geirmundsson much better because he'd been the first to confess—just as Thurídur had predicted. All the robbers' property had now been confiscated, leaving the families of Sigurdur and Shank Jón destitute. Seeing this, Johnsen took in Shank Jón's wife, Kristín, and

Sigga, looking after them as his own, cementing Thurídur's correct assessment of him.

The other three stayed at various farms where everyone liked them. Sigurdur was handy and helped around the place, Haflidi mild mannered and pleasant. Poet Jón wrenched the hearts of all who saw him, lost in remorse and grappling with his faith, composing endless poetry about God and redemption.

One day, Poet Jón and Haflidi's younger brother Thorleifur, who had a growing reputation as a seer, visited Poet Jón, greatly disturbed.[12] He'd had a dream, he said, that Poet Jón would be taken from Iceland and never return.

Poet Jón took his brother's dream as truth. Marry my beloved fiancée, the lathe maker's daughter, he urged him. Take care of her.

Thorleifur promised he would, setting in motion the fulfillment of his teenaged prophecy.

So, the heinous Kambur crime was solved, the culprits all confessed and in custody. CC Thórdur took full credit, neglecting to mention Thurídur or anyone else. "It became popular belief," he wrote, "that I had had help from supernatural powers when I managed to only apprehend the guilty people and no innocent people, and this at a time when no one had admitted the guilt."[13] There is also no evidence Thurídur ever received an official license from the Danish king, or anyone else, to wear trousers.[14] Not a real surprise, since it seems no such licenses were required or even existed.

But if the community or Thurídur thought that CC Thórdur had finished with them and they could now go back to their normal lives, they were quite mistaken.

19

IN THE BELLY OF
THE BEAST

1827–1828

Just as the community thought the whole horror of the interrogations had ended, things took an unexpected and alarming turn.

Instead of leaving, CC Thórdur and Johnsen decided to extend their investigations to the entire community.[1] Sigurdur had during his confession admitted to stealing some planks from the merchant store. He had also implicated another man who'd stolen butter. This, CC Thórdur decided, was only the surface slime of a dangerous and deep swamp. And, he decided, he was the man to clean it out.

In this well-publicized effort, he and Johnsen began to extend their investigation in an entirely new direction, interrogating the four robbers relentlessly about any thievery they—or others—might have done apart from the Kambur robbery. Under duress, the robbers began to admit to stealing wood, butter, food, and other items from the merchant house. Soon they'd implicated their kin and neighbors—whom CC Thórdur and Johnsen quickly brought in for their own interrogations. The investigations now veered away from the Kambur robbery altogether, focusing instead on ferreting out any infraction of thievery or wrongdoing they could find in the community as a whole, particularly against the Danish-influenced legal order protecting the landowning class and the merchant store.

As spring plodded toward summer, CC Thórdur and Johnsen stretched their reach to interrogate more and more people. Under pressure before these frightening officials to reveal *something*, those under interrogation dredged up confessions to anything real or imagined in themselves or anyone they might know, purging their intestines of any moral weakness regardless how ancient or petty. They incriminated others and then withdrew their claims. Like a snake eating its tail, neighbors, kin, and friends turned on each other in mindless terror.

As accusations spread, community psyche slid from fascination with the robbery to fearful self-examination. Who among them had not stolen at some point in their lives? A bit of food, wood for fuel or to make a bed? In such inequality, simple thievery counted as a survival tactic. Who could escape being caught in this ever-expanding vortex?

Fear so easily eats compassion and grief; people became sharply divided in chaotic confrontations of guilt, dread, and distrust. Old grudges now found space to bloom. Fear turned to panic.

Even Shank Jón Geirmundsson's younger brother "Snap it Snorri" got sucked in—an easy target. His accusers acknowledged he hardly had the intelligence to steal unless someone helped him, and most of his thievery at the merchant store occurred while he was still a child. No matter. CC Thórdur added his infractions to his rapidly growing list.

Heady with success, Johnsen and CC Thórdur brought in dozens of local residents, even old women.[2] Few confessions came from this wide net, although Johnsen was convinced he'd uncover unending thievery dating back decades.

In July, CC Thórdur received news that his daughter had died of croup. He brushed this aside and continued the investigations.[3] In late August, "surrounded by robbers and scoundrels I was interrogating,"[4] he received word that now his "beloved" son had also died "along with all joy I could have expected in my senior years." He recorded his reaction to this terrible news. "I don't know if it signifies my calmness, that I continued the interrogation throughout the day so people would barely notice what kind of news the messenger had brought."

Through all this, the one person who refused to confess and told no stories about anyone was Gosi. His equally courageous ex-wife, Kristín, a strong, intelligent, and fiery woman, steadfastly defended him.[5] Gossips now claimed she'd made a pact with the Devil to protect their son Sigurdur.

When CC Thórdur called Kristín in to testify, she turned up her nose as she entered the courtroom and snorted as though she smelled some disgusting odor. When the county commissioner asked her what the problem was, she replied, "I am blowing away the filthy spirits in here—ugh—I hate their stench."[6] Nonetheless, she gave a clear testimony that in no way implicated her ex-husband.

Since Gosi refused to confess to anything, Johnsen decided in mid-August to force him into submission.[7] He placed him in a room on the bare floor with his hands and legs in irons and had him fed almost nothing. Since everyone knew of Gosi's love for chewing tobacco, Johnsen placed a wad of tobacco close enough to Gosi so he could see and smell it but not reach it.

It seemed members of Johnsen's own household found it hard to endure seeing this treatment.

Johnsen shared the key to Gosi's room only with his wife, who was also assigned to bring his meager food. She often secretly took a piece of tobacco, and when Gosi had finished eating, she placed it in his mouth. Once when Johnsen came in while Gosi had tobacco in his mouth, he quickly swallowed it so as not to give her away. Johnsen's teenaged son also gave him tobacco when he could, as did the man billeted to care for Gosi for a time while Johnsen was away. At sixty-five still strong and charming, Gosi impressed everyone with his stamina. Except perhaps CC Thórdur and Prosecutor Johnsen.

Finally, after a month of this treatment, Gosi confessed to at least a portion of the stealing of which he was accused. He stoutly absolved Kristín of any knowledge, claiming—somewhat unbelievably—that she never cooked a single sheep he stole.

On January 21, 1828, the first judgments by CC Thórdur came down. He stipulated whippings for dozens of local residents including women and Snorri. The robbers were to receive torture and imprisonment in Denmark. As was usual, these verdicts were appealed, resulting in some punishments worse, others somewhat less, and a few women acquitted. The Icelandic court then sent these verdicts to Copenhagen for a final determination that would take at least a year.[8]

Meanwhile, news exploded of another crime in the north of

Iceland, this one a double murder. On March 14, 1828, two women together with a nineteen-year-old male companion allegedly murdered two men by hitting them on the head with a hammer and stabbing them twelve times. They then burned the farmhouse in an attempt to destroy evidence—just as Sigurdur had threatened to do in the Kambur robbery. The county commissioner there—certainly aware of the happenings in Stokkseyri District—decried the crime as springing from rising rebellion among the farmhand class. He was convinced the farmhands' motive for these murders was robbery of a wealthy farm owner.[9]

Such an occurrence intensified the determination among those with power over Stokkseyri District to squash any and all lawlessness through harsh retribution. CC Thórdur wrote that he was sure the Stokkseyri District "flock"[10] or "common people" originally "thought they had nothing to fear" from him because he "was a stranger to these parts, but after the investigations started, they saw that everything was not as it seemed." Then "rogues started to fear me and others increased their belief in me... There were no more criminals in my area, people came, knelt before me, kissed me in gratitude." Besides still not mentioning Thurídur, he only acknowledges Johnsen as "loyally following" him.

The interrogations lasted eleven months and resulted in thirty people out of a population of about four hundred being formally accused of various infractions, the largest and longest investigation in Iceland's history. Almost every local resident had kin or neighbors now awaiting punishment. Whether the district ever really healed from this is an open question.[11]

It was now common knowledge in Stokkseyri District that Thurídur had provided the evidence that led CC Thórdur and Johnsen to the Kambur robbers. This might have made her as safe from suspicion as Archdeacon Jakob—at least from the prosecutor and county commissioner—but it made her a pariah in the eyes of many in this now shattered community. The Kambur case and ensuing accusations were now nationally infamous. For the community that had supposedly spawned such lawlessness, it meant humiliation, horror, and grief.

People needed someone to blame. CC Thórdur and Prosecutor Johnsen were off-limits. Móri's shoulders couldn't carry this kind of weight—he'd been only a child when he died. Those who resented Thurídur, or had never approved of her anyway, grew vocal and vicious in their gossip. No matter that Thurídur was not involved with this terrible explosion of trials but only solved the actual robbery—after having been forced by the county commissioner to participate. Unconventional and outspoken Thurídur was a perfect scapegoat.

Because Archdeacon Jakob had decided to no longer have a boat out of Stokkseyri, Thurídur had captained the 1827 winter season on a large ten-oared boat for ship owner Jón Jónsson.[12] Now he began publicly mocking, threatening, and slandering her.[13] He'd also decided not to pay her the required captain's salary, usually two shares or at least a share and a half to the deckhands' one.[14] In this he was going against clear law, which he must have known.[15]

Thurídur, reflecting on her previous success against the slanderous Ólafur, sued him, demanding three Danish state dollars in wages to be paid within three days, and also forty-eight shillings for his slanderous words—paid not to her but to the district's poor. She got two Danish state dollars in back wages but, unlike before, not the fine for slander. Whether this was because the mediation did not consider the slander serious enough or because Thurídur had lost standing, or perhaps because she wished the funds to go to the poor instead of herself, is never said.

Regardless, this was only the beginning of what a community turned bully could do. Now it was not the robbers who threatened her but a menace more amorphous and less easy to ascertain—and with no recourse for protection. Sea storms she could watch and calculate her risk; this increasing danger on land of a human kind was much less predictable.

20

THE DEVILS
ARE DANCING

1828–1830

As the 1828 Stokkseyri winter fishing season started, sixty-six-year-old Valdi gave his children a sobering message: they should prepare for his death, as he knew this season he'd drown.[1] Shortly before Christmas, he'd gone walking after the evening readings eastward along the shore to where they usually pulled up their boat. There he'd seen a vision of his crewmates, including himself, all wearing their sea clothes but holding their sea hats.

Valdi had always been afraid of the sea, but this vision changed him. Instead of becoming frantic now that he knew his fate, he lost his fear of the inevitable. He never tried to stop fishing, but he grew serious, no longer joking or laughing with his crewmates. After a few weeks, he moved from the communal fishing hut and rented himself a solitary cabin where he said he could be more contemplative. There his meditation deepened to acceptance.

One day, soon after the winter fishing season had already started, a young man came by Thurídur's fishing hut asking for a job.[2] Thurídur assessed his measure. People have their untold pressures or reasons they might arrive late looking for a position; life is often complicated. Overall, he seemed a decent young man.

She already had a full crew, she told him, but if he headed west along the shore, he was sure to find some boat that needed an extra hand. She also told him that if ever he ran into trouble, to just say her name and have someone call her to help. He thanked her for her advice and continued on his way.

Winter passed, and spring arrived with its usual complement of mixed blessings and tragedy. The wreck Valdi had foreseen came April 8, all boats out when the weather changed. Captain Thurídur and her crew made it in as well as Captain Gamlason. Even Sesselja's husband, Gísli—risk-taker as he was—made it. But one boat did not.[3] Ten men drowned, including the captain who was the younger brother of Margrét's second husband Gudmundur, one of Sesselja's brothers, Gudmundur's sister's husband—and Valdi.

People said the captain had "smoke on him," meaning he later returned as a ghost to check on money he'd gathered while he'd been alive. Perhaps. Or perhaps he just regretted a life cut too short.

Then May 5, on a deceptively bright spring day during the final days of the fishing season, came a second wreck as bad as the first.[4] Among the nine who drowned was Kristín Brandsdóttir, forty-two years old, the youngest daughter of the cantankerous singer and shipwright Brandur.

From this already ravaged district, nineteen people died, the worst year for drownings in Stokkseyri's history. One by one, the bodies drifted ashore to be found among lava, seaweed, and stretches of sand. On June 29, the sea belched out four at once, their souls sent forth in a single funeral.

Can even a vengeful God turn so cruel? How can He expect even ironclad faith to remain impervious to fracture? We cannot all be Job.

And who would choose to fish from Stokkseyri now? Perhaps these rich and accessible fishing grounds came with a price too high. Thurídur, Gamlason, and Sesselja's husband, Gísli, continued, brave, confident, or foolhardy, but many others began a migration to the much safer landings at Thorlákshöfn.[5]

At the end of the winter fishing season, Thurídur heard that the young man who'd come by her fishing hut near the start of the season and who, as she'd expected, had later found a job, was now being accused by the boat's owner of stealing. He'd gone from Stokkseyri to Eyrarbakki, where people sent him on to Thorlákshöfn. A man there needed crew; as he had a bad reputation, no one wanted to work for him, but it would be a place the young man could get a job. He did, receiving one-fifth share, giving four-fifths to the boat's owner.

Deckhands cleaned their own fish, but the youngest crew member, in this case the young man, took care of the guts of the owner's fish as well. As the young man's pile was noticeably larger than anyone else's, the owner was sure he'd cheated on counting the owner's share and called in CC Thórdur to complain. When CC Thórdur arrived, the young man gave him Thurídur's name, just as she had told him, asking someone to send for her to help him.

When Thurídur heard, she went immediately, arriving to find various piles of drying fish stacked separately for each crew member. Indeed, the stack of the young man, whom no one really knew, was considerably bigger than anyone else's—except the owner's, of course.

Thurídur carefully examined in turn the young man's fish, the owner's pile, then everyone else's. She held up one of the young man's fish.

It's cut differently from those of the others, she noted. Using this difference, she calculated the ratio of his fish pile to those of a similar cut on the owner's pile, the comparison revealing an accurate division.

Skeptical, the owner asked Thurídur how she knew the young man's fish would be cut differently.

Simple, she replied. When the young man had earlier come by her hut asking for a job, she'd noticed he was left-handed. Since all the other deckhands were right-handed, they cut their fish from the opposite direction.

Faced with this kind of evidence, the boat owner had to back down. The young man was innocent; he kept his fish. Thurídur's reputation for looking after the welfare of others, being a keen observer, and having deductive intelligence rose another notch.

At the fishing hut over the winter, Thurídur had begun to reconsider her off-season living arrangements. She'd been living as a lodger for a couple years; this didn't give her the security of a farm but had allowed her to save. At fifty-one still strong and vigorous, why shouldn't she invest her savings in a leasehold again? She didn't have the funds for a full farm leasehold but could work a share. She could build on that, maybe eventually able to get a small place like Gata again.

She approached her friend and former deckhand Sesselja and her husband, Gísli, to see if she might sublease part of his inherited, large

Kalastadir leasehold. Gísli was amenable. Thurídur could lease one-fourth of the farm—in exchange for farm goods.[6]

Great! On her way to being a farmer again.

When she moved to Kalastadir in May, she looked around the property. It was in terrible shape, having been neglected for at least thirty years. Well, she'd seen that before. She had funds and would start fixing it up immediately, removing stones, building a proper stone wall, putting in a vegetable garden. It was good land, near the sea; it just needed some hard work to get it to the level it could be.

Then she saw a figure in the distance. She shaded her eyes against the high spring sun.

Who was that walking her way? Jón Egilsson. Well, well, what might he want?

A formal divorce, it seemed, now possible, since they'd been legally separated for three years. Thurídur looked at him, his face reflecting urgency. He had some reason he wanted this now.

Yes, Jón Egilsson replied to her inquiry. He looked at the ground. The husband of Gudmundur's sister had just tragically drowned...

Ah. Thurídur got it immediately—complicated relationships that she, like everyone else, had neatly cataloged in her head. The drowned man had a very good farm near his wife's brother Gudmundur and Margrét; Gudmundur was looking after the interests of his sister—now a young widow with three children to support and in need of a husband. He knew and liked Jón Egilsson as their farmhand of eight years and, even with the husband barely cool in his grave, was pressing for a quick match between the two. The prospective couple, both of a similar age, also liked the idea. There was only one hitch—Jón Egilsson was still officially married to Thurídur.

Thurídur's smile broadened while Jón Egilsson began to blush.

Jón Egilsson had hit it lucky. Through this new marriage he now had an opportunity for all he'd wanted with Thurídur and more. This was a well-off family. No more being a farmhand for Jón Egilsson.[7]

Well, wasn't this an interesting turnaround? Certainly, Thurídur would divorce him.

They set up the formal proceedings as soon as possible, on June 6, 1828, with Archdeacon Jakob presiding and Jón Rich sitting in as second witness. Only about one percent of Icelanders officially divorced, mostly the wealthier class, but when they did, unlike in most European countries, their assets were divided equally between men and women.[8] Having been apart so long, Thurídur and Jón Egilsson were both declared without joint property, able to keep whatever assets each might have. The official reason, "so they can get married again," clearly meant Jón Egilsson.[9]

He did, and according to accounts, this marriage was a happy one. Exactly what he'd clumsily tried to force with Thurídur. All's well that ended well, it seemed, despite the tragic death that precipitated it.[10]

Thurídur set to work on her section of Kalastadir.[11] She hired some workers to help and began leveling the fields, adding to the soil, putting in a proper track, and preparing land for the vegetable garden. With her helpers, she collected stones from the surrounding meadowland to build a wall around the garden.

As the weeks passed, she noticed Gísli getting annoyed with her, more than annoyed. Angry. Why? She was improving the land, better for all of them. But even Sesselja was becoming cool toward her, presumably influenced by her husband. As summer darkened to autumn, autumn to winter, Gísli's anger continued to grow. Thurídur had no idea why.

Then, one day during winter, as she was busily digging up rocks and working on the stone wall, Gísli walked up to her with two men he called his "witness." He was livid. About what? That Thurídur was building a wall?

I forbid you to do this kind of maintenance! he ordered. If you do, I'll just tear it down.

Why? Because she was expanding the vegetable garden? What was his problem? Thurídur continued working.

A few weeks later, she returned to find the wall destroyed. Gísli had torn it down.

Now Thurídur was angry. What was this all about? Was Gísli afraid that since he and his brother, both young, strong men, had taken their leasehold for granted, neglecting the property for so long, the owner might notice and prefer Thurídur as his tenant? That was not her intention, but possible.

None of them were now on speaking terms.

In March, Thurídur began noticing something very odd in her hay crib. Her winter hay had begun disappearing at a rapid rate, much faster than she was using it. She also noticed hay scattered around the barn in a way she never left it. This was serious. If it continued, how was she going to feed her animals? Who in the world would be stealing hay?

She began asking others in the area: was this happening to anyone else? Yes. Particularly a poor neighbor named Pétursson,[12] his hay also disturbed, and once he'd found his hayfork in the home field, when he always left it in the barn. He had five children—his wife, in both a blessing and a curse, had recently had triplets, all of whom lived—and only one cow, leased to him by Archdeacon Jakob. How was he going to feed it?

Thurídur decided to take action. If this wasn't halted it could quickly destroy people's food supply, including her own. She'd go to the county commissioner, ask for an investigation. In order to do that, she had to go through Jón Rich, their district deputy.

Jón Rich agreed they should write a letter outlining the issue and, at Thurídur's suggestion, ask the county commissioner to assign four "respectable men" to visit the various farms, look to see where hay might be missing, and try to determine if someone was in fact stealing it.[13]

CC Thórdur thought this sounded like a fine idea and wrote back telling them to do just that. He wanted the four men to then send him a report so he might "punish those who are guilty of despicable hay theft."[14]

The men did as he asked and sent him the required report ten days later.[15] In it, they stated that they thought Thurídur was correct, some farms did have considerably less hay than they should, while others had more—the least at Pétursson's and the most at Símon's House, where Erlendur's elder half sister Margrét still lived. Unfortunately, there was no way to determine who might be stealing.

CC Thórdur's response was to ask Thurídur to name people she thought were likely hay thieves. When she couldn't—or wouldn't—he decided to just drop the entire affair. Already in a precarious position, Thurídur had taken action not just for herself but also on behalf of the entire area, since she had previously determined that the hay interference appeared to be a wider concern. By giving

Thurídur, and those who were losing hay generally, no support at all, CC Thórdur undermined all of them.

For Pétursson, all this noise about stolen hay made things immediately worse. Archdeacon Jakob, on hearing that Pétursson no longer had enough hay to feed his cow, demanded it back. Without the cow, Pétursson had no milk for his children. He wrote a desperate letter to CC Thórdur asking for help.[16] The old documents are silent on whether he ever got a reply or if the Archdeacon let him keep the cow.

Everyone seemed to make it to summer despite their hay losses. In mid-June, CC Thórdur received a letter from the Kalastadir landowner, Ingjaldur Ottason,[17] stating that he had decided he wanted Thurídur to take over leasehold of two-thirds of Kalastadir. He authorized CC Thórdur to inform Gísli he had to vacate by the next May Moving Days, giving him a full year to find a new leasehold.

It seems Gísli's concerns about the owner's favoring Thurídur because of all the improvements she was doing were well founded.

Gísli did not react well to this news. He hadn't maintained the farm, but he'd also lived there since childhood. With the family's long-standing leasehold and Gísli's contentious reputation, Ingjaldur might have perhaps handled the situation differently. But when the landowner had kicked Jón Bjarnarson with Thurídur off his land, he'd hardly given them any notice at all. It was his land; he could do what he liked. But in this case, instead of preparing to leave, Gísli forcibly drove Thurídur from the farm.

With nowhere to go, Thurídur took refuge at her sister and Kristján's. She wrote a confused and distraught letter to CC

Thórdur. "What is my crime?" she asked.[18] To work hard improving a property? Expanding a vegetable garden? Gísli had treated her badly, tearing down everything she had built up, but what had *she* done wrong? Could CC Thórdur assign someone to represent her?

In response,[19] CC Thórdur wrote Deputy Jón Rich, announcing Ingjaldur's intentions and telling him to determine if Gísli planned to leave amicably the next Moving Days; otherwise he'd have to assign a representative for Thurídur. In reply, Jón Rich stated that Gísli had no intention of leaving.[20]

To this, just as with the suspected hay stealing, CC Thórdur decided to do nothing.[21] He did not assign Thurídur a representative. Instead, in late September he decided to pass the entire responsibility for any mediation or resolution to his district deputy—Jón Rich.

With this act, he handed Jón Rich the power to exact on Thurídur any vengeance he chose. Finally, he had her exactly where he wanted her. Further stacking the balance, Gísli was Jón Rich's wife's nephew, her sister's son. And Gísli's brother—with whom he owned his boat was married to the Kolbeinsson brothers' sister, while Jón Rich was close friends with the robbers' father,[22] all these people kin to the brothers now imprisoned directly due to Thurídur's clever observation.

Left completely free to do as he chose, Jón Rich ruled that Thurídur had slandered Gísli, that in improving the farm it had been her intention to take it from him. Thurídur protested that this was not at all her intent, that she'd just wished to improve the farm for all of them, with Gísli always as primary leaseholder.[23]

This fell on deaf ears; what she might say was of little interest to Jón Rich. He first ordered her to apologize, which she did, saying she never meant for this to happen. Jón Rich then ruled that Thurídur should forfeit all her belongings, everything, hay and all her savings, as his determined fine, leaving her homeless and completely impoverished. He ordered her to formally vacate Kalastadir in three days. Finally, Jón Rich had the opportunity to destroy Thurídur.

He soon changed part of his ruling: instead of insisting she leave in three days, he'd give her until May Moving Days—probably because he realized that was the only legal option he had. A moot point really, since there was no way Thurídur could now stay at Kalastadir anyway.

Deputy Jón Rich effected his revenge well. Thurídur was left destitute and homeless at the beginning of a long, dark winter in a community where many would have considered his actions just fine.

21

STAND PROUD, MAN ALIVE!

1829–1830

Like long-armed shadows, the murders in the north and the robbery in the south magnified each other. Such pockets of crime among Iceland's impoverished populace would metastasize if not immediately crushed. Examples needed to be shown, harsh sentences paramount.

In the north, investigations of the murders had also expanded to the general local populace, with forty people interrogated about thievery, including sheep stealing. "I rarely have any peace from thieves and rascals around here," stated local county commissioner Björn Blöndal.[1] The three convicted of murder there received death sentences by beheading, their heads to be speared on stakes.[2]

In due course, on January 12, 1830, using a special axe imported from Denmark, a brother of one of the murder victims in north Iceland beheaded the man and one of the women accused of the crime. As promised, their heads were speared onto stakes for all to see. CC Björn Blöndal ordered local farmers, 150 in all, to watch this grisly spectacle as a warning to others, especially servants who might consider rebelling.

Despite this warning, the two heads did not stay on their stakes long. Very soon they disappeared, seemingly by magic, rumor contending that a compassionate farm woman removed and buried them.[3]

On June 15, 1829,[4] judgments against the Kambur robbers arrived. Sigurdur Gottsvinsson and Shank Jón Geirmundsson received sentences of flogging and a life of slavery in Danish prison, Jón Kolbeinsson twelve years and Haflidi eight. Once they left Iceland, none of them expected to see the shores of their homeland again. In a desperate attempt to save them, their neighbors and kin immediately began petitioning the authorities for clemency.[5]

More than a dozen Stokkseyri District residents received sentences of flogging. Gosi's clever, "sassy" daughter[6] they whipped fifteen times, Gosi's younger son fifty-four. Even "Snap it Snorri" received fifteen lashes, another man the same for stealing butter. Amid the cries and slashing snap of whips, a sickening grief spread through the community; in their years of disease and natural devastation, this was a new kind of plague.

Gosi's sentence of two sets of twenty-seven lashings—almost one for each of his sixty-six years—he declared he would take all at once.[7] Set up to be humiliated, in an example watched by a large audience, he remained completely calm. They pulled up his shirt and slashed his back with the first biting stroke.

"An old man becomes a child twice, man alive!"[8] Gosi shouted to the crowd, reframing his familiar phrase in open defiance, meaning that this flogging was to him no more than a mere thrashing one might give a child—then considered beneficial in child rearing. Regardless of Gosi's transgressions, such courage and resistance could hardly be considered anything but admirable.

All pleas for clemency for the Kambur robbers eventually failed. With news of the northern beheadings still ringing in his ears, CC Thórdur had the four men tied together and moved to Reykjavík, where they'd await the spring postal ship for transport to Denmark.[9] To handle Sigurdur, recently back from his third escape exploit— one time just to see his favorite horse—CC Thórdur assigned five specially selected men, tying his hands behind his back, him to the horse, and men on each side holding the ropes to keep him in place.

As they carried Sigurdur to be loaded aboard the ship, he suddenly sprang free from their grasp and leaped straight from their arms up to the ship's deck, landing lightly on his feet as if such prowess and agility were child's play.

While the ship was on the high seas to Denmark, a dangerous storm blew up, damaging the narrow bowsprit that sticks like a slender wand straight out from the bow, vital for positioning the sails. The captain stood in a quandary of life and death. Any man he sent out to fix it would almost certainly get immediately thrown into the raging sea. But without the bowsprit, they couldn't control the ship.

I'm dead anyway, Sigurdur told him. I'll go. What do I have to lose?

The captain agreed and had him untied. Sigurdur climbed out onto the bowsprit, successfully fixed it, and slid his way back again.

You've saved us, the grateful captain said. When they got to Denmark, he'd request a pardon for the agile Sigurdur.

Safely at Copenhagen harbor, the captain threw a party for his crew, including the prisoners. Sigurdur got drunk and, as was his wont, grew violent, hit one of the crewmen—and destroyed his single chance at freedom. The captain rescinded his offer. Through his own lack of self-restraint, Sigurdur would not escape his predetermined fate.

Both he and Shank Jón Geirmundsson received floggings in Denmark. Now sober, Sigurdur, like his father, controlled himself, not even appearing upset, remaining silent as they tied him to a post and whipped him.

As they loosened his bonds and he turned his back to the post, he spoke, his tone provocative defiance. "Ah, my back itches a bit, guys!"

In Denmark, his unbroken will infuriated the commander, who immediately ordered him retied and lashed again. Sigurdur remained silent. The commander only halted that flogging when the flesh fell from Sigurdur's back.

In the hospital, Sigurdur recovered much more quickly than people expected.

CC Thórdur personally did very well off this entire Kambur episode and the ensuing Stokkseyri District trials, later made a senior judge, went into politics, and eventually became head of the national parliament. He translated a group of laws into Latin and was made an honorary member of the Icelandic Literary Society.[10]

The fallout for Thurídur continued to be quite different.

After being evicted from Kalastadir, Thurídur stayed for a time with her sister and Kristján, wandering with no fixed place to live, skippering for the autumn season as she had for the last eight years on a six-oared boat owned by Student, who remained her solid friend despite Thurídur's now tarnished standing in the community. She was still an excellent captain any boat owner would only profit to have.

One morning in October, Thurídur walked toward Student's Eyrarbakki boat shed after spending the night at Loftstadir seaside farm just beside Gaulverjabaer, home of Gamlason and his family, who had also steadfastly remained her friends regardless of what others said. She went as usual to check on the boat before the day's fishing, opened the door, and stopped in shock. During the night someone had broken in and smashed the boat to pieces. Someone who hated her.

No one claimed to know anything. But, of course, they did; people generally hung around the boat sheds, and very little escaped their eye. Having the powerful Deputy Jón Rich dead set against her, and Gísli still firmly settled at nearby Kalastadir, meant everyone knew any action they might take against Thurídur would most likely lead to no legal consequence at all. Instead rumors circulated that Thurídur had done it herself, regardless of how unlikely—especially since she hadn't even been in Eyrarbakki.[11]

The violent warning was clear: fishing out of Stokkseyri District was now dangerous for Thurídur in ways beyond turbulent surf. Virulent gossip had crystallized to action. Anyone who now hired her endangered their boat on shore even more than at sea. She was already destitute with no home, and now someone had in mind to stop her fishing career. They'd crush her completely.

Student had other ideas. Despite the financial loss of his damaged boat,[12] he offered Thurídur—and himself—a creative solution. Since Thurídur had already been skippering for him during autumn season, why not extend that to winter season on the same boat—once he'd got it repaired—not from Stokkseyri District—but from Thorlákshöfn? Fishing was on the decline in Stokkseyri District and starting to boom in Thorlákshöfn.[13] His proposal protected his boat while keeping his lucrative skipper. It also meant he was publicly demonstrating his support for—and thwarting revenge against—a woman others, who he would continually meet at the merchant shop, clearly now detested.

For Thurídur, this proposition was a godsend. A smaller winter boat than she was used to, but so what? She was sure she would still get excellent catches. His proposal gave her a lifeline out of Stokkseyri District for several months a year and allowed her to continue working as a captain. She gratefully accepted. She still had some friends, and they were being very kind.

But even with Student's vital intercession, Thurídur still faced a sobering realization. CC Thórdur was not going to press Gísli to leave, and without that official support, neither would the landowner.[14] After this kind of official trouble, even if she could ever raise the funds, she would never again acquire a leasehold, never have the security of a farm for her old age. At fifty-three, she'd been left with nothing and little way to sustain herself. Her fishing, dependent on the temperamental sea, was now her sole resource, and that would last only as long as her body could take the arduous, dangerous work the profession required. For how long? She had no children or kin who might support her in her advancing years. How soon would she become a pauper, homeless and penniless, living off the county? That seemed to be the intent. How would Deputy Jón Rich, in charge of the pauper funds, treat her then? It didn't bear considering.

In this moment of desperation, both Student and Archdeacon Jakob came forward with their public support. They'd help her apply for a pension from the Danish Crown, sometimes given to respected captains. She certainly deserved one; regardless of gender, she was one of the best, and she'd done great service for the Crown solving the Kambur case.

Student told her that if she dictated the application, he'd write it in the necessary formal Danish. Archdeacon Jakob would throw his not inconsiderable weight behind the effort by writing a letter of support. When Thurídur approached CC Thórdur for an additional support letter, he said he would write one. With a pension, she could keep her self-respect, regardless of those intent on destroying her.

In mid-January 1830, she and Student sat down to compose the application letter.[15] This is "[m]y humble application for support in my old age of a small yearly pension for my successful fishing here in Eyrarbakki," Student wrote on her behalf. Since her childhood, he wrote, she'd contributed through fishing while at the same time, "without ignoring important women's duties." For the last ten years, she'd fished both summer and winter seasons, managing "boat and crew with great success and luck, courage and Godly presence in greatest dangers at sea, uncommon for women to do." As she was getting older, she could no longer provide for herself by fishing and as a result, had become "very poor especially after helping her relatives in need."

They did not mention the recent conflict but did note that she had left behind three improved farmsteads. "I made vegetable gardens and over the last year at the last farm I have, at great cost, made a stone fence fifty fathoms long." They ended the letter, "Your most submissive, Thurídur Einarsdóttir," with Student signing as having penned it.

A few weeks later, February 6, Archdeacon Jakob sat down to write his support letter. He briefly introduced Thurídur, noting her constant help to others and that she had fished "in difficult conditions and good luck for almost forty years." Her "exceptional" sea skill, although "necessary here," is "rare in women." In addition, "she has for some years been entrusted as one of the most capable captains of an eight-oared boat." Here he knew what he was talking about, since the boat had been his own.

On land, he continued, she had "advantageously inhabited one farm after another with strength and sacrifice in the construction of houses, gardens, and stone walls," but now she lived "like a very poor farmhand and is losing her strength." Because of her "diligent," "hard working, well organized, sensible, and efficient" contributions, the Archdeacon wrote, "[t]his pious person is most humbly recommended to be graciously taken into consideration to enjoy being provided for in her last years."[16]

Then came the February 15 statement from CC Thórdur, supposedly an additional support letter.[17] He first noted that he accepted what the Archdeacon had written about Thurídur, but then his letter took a very different tone: "[W]ithout wishing to dis-recommend this application, I must note however that it is not uncommon in Eyrarbakki for women to fish, an occupation done by both men and women, who do this all the time to support themselves, but not so much for the benefit of the public or their descendants." This was different from land work, he wrote, because farms profit not only the farmers but "such work can be fruitful both for the descendants and for the public in general."

He ended his letter not by supporting a pension, but with, "In this light, I will recommend that this applicant, who is old and needy, receive a small monetary gift from the public."

Why did CC Thórdur, after agreeing to write a support letter, instead damningly undermine the application, both by putting down fishing folk in general and then managing—in a rare contemporary confirmation of the numbers of women working at sea—to twist it so it diminished Thurídur's accomplishments? One doubts he would have said the same of a male captain, that the presence of other men also working at sea took away from his applicant's excellence.

Gender aside, both his tone and words make it clear he did not want Thurídur to receive any kind of public accolade or sustaining pension. His reasons are not clear, but this, on top of his having dropped the hay investigations she requested and then tossing her to the nonexistent mercy of Jón Rich, are the actions of a man doing the opposite of supporting a woman who'd solved a major crime for which he was claiming credit.

Unaware she'd been so betrayed, Thurídur left for Thorlákshöfn to try fishing among people she didn't know, in a smaller boat on waters she knew only because it was where they landed now when the weather turned too rough in the Stokkseyri area. It would be a test of her abilities. Could she manage to retain her sterling sea reputation?

22

ESTABLISHING ESCAPES

1830–1831

Thurídur surveyed the calm water as she and her crew headed out of Thorlákshöfn. Such a better landing place than Stokkseyri, allowing ten- and even twelve-oared boats[1]—she was one of the smaller ones now. But she was fishing well, had a good crew, and was meeting new people and learning new cultural norms, each area having its own. As with others in Stokkseyri, she'd always had her crew say the Seaman's Prayer as they'd clambered into the boat; in Thorlákshöfn they said it after they'd already started rowing.[2] Local differences. Including a whole new set of fellow captains—all male—who didn't know her and looked at her skeptically. She could adapt. An interesting new adventure—away from Stokkseyri District.

For the last several weeks, she'd been promoting a competition between her crew and that of the local District Deputy Árni Magnússon—even though he had a much larger boat, superb crew, and was considered the best captain in the area.[3] She smiled to herself.

His advantages were a big reason *why* she was doing it. Anyway, a bit of competition added fun to the day and gave her crew more energy to pull in larger catches. She was pretty sure her crew could row as fast as Árni's. Proving herself in this new community wouldn't hurt—and perhaps she also had a distaste for deputies these days.

Let's head east of the cove,[4] Thurídur told her crew. They'd fish there for the day, same as most of the other boats. It was a slow fish day, no one catching much. She watched the weather: a north wind blowing offshore, light at present, likely to rise. But not for several hours.

When the north wind did freshen, most boats headed in. Except Deputy Árni. And Thurídur.

Her crew glanced at her.

Let's row over until we're in the lee of Deputy Árni's boat, she told them. That will protect us from the wind.

And annoy Deputy Árni no end, one might add.

Once behind Árni's larger vessel, Thurídur's boat sat steady on calmer seas.

We'll just stay here, she told her crew.

Both boats fished for a time but caught little. Meanwhile the wind stiffened, the weather growing worse. Deputy Árni's helmsman gestured toward shore. They needed to head in, he told his captain.

"I'd prefer not to go in before Thurídur," Deputy Árni replied.

"Then you'll have to sit a long time," his helmsman said, "because it's clear she intends to be in our wake." Meaning Thurídur was waiting so she could row into the cove protected behind Deputy Árni's boat.

When Deputy Árni heard this, he commanded his crew to pull up their fishing tackle and head for shore. Thurídur immediately had her crew follow suit, telling them—as predicted—to stay protected in the other boat's wake.

Her crew flexed their muscles and eagerly put their shoulders to the oars. A competition! Good. A thrilling if rather dangerous end to a slack day's fishing.

With fewer rowers and a smaller boat, Thurídur and her crew stayed right in the wake of Deputy Árni's boat. As both boats rowed through the waves, the distance between them never changed.

When they were east of the tip of the inner peninsula on which Thorlákshöfn lies,[5] Deputy Árni told his larger crew to buck up, get a move on, show this smaller boat they could leave them behind. His crew complied, now rowing as hard as they could.

"Oh, they're toughening their stride," Thurídur told her own crew. "Try to follow them." So they did, putting their backs into keeping the boat shooting through the swell.

They kept the distance between the boats the same, and there it remained no matter how much Deputy Árni exhorted his crew. Only when the boats reached the safety of the cove and were out of the force of the wind did Thurídur have her crew slacken their pace.

Deputy Árni's crew stared at them in grudging acceptance and admiration. It was clear Thorlákshöfn had gained itself an excellent new captain. Good enough to give Deputy Árni stiff competition as the best.

It didn't take long before verses about Captain Thurídur and her Thorlákshöfn crew appeared:

> *In a storm's fierce contest of war*
> *sea wolf whipping stern to the fore*
> *Thurídur fear will ignore*
> *while unkind tempests roar.*

Submissive as expected
eyes on their maiden king
asleep but weather awake
virile goddess and crew.[6]

May arrived, marking the end of the winter fishing season—also when Thurídur would have to return to Stokkseyri District, back to Jón Rich and Gísli, people smashing up boats she was captaining—and what else? She had nowhere to live and only her fish shares saved from that winter season to sustain her. Her application for a pension had come to nothing. The Regional Governor (*stiftamtmaður*) Krieger,[7] in considering it, had reviewed Thurídur's land and sea work, noting that although he did not know her personally, he supported the county commissioner's much cheaper recommendation to give her one small payment, suggesting eight to ten Danish state dollars.

These small cash awards, given mostly for land contribution in "making the land more fertile,"[8] were acceptable to present to outstanding women; Jón Rich's neighbor Sigrídur Hannesdóttir received one in 1832.[9] CC Thórdur's assessment gave Regional Governor Krieger an easy and inexpensive recourse. In the end, Thurídur was awarded a single payment of eight Danish state dollars, a token but no long-term help at all.

The only housing option she had that would keep her independent and not a farmhand was to rent one of the rustic cabins (*tómthús*) often used by itinerant fishing folk who did not have a farm leasehold but could pay rent through their fish earnings.[10] She'd done that before with Ingibjörg's brother; she could do it again. But she'd go to Eyrarbakki, a few miles from Jón Rich and Gísli, where at least she wouldn't have to confront them each day.

In the middle of Eyrarbakki, very near the sea, stood just such a cluster of cabins, called Gardbaer. It was a place to live—and she wasn't planning on staying there much of the year anyway.

Now she had to find some kind of paying work.

Although working independently was technically illegal, some did it, just as Thurídur had for then Pastor Jakob so many years ago after she'd left Jón Ólafsson. Now she hired herself out[11] as a freelance laborer during late summer, scything hay on farms near Reykjavík.[12] Usually considered "men's work," scything hay paid comparatively well, particularly for women because, unlike for almost everything else except fishing, haying generally paid women equal wages to men. These few weeks of arduous labor earned them sometimes as much as an entire year as a farmhand.[13]

By spending the winter and spring living in a Thorlákshöfn fishing hut and late summer cutting hay elsewhere, Thurídur could wrangle being away from Stokkseyri District six months at a time. That left less than half the year she had to worry about someone attacking her.

23

FURY UNBOUND

1831–1834

Thurídur stood beside her Gardbaer cottage in Eyrarbakki, looking around, lost in thought. No one heard much of the robbers these days, imprisoned in Copenhagen for a year now. She hoped this would keep resentment against her at least to a low simmer. Her living arrangement was holding steady at present, fishing out of Thorlákshöfn, staying here during the summer until the haying started. She could do it for a few years. During these summer months, she visited friends, Ingibjörg now pregnant with her ninth child—of whom three had already died, including her first-born, Thórdís. With luck and God's will, this one might survive.[1]

She also stayed with Archdeacon Jakob at Gaulverjabaer and Gamlason at his nearby Loftstadir farm. There she sometimes saw his son Ari when he came to visit. Ari was now living in the booming trading and fishing hub of Hafnarfjördur (Harbor Fjord) near Reykjavík. He'd handled himself well during the relentless 1828 interrogations, but soon after that he'd left Stokkseyri District, managing to get himself hired as an assistant with the Danish merchant Thomas Thompsen in Hafnarfjördur, an impressive feat for an Icelander; such positions almost always going to interconnected Danish families. Now married to María, a midwife and respected herbalist,[2] with children of their own, Ari was clearly a local success story—even if he had decided to decamp. Who could blame him?

Thurídur remembered when Ari as a boy, close to the age of her daughter—had she lived—had come to the shore to visit his father, when he was working at the Eyrarbakki store alongside Student. She'd watched him grow up; they'd always liked each other. He'd even hired Thurídur for a while to skipper a small spring boat he'd acquired.[3]

Thurídur's quiet contemplation was suddenly broken as a woman emerged from one of the nearby cottages, running toward her as though being chased by a ghost. Thurídur immediately recognized her.

Gudrún Jónsdóttir. She'd escaped from her husband and was coming to Thurídur because she needed help and had nowhere else to go.

When Thurídur saw Gudrún running in her direction, she didn't hesitate. She had no farm, no standing, and more enemies in the area than friends, but she'd help however she could.

She knew the history and reasons Gudrún might be seeking protection. Now about forty, she had in her early twenties been a housekeeper for the older, married farmer Jón Haflidasson, who had drowned on Farmer Jón's boat in 1812.[4]

In 1815, Jón's younger brother Páll, himself a fishing captain, had applied for permission to marry Gudrún, whom he described as his drowned brother's pregnant housekeeper.[5] Since his brother had been dead three years, it seemed that he was himself the child's father, although, while taking responsibility, he did not claim paternity. This did not bode well for a happy marriage.

In 1825, Gudrún went before the mediation committee, desperately wanting to divorce Páll. But because of their by then ten-year-old child, whom Páll claimed he wanted to raise, the presiding Archdeacon Jakob and Lambert determined they should stay together. Given no choice, Gudrún agreed, but only until Moving Day, which that year was May 14.[6]

Hard and in general "not a good man,"[7] Páll was disliked by almost everyone—the same person Shank Jón Geirmundsson had dreamed cut open his stomach to let the Devil eviscerate him. One of many interrogated during CC Thórdur's protracted court hearings, he was somehow acquitted even though locals knew he'd often stolen goods from the merchant store.[8]

Páll beat Gudrún. Although most people knew this, they did nothing; it was between husband and wife. At some point during or before their marriage, Páll also entered into an adulterous relationship with a farmhand named Margrét Jónsdóttir.[9]

In 1830, Gudrún, not having managed to get free of Páll, went to court again, this time to stop Margrét from continuing the affair. Brazen Margrét, beyond engaging in an overt relationship with Gudrún's husband, accused Gudrún of being the "thief" stealing "her" Páll.[10] Blatant adultery being less acceptable than male marital abuse, Archdeacon Jakob ruled that if Margrét wished to remain in the Eyrarbakki area, she had to get married to someone else. This she promptly did. One speculates this marriage of necessity was not great either.[11]

Gudrún then applied for an official separation, "of bed and table," the same as Thurídur had previously done with Jón Egilsson; the reasons here were adultery and abuse.

But when the separation came through, Páll refused to let Gudrún leave, keeping her a prisoner. To get out, Gudrún needed, beyond escaping the physical cottage, to find someone who would take her in and accept responsibility for her—as Student had for Halla when she left Shank Jón. For Gudrún, the trusted person she chose was Thurídur.

Thurídur's cottage was small, but she could squeeze in Gudrún. She also somehow convinced the authorities she could support Gudrún, having her work in return for room and board—and a safe haven.

Most people—and the law[12]—considered a man's wife his possession within his household; outsiders shouldn't interfere, regardless how he treated her.[13] But Thurídur decided to guide Gudrún in applying for a divorce from Páll, also suing him for abusive treatment. They asked the return of a chest—one of Gudrún's very few possessions— her clothing and, knowing this was a very large sum, twenty Danish state dollars.

Perhaps Gudrún alone could not stand up to Páll, but Thurídur would; she now had experience with the mediation court and knew that it was a space where even a woman could demand a hearing. Thurídur might now be poor with almost no assets, but she could stand up for justice. She'd go to court for Gudrún even knowing that this was unlikely to improve her own already tenuous standing in the community.

The settlement of their suit[14] didn't require Páll to pay any money, but he did have to return Gudrún's chest and clothing. It also left her legally free to choose where she wished to live—which was with Thurídur.

This sent Páll into a rage, spitting slander at Thurídur. Unfazed, she immediately sued him. What else was she supposed to do?

Páll was ordered to beg her forgiveness and retract his words.[15] Being forced into such submission, especially to a woman, enraged him even more.

Then, in a bizarre twist, a fellow farmhand of Páll's mistress Margrét, a woman named Vilborg Bjarnadóttir, also became furious at and slandered Thurídur, supposedly for helping Gudrún get free. Presumably a friend of Margrét's, she for some obscure reason approved of Páll's keeping Gudrún an abused prisoner while at the same time having an adulterous relationship with Margrét. Perhaps she was one of those in the community who disliked Thurídur. Perhaps she did not believe that others should interfere in matters between wife and husband. In slandering Thurídur, Vilborg was joined by Páll, who had clearly learned nothing from his previous experience.

Thurídur promptly sued them both, really her only option to curb their mounting abuse.

This time[16] Archdeacon Jakob and his fellow official decided after mediation efforts that Páll's words were perhaps misunderstood, not to be taken seriously and now considered "dead." But Vilborg's were slander. Thurídur and Páll both agreed to the ruling, but Vilborg refused until a month later when, presumably under pressure, she admitted her words were spoken in a fit of anger.[17] For this she had to pay Thurídur three Danish state dollars and apologize.

These court proceedings did nothing to temper Páll's behavior. He endured seeing Gudrún freely living at Thurídur's for a year and half, but in the spring of 1833, unable to stand it anymore, he stormed over to Thurídur's cottage, grabbed Gudrún, and tried to drag her away. When she resisted, he punched her, using his fist armed with a large metal key. Then he kicked her legs black and blue.

Luckily for Gudrún, Thurídur arrived. Although slim and in her fifties, Thurídur's broad rower's shoulders bespoke strength while her angry eyes darted their telltale flames. She would do whatever it took to keep Páll at bay. Páll's reaction was to throw a punch at Thurídur, knocking off her signature short top hat and sending it flying into a vat of fish oil.

This act made another court case inevitable. In it,[18] Thurídur sued on behalf of herself and Gudrún, asking the considerable sum of one silver Danish specia for Páll's violence.[19]

Páll contended that four Danish state dollars should be enough, since, despite physical evidence to the contrary, he hadn't hurt his wife, claiming there hadn't been other witnesses to contradict him— the two women's words meant nothing. He also defended himself by noting it was his right to do what he liked to Gudrún, since their divorce was not yet final.

In response, Thurídur challenged him to give them four Danish state dollars right there so they could make the divorce official. He did not take her up on this offer.[20]

Mediation had now clearly broken down, so Archdeacon Jakob, assisted by Student, used an old law from 1798 to give Thurídur and Páll three weeks to work out their differences and come to some agreement. This they somehow managed to do, Páll paying Thurídur six Danish state dollars within twenty-eight days for destroying her hat. Notably, the settlement paid nothing for Páll's violence toward Gudrún. It seemed Páll had been correct to contend he had every right to beat a woman who, although legally separated, was still his wife.

But Thurídur had begun to realize a renewed strength. She'd previously used the court to stand for herself; this time she'd sued on behalf of someone else's rights. Why not? It was, she decided, the right thing to do, no matter what public opinion might say.

The past three years had slid by slowly for the Kambur robbers as they rotted away in Danish prisons. Shank Jón Geirmundsson fared the best because Johnsen, true to his word and Thurídur's prediction, periodically sent him care packages of clothes and butter. He also looked after Shank Jón's wife, Kristín, and daughter Sigga.[21] At one point Johnsen wrote Shank Jón with a request. Kristín had become pregnant by a local man. Would Shank Jón consider divorcing her so she could marry the child's father?[22] He readily agreed.

Sigurdur's family had not fared so well. The authorities had confiscated their possessions, including all property. Jón Rich bought Sigurdur's half of their farm at auction, while Archdeacon Jakob bought Vilborg's (which, being married to Sigurdur, she had lost), later selling it to Jón Rich—adding to his ever-expanding property empire.[23]

In prison, Sigurdur had soon got a hand wound that never healed, causing him constant pain and permanently disabling him.[24] Because of this he was moved to another location, given less hard labor, and the doctor ordered that he receive a daily half liter of milk even though another prisoner told a supervisor he thought Sigurdur was too strong to deserve this. A prison guard named Reimann also constantly goaded Sigurdur about his injury.

Otherwise, no one made any complaints about his behavior, except fellow prisoners saying he kept them awake with his loud prayers and singing of hymns, this powerful man clinging to his fractured faith as piece by piece he steadily became broken.

Then in 1833, one of the other prisoners challenged Sigurdur to a fight. Sigurdur at first declined, but the other prisoner taunted him, saying this was only an excuse because he was disabled. Unable to resist the baiting, Sigurdur accepted the challenge. Almost immediately as they began to fight, Reimann entered and stopped it—so quickly one wonders if this might have been the plan.

All the prisoners stated that Sigurdur had not started the fight, except for the other combatant, whom Reimann seemed more inclined to believe. As a result, Reimann sent Sigurdur to the foreman, who ordered him not to leave his workstation.

Shortly after, Reimann told Sigurdur to help with the food, something that gave Sigurdur a great deal of pain in his hand.

I've been ordered to stay put, Sigurdur replied.

Hah! Reimann taunted him. He continued until Sigurdur became riled, ran at Reimann, and stabbed him twice with a knife.

Although Reimann recovered within a few days, the stabs were ruled potentially life-threatening—carrying a penalty of death.

The judges argued over this sentence because the paper Sigurdur had been given to read warning him about this law was in Danish, a language Sigurdur did not understand, meaning he never knew about it. Regardless, eight out of the ten ruled against mercy, making him pay both court costs and for his own execution from his meager prison laboring wages.

I don't care if they kill me or not, Sigurdur said when he learned this.

On March 4, 1834, they beheaded him. On the postal ship, this sad news made its way to Iceland. The first, and most legend-worthy, of the robbers had died, the final destruction of this extraordinary man, powerful, intelligent, agile, charismatic—and tragically flawed.

One night while Thurídur was alone in her Eyrarbakki cottage, a gunshot shocked her awake.[25] The membrane window above her bed blew to shreds as a bullet flew by and hurtled into the floor beside her. Had she been elsewhere in the room, it would have killed her.

No one seemed interested in discovering who'd fired the shot, least of all Deputy Jón Rich. Perhaps the shot came from Páll, perhaps Gísli, perhaps Sigurdur's kin or friends who blamed her for his untimely death. Too many potential suspects with no one to investigate.

The broken boat had been a warning. This was attempted murder. The threats before had been amorphous; now someone—or a group of someones—was intent on seeing her dead. They were telling her in violent terms that if she wanted to stay alive she'd better leave. Having so often helped others, she now needed protective sanctuary herself.

But what could she do? Merely moving to another household would only endanger the friends who took her in.

Her salvation came from Gamlason and his son Ari.

Come to Hafnarfjördur, Ari invited her. I can give you a job at the merchant house.[26] A considerable distance away, Hafnarfjördur would be safe among people unrelated to all that had happened in Stokkseyri District and who didn't know her. She'd still fish out of Thorlákshöfn, but the rest of the year she'd work for him.

Thurídur considered his incredibly generous offer. If she accepted it, she was jumping into the unknown. Except for fishing out of Thorlákshöfn and going on a few other short forays, she'd never lived anywhere but Stokkseyri District, hardly traveled beyond its borders. Thorlákshöfn had been a culture change, but Hafnarfjördur? She would be leaving everything, and everyone, she knew behind.

But Ari was also offering her an escape few others ever had, again a godsend from a friend willing to publicly stand up beside her regardless of consequence.

She gratefully accepted his proffered helping hand, packed up what possessions she still had, and left, thinking never to return. Her home had effectively expelled her. Where she was going could be better—or it could be worse. At least she wouldn't be cowering like an eider duck waiting for some lurking fox to attack.

24

IS PEACE POSSIBLE?

1834–1836

Thurídur gazed around in wonder.[1] Hafnarfjördur's natural harbor was so different from the filigreed skerries and channels of Stokkseyri or even the cove at Thorlákshöfn. Beside a rocky beach, deep waters reflected dancing patterns of an ever-changing sky; small fishing rowboats packed the harbor, not the dozens of Stokkseyri and Thorlákshöfn but hundreds.[2] Scattered among them rode tall-masted schooners, their white sails as graceful as swans. What things of beauty they were!

A new world. Every day busier than Stokkseyri at the height of its fishing seasons, foreigners wearing strange clothes, speaking strange tongues. Danish, she recognized of course—she'd have to learn it here, at least to some extent. That was all right; she could do that.

She turned from the water to the land, lava rising directly from the shore in tumbled erratic columns ten to fifteen feet high. Precarious stone slabs formed natural bridges from pillar to pillar bridging hidden caverns, all cloaked in shimmering lichen and moss of umber, chartreuse, and scarlet. Snowcapped mountains, new from the ones she knew so well, glowed white-blue on a distant horizon. She smiled in pleasure. Such tranquil beauty encircling this growing bustling community.

Tucked one above the other among the lava crevices huddled dozens of familiar, low, mound-shaped, sod-roofed stone houses almost indistinguishable from the surrounding landscape. Thurídur counted at least fifty. Must be two hundred people living here or more, all for the fishing and merchant trade. Few farms in sight, a completely different kind of community, one of the only places in the country besides Reykjavík you could call a town. Very strange, at least to her—with its natural harbor, this area had been a trading hub for centuries.[3]

Thurídur took a quiet deep breath. The place was a magnet, new people just like her arriving every day. A daughter of her brother Bjarni now lived here, a nephew of old Brandur.[4] And Margrét, Deputy Einarsson's girl she'd so liked, now married and a mother herself, was here, a welcome familiar face.

And what wealth! Set along the lower land between the shore and the lava outcroppings stood several large timber merchant warehouses and no fewer than four timber houses—amazingly one of them Ari's![5]—he'd named it Street Splendor (*Götuprýði*); it was indeed splendid, but most people called it simply Ari's House (*Arahús*).[6] Any one of these houses was as impressive as The House of Eyrarbakki; tall glass windows through which she saw wooden floors and paneling, imported furnishings—beautiful rugs, cut glassware, mahogany tables and chairs, paintings on the walls. Was this what Europe looked like?

Who could have ever imagined Ari could have done so well?

His wife, María, had recently had another healthy child, more blessings to them.[7] They were also fostering María's sister's children, taking them almost as their own after first the children's father died well over a decade ago and then María's sister in 1826.[8] It felt comforting to see this good man she'd known since childhood, and to whom she would always be grateful, doing so well.

She'd already found a place to live, Skúmsstadir, lodging with a couple also in their fifties, paying with her fishing and new wages.[9] Unlike most people, she was now accustomed to paying rent as a lodger. But this was different. On a farm or with fishing, she had worked with living beings, sustaining—or trying to survive—for herself and others through whatever bounty the earth and sea might give. But here people mostly traded inanimate objects for profit, an odd concept that in Stokkseyri District was contained within the confines of the Eyrarbakki store and a very few men, like Shank. Equally strange on so many levels was being on the opposite side of the merchant-store counter.

Thurídur smiled. She could get used to this. Working for wages and living independently as a lodger meant she was free, at least as much as anyone could be. And here no one knew her, no one would harass or jump at her out of nowhere. Her home may have exiled her, but thanks to Ari, she now stood on the brink of a life transformed. Where, she wondered, would it take her?

As Thurídur approached the store, she saw Ari, so well dressed, clearly managing everything no matter who really owned the place. She knew he'd invited her to come because of the concern both he and his father shared for her safety, but regardless of what precipitated his actions, she could see that he was happy with her work already.

He'd assigned her to the outside job of selling timber, iron, and other items. It required strength, accuracy, careful attention to detail, reliability, and trustworthiness, since the goods were valuable and easy to steal. She could certainly do all that. He told her he'd had the idea seeing other women who worked outside the shops[10] and with the unloading of ships, heavy work they did well.

The outside work also paid women equal wages to men. She would have expected that, and she knew she deserved it. Still, she appreciated his consideration, since he must have known he could have offered her most anything and she would have had little option other than to accept it. The women unloading the ships were treated badly, almost like slaves, paid a third less than the men.[11] She'd already heard reports of their getting harassed.

Thurídur did not expect any trouble from men herself. From her years of being a captain, she had developed an unmistakable aura of authority; her trousers also sent a strong signal. And she was used to working around men.

She found herself working, as Ari did, twelve hours a day or more,[12] an easy load for her, much less than she was used to fishing. In many ways it was not a surprise Ari had chosen trade instead of fishing when he'd had the chance. Fishing could be freezing cold, wet, dangerous, exhausting, with an uncertain return. Trade was much safer, something over which he had more control. He was very lucky Student had taken him as an assistant and taught him what he needed to know to get this position. And now he was passing that luck to her.

In Hafnarfjördur, Thurídur quickly learned the lay of the land. The owner of the Nordborg store where both she and Ari worked was Thomas Thompsen; in the usual practice, he'd inherited it from his father. Thomas had been comfortable with Ari's hiring Thurídur; even he'd heard about her. Here, Thurídur realized, she was almost a celebrity, not a deterrent but a draw with her jaunty tailcoat and short top hat, right in the heart of town. A pleasant change indeed.

Ari had placed her at the front of the store, telling her an important part of her job was to chat with the men strolling by and get them to enter. Clearly being social was important in this business. She saw quickly that much of Ari's success was that people liked and trusted him.[13] It helped being the lone Icelander with whom his customers could trade in their native tongue; clever Ari now spoke both languages.

Even though Thomas owned the store, everyone had started just calling it Ari's Store—after all, he was the person they knew and who they saw doing everything. He'd learned his conversation skills from his father and knew how to get along with everyone regardless of standing, nationality, or wealth, treading lightly that unstable bridge between Danes and Icelanders. It was an ability Thurídur also had; after all, she'd been doing essentially the same thing for years as she wandered among her fellow fishing folk along the shore. Now she could use it consciously in her work at the store.

She took her place outside the shop and started talking and laughing with a group of men passing by, amusing them and consciously drawing them in with her witty comments. She saw Ari watching her with a smile. She knew people were coming to the shop now just to chat with her and that this gained the store respect.

This move to Hafnarfjördur was turning out better than she could have possibly hoped.

As Thurídur amused some potential customers with a comment, out of the corner of her eye, she saw Ari approaching. She finished with the customer and turned to see what he might want.

I'm thinking, he said, that if you're interested, I could put you also in charge of the alcohol.

Thurídur recognized why he was asking her. Handling the alcohol was a very tricky position to fill. First of all, you needed someone who wouldn't guzzle down all your product, not easy to find among men. He would also need someone with whom the thirsty farmers who came in to trade their farm goods could relax and be happy to dally. She'd already figured out that brennivín gave a much better profit margin than other imported goods—quickly learning the myriad details of this complicated profession.

Handling the alcohol was convenient to Thurídur's other duties, Ari pointed out, since they kept the barrel of brennivín[14] near the door—an enticement, one might say. The merchandise he didn't display in the windows—the temptation for thievery was high enough already—but alcohol was a different matter. And from here Thurídur could easily move between handling the alcohol and outside work without missing a thing.

Thurídur considered. She had observed that the shop catered to a variety of customers including foreigners, so the alcohol selection was extensive: customary brennivín but also small bottles of schnapps, rum, port, sherry, all kinds of light wines and spirits. She'd have to learn all that. The quality of the brennivín, which they sold directly from large casks, was inconsistent at best—customers talked about "corn brennivín" or "human-shit brennivín."[15] The difference was because, as the cask levels lessened, Ari—and all the other merchants—topped them off, not with brennivín but with spirits and water to re-create the alcohol content of brennivín. Everyone did this. The customers didn't seem to care much, as long as it was strong enough.

From her position handling the outside wares, Thurídur had observed and become familiar with the social scene around the selling of alcohol, not so different from at the shop in Eyrarbakki. Men—always men—drank at the shop while they bought the items they'd actually come for. Her job, Ari told her, was through her entertaining chatter to encourage them to have a drink as they stood—or sometimes sat—on the square counter beside the barley, rye, and other goods. This was often distracting for Ari behind the counter, but both he and she liked it. The men were amusing, livened up the place, and made the day pass more pleasantly.

Sweetening this already attractive proposal, the job had the added perk of a free eighth of a liter of brennivín each morning,[16] very welcome for heating up the innards and toes during long days standing in the unheated shop and outside.

To Thurídur, this sounded excellent. She was sure she could handle it well. It sounded interesting. And she liked a nip now and then—never to excess, mind you; all things in moderation.

Accepting Ari's proposal, Thurídur became a central presence as the shop prospered. Things were turning out far better than she ever could have expected.

25

ASCENDING MOUNTAINS

1836–1839

Thurídur said goodbye to her latest customer. Then she turned toward the Norwegian-born and Danish-reared merchant P. J. Knudtzen, who'd just entered the store.[1] He'd clearly come to see Ari, or perhaps the shop's new Danish owner, but more likely Ari, since he handled most things. The new owner had recently promoted Ari—an Icelander—to official store manager.[2]

But Knudtzen! He was an important merchant, but most locals saw him as arrogant, aggressive, stubborn, and unreliable. Icelanders gossiped about him behind his back—too dangerous to risk otherwise. Not even the Danes appeared to like him. Following Ari's example, Thurídur made it a point to be always very pleasant, using the mix of Danish and Icelandic she'd learned.

Through chatting with their customers over the few years she'd now lived here, Thurídur had learned a lot about Knudtzen and the other merchants of the various shops. First of all, they were all related. No Icelanders except Ari—although it hadn't always been that way. Until recently an Icelander had had as much influence as Knudtzen had now. That was Bjarni Sívertsen,[3] who had, as a young man of humble means from near Thorlákshöfn, worked for the vice governor and had later married the vice governor's widow. Bjarni had then managed the seemingly impossible—for an Icelander—of negotiating trading rights from the Danes. In the late 1700s, he had partnered with an independent Danish merchant, Westy Petraeus, together acquiring several schooner-style sailing ships. Then, in his final years Bjarni's fortunes had slid rapidly downward, and he'd died the year before Thurídur arrived, leaving a gaping hole in the Hafnarfjördur business market.

The person who jumped in with both feet was...P. J. Knudtzen. Among other properties, he bought at auction Merchant Bjarni's large store and lovely timber house, quickly becoming the biggest merchant in the area, a kingpin.

Already a connected businessman when he came to Iceland, Knudtzen was married to the sister of the same Thomas Thompsen who'd previously owned the Nordborg store where both Thurídur and Ari worked. As his first Hafnarfjördur manager, Knudtzen hired the young Peter Christian Petraeus, a young man already familiar with the shop, since he'd worked there as a teen for Merchant Bjarni.

This consolidated all the power of the community into the hands of a very few closely related Danes.

Except Ari.

As Thurídur greeted Knudtzen, she kept her thoughts to herself and put on a smile, adding a complimentary joke in Danish. They stood together bantering until Ari saw them and came over. He gave Thurídur a grateful nod and invited Knudtzen to his office.

Thurídur turned to a group of men who'd just come in. They looked thirsty for brennivín, she could tell; she knew them. They'd started coming by often, chatting while having a drink. She was learning how to socialize with everyone—regardless of their social standing. It was an illuminating experience. She was learning a lot through this job and new life.

So passed for Thurídur five peaceful years. People liked her; she was even popular. A delightful change after her last years in Stokkseyri! From time to time, she visited her dear friend Margrét, Deputy Einarsson's daughter, who was still living in Hafnarfjördur and now had a small son they called Brynjúlfur.[4] A bit weak this boy, pale. But Thurídur liked him—she liked most children. Ari's family kept growing as well, welcoming a fifth child in 1837.

Between her fishing, living as a lodger, and working at the shop, she had an independent and vibrant life, a future she could scarcely have envisioned during those desperate times so few years before. She had abandoned the idea of ever again having a farm leasehold— here having a farm didn't hold the same power of status and hier-archy, since instead, most people worked for wages. All the same, she yearned for a home of her own rather than being someone else's lodger. Simple was sufficient—as long as it was hers.

But for that she needed more funds. She soon understood that Hafnarfjördur brought the possibility of becoming an entrepreneur—even for a woman—in a way almost unthinkable in Stokkseyri District. She'd observed the society around her and, after a short time, saw an opening for a good opportunity.

Few of the Danes knew much, if anything at all, about the

Icelandic countryside or how to travel through the landscape. Most remained as urban as in Iceland it was possible to get. They came by ship and traveled by ship. If they needed something delivered by land, they had to hire someone to do it; if they wanted to go somewhere outside the narrow confines in which they lived, they needed a guide.

Who better to do this than Thurídur? She'd discovered that she loved traveling, exploring new places. This was an activity she could enjoy and at the same time make extra funds.

Her idea worked. The Danish merchants quickly realized she was not only strong, energetic, clever, and reliable, but also intrepid. They began to hire her to deliver important messages to various people.[5] For Knudtzen, now the most powerful man in town, she did a number of jobs. Even though few people liked him, Thurídur and he got along well enough. For him, she traveled to the Westman Islands (*Vestmanneyjar*) off Iceland's south coast; she also delivered for him a letter to the county commissioner in Borgarfjördur, two days' distance to the northwest. News of her abilities spread. Soon an investor named Gran asked her to guide his brother east to Eyrarbakki, where he'd never been. She not only accomplished this with no difficulties but stayed on as the brother's guide for the rest of his stay in Iceland.

One late autumn, a merchant asked Thurídur to go north and west to a farm at Grafningur, so called because it lies between the hills and the lava. She was to make a deal with the well-known hunter Grímur for some rock ptarmigan, a prized Christmas holiday dish. Grafningur, two days' tough walk from Hafnarfjördur, also lay beyond a pass already covered with trackless snow.

Undaunted, Thurídur said she'd do it. Magnús, a man going

that way, would accompany her, as he'd been along the route before. Thurídur had not, so this sounded good. But Magnús, a drifter (*lausingi*) with no permanent position, had the unsavory nickname Kastról[6]—conveying a reputation as a boozehound. Also, the only shelter along the way, where a number of frozen travelers had already died, was notoriously haunted. Everyone had heard of the horrifying experiences of Grímur, the very ptarmigan hunter they were on their way to see.

Most people refused to stay alone in the haunted shelter that sat beside the now frozen, ominously named Ghost Pond (*Draugatjörn*).[7] A cairn-marked route passed very near the shelter, but, particularly during the snowy months on this frozen, wind-swept, barren lava plain, the hut melted into its surroundings, becoming just another lump of endless snow-covered lava.

Travelers had too many times wandered exhausted in the area of the hut unable to find it; when they finally did, they'd became so cold they stumbled inside and died. Such doomed travelers included good friends of the hunter Grímur.[8]

Before Christmas each year, Grímur traveled alone from his farm to Reykjavík to sell his much-prized ptarmigan, having to traverse this same route in order to get there. Known for ice skating across Lake Thingvellir[9] to capture the best trout around, Grímur was also afraid of the dark and always avoided staying in this hut where his friends had died.

About 1820, he'd set off with his dog and horse as usual, planning to make the trip in one long day. He made it over the pass, but once he reached the lava plain, the weather deteriorated, darkening until his dog became afraid. A storm was coming. Turning around meant he'd have to struggle up and over the high pass against a freezing headwind currently pushing against his back, sure to lead to disaster. The lava uplands on the way forward stretched desolate for miles. The only shelter was the windowless hut beside Ghost Pond.

He left his long-haired horse, used to subzero temperatures, outside and gave it some hay. Then with his dog, he entered the hut, securing the door with a piece of wood. His dog stationed itself near the door to sleep, while Grímur settled on the stone-and-sod bed at the back of the cavelike hut. He always carried his gun with him when he traveled in case he might come across some game; this he now set beside him, loaded with its two shots. For a long time, he lay staring into the pitch black, until finally he fell asleep.

Suddenly he started awake. He heard people outside talking, a number of them with horses. His first reaction was delight. Company.

Then a chill of horror stabbed his spine and spread quickly to every part of his body. He recognized the voices of his friends, the ones who'd come here and died. He grabbed his gun, finger on the unlatched trigger.

The door smashed open, tossing his dog like a feather and slamming it against the far wall. Through the yawning doorway, he heard the movement of a large group entering, talking and laughing as though at a party. But there was no one there.

For a long time Grímur did nothing, just lay frozen in terror, staring into the noisy, empty dark. At the far end of the room, he then saw some sparks, as if from a fire. The sparks began to glow like two orbs of burning coal that gradually transformed into glowing human eyes—he could see veins in the eyeballs. They had an evil stare. Slowly they moved toward him, approaching closer. And closer.

When the eyes reached the bed, he shot them. Suddenly every-thing turned silent, the voices gone, only the solitary sound of the storm still raging outside.

Grímur got up and checked on his beloved dog. It lay dead, killed by the door or whatever force had come with it. Since the door itself wasn't broken, he shut and secured it again, hoping for peace until dawn.

But no. Soon the door burst open again; in came his dead friends, then the eyes. Again he shot at them, and again everything went silent. But that was his last bullet.

Terrified beyond sense, Grímur ran from the hut, leaving his belongings behind. The weather was better, so he could somewhat see, and he knew the way. He grabbed his horse, riding as fast as he could, leaving the cursed hut behind. Still he rode. He rode so hard that when he finally reached safety, his horse died from exhaustion.

Grímur lived many years after this, still a respected ptarmigan hunter, but he was never the same. People said he was all right most of the time, but sometimes, particularly in the dark months, he went insane.

The day for Thurídur and Magnús's journey dawned with a light wind blowing out of the north and carrying cold, clear weather that left the snow hard and good for walking. Perfect for their long trek across the lava uplands to reach the rudimentary shelter where they planned to spend the night. The next day they'd climb over the mountain pass leading to Grafningur beside the enormous Lake Thingvellir and the inland farm of the ptarmigan hunter Grímur.[10]

Using their sturdy, spiked wooden walking staffs,[11] Thurídur and

Magnús traversed the long miles to the dilapidated stone-and-turf shelter set in the shadow of the steep slopes they would climb the next day. Despite the snow, they found the hut without difficulty, grown even more dilapidated over the years but still the only shelter on this frequently traveled route. At least there were two of them.

During the night a moaning low wind arose. No glowing eyes, but the next morning's late dawn arrived filtered through thickening cloud that descended like a heavy quilt. Climbing over the pass, they'd make Grafningur before the early nightfall.

As they trudged up the steep, snowy mountainside, the nothingness of thick cloud soon enclosed them. As they continued to climb, it started to snow, filtering through the cloud, softly at first, no wind. Then a cold north wind stirred, first in deceptively gentle tentacles curling dangerous fingers around them. As they reached the pass, it rose to buffeting fists. They now walked bent against the wind along a cliff-littered ridge able to see mere feet on either side. The route led along the ridge for some miles until they would reach a spot where they were supposed to descend toward Grafningur. For a time one side of the ridge rose in a protective and defining slope, but then it flattened, completely unprotected on all sides.

"We'd be wiser to turn back," Thurídur said at this point. "Soon we won't be able to see our way at all. Better to turn back than risk getting lost and freezing to death."[12] From where they were they could still find their way back to the hut.

Magnús scoffed. Only losers turn back, he said.

Perhaps his terror of spending another night in the ghostly hut outweighed his fear of getting lost. He'd gone this way before, he assured Thurídur; he knew the way. She could trust him.

Such brazen boasts seldom turn out well.

26

FATE LISTENS TO NO ONE

1836–1840

Despite his flagrant boast, what Magnús said was true—he had apparently walked this route before, and Thurídur had not.[1] But she knew mountains. And she knew weather.

They struggled forward, seeing nothing, using their staffs to steady themselves, supposedly north and west along the ridgeline toward the route down. The wind blew in gale-force gusts. They could walk off a cliff and never know it until they fell.

Suddenly Magnús stopped, sagging on his staff. "I don't know anymore where we are or where we should go," he said. "We'd better return to the hut."

Thurídur stared at him a moment in silence. "It's too late for that," she said. They'd now been walking along the unseen ridge for hours. "We'll never find the pass, let alone the shelter. And we've gone so far now, it's closer for us to go forward than back." They should be getting fairly close to the descent by now. Even if they could retrace their steps, they'd never reach the hut by nightfall.

Instead of trudging forward, Magnús stared at Thurídur's bag, where he knew she carried an emergency bottle of brennivín. "I have no courage to go forward," he told her. "Unless I get some refreshment."

Thurídur set her jaw. "I'll not open the bag in this storm."

"Well, then, I won't move one foot from here," he replied obstinately. "I'll die where I am."

Both their lives were at stake; they could stand here arguing until they died. Her eyes flashing, Thurídur pulled the bottle from her bag and passed it to Magnús. He grabbed it, drinking long and deep before passing it back.

Thurídur took a small sip herself—fortitude for dealing with this idiot. She'd never be able to keep the bottle from him now, and he'd soon drink himself incapable of walking.

With great deliberation, she held up the bottle and smashed it into a million pieces against her walking staff.

"Even though we may now get into very serious circumstances," she told him, "it will not be the bottle that kills us."

Furious, Magnús declared he wouldn't go another step.

Thurídur had had enough. "You can choose what you want," she said. She walked forward through the snow and blasting whiteout in the direction she considered best.

After a few minutes, Magnús followed. It seemed he wasn't yet ready to die, regardless of what he'd said or the lack of drink.

They walked a long time along the ridgetop, still unable to see, Thurídur in the lead now, Magnús trailing behind. The impenetrable white dimmed gray as afternoon edged toward autumn's early dark—once that happened, they'd freeze to death. Like so many lost travelers before.

Suddenly, indistinct, sliding through the wind, came a dog's bark, somewhere off the ridge, a long way away. But in this country where the largest wild mammal was the arctic fox, they'd definitely heard a dog. A dog meant a farm. Somewhere. Thurídur shifted direction and headed toward the sound. Maybe they wouldn't die after all.

Then right in front of them, the ground fell away in an abrupt drop. They stood on the edge of a very steep slope covered with hard snow. They'd climbed up a long way, the drop before them could be a thousand feet, it could lead to a sheer cliff. Below, unseen, could be anything.

Magnús gave up. "We can't possibly pass this," he said. "At the bottom there's probably a valley full of outlaws anyway. We have to turn back."

But they couldn't turn back; that way led to certain death.

Thurídur stood at the edge. Through the murky gloom and shifting snow she assessed the slope and conditions. What she was thinking might mean a quick demise. But turning back had no "might" about it. She secured her bag and placed her walking staff between her legs, clutching its top in front of her, with its metal spike digging into the hard snow behind. "Don't speak, Magnús," she said, "and do what I do."

With that, she shoved herself off the edge. Sliding into a rapid glissade, she pulled the front of the staff up, digging the sharp spike into the snow behind. She and other Icelanders often did this as children on much shorter and safer slopes. The staff became a brake, allowing her to control to some extent her direction and speed. But if she fell, it was all over.

Magnús watched in dismay as she flew down the slope and out of sight. Unless he followed her, he was now alone. His decision didn't take long. He grabbed his own staff and shoved off.

From the bottom, where Thurídur had arrived just fine, she watched Magnús slide to a halt without serious injury. They'd made it. Off the ridge, but not to safety.

In front of them, parallel to the mountainside, ran a river, its water fairly low now but swift-moving, its ice broken and unstable. Clambering along its bank for some distance, they finally found a place they deemed safe enough to cross. They heard the dog bark again, considerably closer this time. A farm was around—somewhere.

"Where do you think this is?" Magnús asked in trepidation, still worried about outlaws.

"Reykjakot farm in Ölfus is the most likely," Thurídur replied. This was not in the direction they were supposed to have headed, too far east and way too far south, back toward the coast instead of north.

Magnús shook his head. "No," he contended, "we've kept the direction more to the north, so that can't be right."

Thurídur shrugged. "We should try to get there, whatever farm it is."

They continued in the direction of the bark over seemingly endless hills and valleys, up and down, over and around. The wind blew from all directions at once, shooting down the mountainsides beside them. Full dark fell. The air, already freezing, grew colder. Still, Thurídur walked steadily forward into the ebony night. They heard the dog again, now even closer.

Finally, they saw the dimmest glimmer of light, a barely discernible farmhouse. It was late; people having their evening readings would be just about finished. Had they been any later, the farmer would have extinguished the oil reading lamp, making the house invisible, an indistinguishable mound of snow in the dark. Thurídur and Magnús could have frozen a hundred yards away from safety. Many had.

The farmer and his family opened the door, drew them in out of the snow, and fed them.

"Where are we?" Magnús asked.

"Reykjakot," the farmer replied. "Was that where you meant to be?"

No, not really. From the pass, Magnús had led them in completely the wrong direction. They were now halfway to Eyrarbakki, as far from their destination as when they'd started. But Reykjakot farm was precisely where Thurídur had expected they were headed. Once she'd taken over the lead, trying only to guide them off the mountains to safety, she'd figured her direction exactly.

The next morning again dawned bright and clear, excellent traveling weather. Exhausted and traumatized, Magnús declared he was sick.

So Thurídur set out alone, reached Grafningur without incident, met the hunter Grímur—adding to tales of this formidable route— negotiated her business there, and returned to Hafnarfjördur. Even though she was almost sixty, by herself Thurídur had no problems at all.

After an urgent request, Thurídur was headed back to Eyrarbakki to embark on another adventure. A boat owner apparently wanted two boats moved from Eyrarbakki to the community of Gríndavík, way out on the tip of the Reykjanes Peninsula, a long distance past Thorlákshöfn along a dangerous exposed coast.[2]

After discussing their unprotected role in this venture, all the deckhands of one of the captains assigned to take the boats had walked off the job—a shocking rebellion. They wouldn't go unless Captain Thurídur led them. Everything sat at a standstill as they waited for Thurídur to arrive.

As she approached the community that had exiled her and was now seemingly forced to ask for her help, Thurídur considered. The route held currents and reefs she didn't know. She'd also never been that way before. But the urgent request came from deckhands, whose safety might be at stake. The weather looked good and likely to hold for the long row. She was up for a challenge. Sure, she'd give it a try.

As they set out, the second boat fell behind, letting Thurídur lead both boats. In that fashion, they made it safely with no reported incident.

Cautiously, Thurídur had caught up with those she'd known for so many years in Eyrarbakki and Stokkseyri District. She heard from Ingibjörg the sad report that her husband had died on the Ides of March 1836,[3] only forty-four years old, leaving Ingibjörg a widow with five surviving children, the youngest only five years old.

But Ingibjörg was fully capable of taking care of herself, managing the farm with her children. Jón Rich had recently added their farm to his stockpile, and he let her continue the leasehold. Why not? She was an excellent manager. Thurídur smiled, remembering a story she'd heard. When Ingibjörg was pregnant with her last child, her other children had come running up from the estuary. A seal! they shouted. They'd come across a seal just sitting there!

Many Icelanders considered seals ancient soldiers of the Pharaoh from the Red Sea returned to mortal realms.[4] As a renowned sealing woman said in referring to seals, "We have eaten a lot of ghosts. Do you suppose the sons of the Pharaoh were any more beautiful than them? What would we have to eat on our farm if not for the blessed seals?"[5]

The seal was a gift that Ingibjörg, even heavily pregnant, wasn't about to let waddle away. No matter that seals were dangerous and attacked people. She ran to the shore, grabbing a heavy wooden plank along the way, and knocked it dead. Then she and the children dragged it up to the house to butcher. Thanks to the seal, they had plenty of food.

It seems she hadn't lost any of the nerve and strength she'd shown at sea with Thurídur.

Thurídur's sister Salgerdur and her husband, Kristján, were not doing so well. Since their daughter Helga had left her farm service before the end of the contract, they were now obliged to compensate the farmer for whom she'd been working.[6] Kristján—in a role he seemed to take often—told the mediation court he just wanted to do what he could to make everyone happy. Hopefully they'd sort it out.

Although Salgerdur still disliked her, Thurídur had little cause to feel resentment anymore. They'd given her refuge when she'd needed it, and Thurídur had hired one of their sons as a deckhand, a likable young man.[7]

They had a hard lot, her sister and brother-in-law. They'd never been able to get rid of old Móri.[8] By now, dozens had encountered him, still omnipresent and pestering people. He'd decided to shadow their son Einar. Poor Einar, perhaps ill-advisedly named after his grandfather, who'd caused this mess to begin with. Móri followed Einar first to one farm, then the next. Three generations down, six to go.

Not that the community was showing much more compassion than Thurídur and Salgerdur's father had over fifty years before. A woman currently living in Eyrarbakki, who everyone knew was on the insane side, had recently hit another woman who took care of local children. In reaction, a mob of residents had attacked her, robbing her of all her meager possessions.

Thurídur was not about to let this action pass. Demented and not responsible for her actions, the woman had been left with nothing, as good as left to die—echoing Deputy Jón Rich's treatment of Thurídur herself not so many years before. But Thurídur—thank God—had friends. This woman had no one to defend her—except, it seemed, Thurídur.

Despite knowing she herself still faced threats in the area, Thurídur quickly dictated a letter to Archdeacon Jakob, her powerful friend of almost forty years.[9] She didn't bother with formality but, in a way few would dare with an archdeacon, told him exactly what she thought.

It was his responsibility to deal with this. "It looks to me as if the Devil has come from beyond with great wrath" to incite people to act in this way, she wrote. Surely, Archdeacon Jakob would not, "like Pontius Pilate, wash his hands in the care of one of his parish." If the woman had done wrong, Thurídur challenged him, let the courts decide. "[S]urely they lived in a land of law, not uncontrolled mayhem."

She had confidence he would do what he could. But if Gudrún and Páll were any example, justice did not favor women with few friends. Despite Thurídur's advocacy, dominance-fixated Páll had managed to keep Gudrún from being able to divorce him.[10] Only when, at the age of forty-seven, she'd become so sick she couldn't take care of herself—when Páll as her legal husband would be obliged to pay her support—did he, seemingly with no impediment, decide he would divorce, leaving her alone, sick, and destitute.[11]

Then last year, Páll had gotten himself into some trouble, being caught for a thievery spree with his housemate, stealing coal, butter, bread, rye, barley, wool, lard, and beans from the merchant houses in both Stokkseyri and Eyrarbakki. For all this, he got "only" twenty lashes, considerably less than meted out to men convicted of much less during the infamous 1828 trials.[12] But by now, CC Thórdur had moved on to a more elevated role as a national high judge,[13] replaced by a less harshly minded man.

Páll's own obstinacy had got him in the end. At forty-six, he caught smallpox. Iceland had been vaccinating for this since 1800, but Páll claimed vaccinations were just a superstition. The only thing you needed to do when you got sick, he claimed, was to curse and suck it up. He apparently tried this on his death bed. It didn't work.[14]

27
FIERY REINS OF THE SEA

1840

Amid the news from her home district, Thurídur could hardly avoid hearing of Jón Rich. At sixty-eight, he'd recently retired from being deputy after holding the district largely under his dominance for thirty-three years.

A relief, even if she no longer lived there. People said that recently his health had started to deteriorate; he had shaky hands, poor eyesight, and respiratory problems.[1] Thurídur had often seen such respiratory issues, arising from living in smoky, poorly ventilated houses. Jón Rich could have built himself a house to rival Ari's, she noted, but he never had, never improved his own house, never made life easier for himself or his family. Why he didn't was a mystery. Instead he used his money to buy more property, always paying cash and never selling, collecting more and more farms like playing cards before a storm.

Thurídur had heard that he'd ensured his continuing connection to the official role, since his favorite daughter's husband, Adolf, had immediately taken over the deputy position upon Jón Rich's leaving. So perhaps he hadn't given up complete control after all. And in buying up all these farms, Jón Rich was now landlord to almost anyone who held a leasehold in the area, giving him a huge amount of power over their lives. He had bought Kalastadir where Sesselja and Gísli lived, so their leasehold was presumably now secure no matter how they maintained it—at least for as long as Jón Rich lived. He had bought East Peathouse, where his neighbor Sigrídur lived, and Símon's House, the dilapidated hovel of Margrét, Erlendur's half sister, who'd recently died. He had also bought Ranakot, where Thurídur was born, and then Gata.[2]

Had Thurídur stayed at Gata, Jón Rich would have by now been collecting her rent, able to tell her how to manage the farm—or demand she leave as he chose. It seemed that, finally, this was a regret she could leave behind, especially now that she'd found a new and exciting life in Hafnarfjördur.

Meanwhile, the merchant Lambert had lost the formerly prosperous Eyrarbakki store with his drunkenness and mismanagement.[3] In a sad demise, it had recently sold through auction, leaving Lambert, born to all kinds of opportunities given only to the very few, a pauper dependent on the district.

One person doing very well, against every expectation, was the youngest Kolbeinsson brother, Thorleifur.[4] Like Shank Jón Geirmundsson, Thorleifur had early gone into trade alongside his farming. He'd charged high prices for his wares and grown prosperous. Thurídur had also heard that he now always treated with equanimity those who stole from him—after all, both his older brothers sat decaying in a Danish prison. He'd seen enough pain.

Keeping his word, Thorleifur had married his brother Poet Jón's fiancée and taken over the leasehold of half the Stéttir farm when Shank Jón Geirmundsson lost it after being convicted. He'd then taken over the leasehold of Ingunn's Big Lava—the former home of his other brother, Haflidi. There he'd generously hired Jón Geirmundsson's timid younger brother, Snorri, as a farmhand, just as Thurídur had done at Gata some years before.[5] She heard the sad news that Haflidi's young wife had died, leaving their child to be raised alone by Ingunn, who in her advancing years had become essentially Thorleifur's farmhand even though she still owned the land.

Thorleifur, with his hawkish nose, wide mouth, and sharp bright eyes, had grown thick in the waist, sported luxurious thick hair, and had large muttonchops. Thurídur smiled to herself. Although he was still short in stature, no one called him miserable anymore.

Of the families of the Kambur robbers, the news was grim. After the 1828 trials, people had placed much blame for the robbers' actions on their parents. For Shank Jón, it was his father. For Sigurdur, his mother, Kristín, bore the brunt of the blame. This did not surprise Thurídur. Rejected and reduced to poverty, Kristín and her daughter were now eking out a meager existence going from farm to farm begging. Now in his late seventies, Gosi hadn't fared much better, doing essentially the same thing and completely destitute.

The news of Poet Jón was the saddest of all.

In Denmark, he'd spent much of his time composing poetry and reading psalms, mired in unending remorse. Depression had overwhelmed him until he was unable even to pretend an interest in life.[6] Recently people had heard reports from Denmark that he was dead—by suicide. Haflidi, still in Denmark despite his sentence having been supposedly finished at least two years ago, was apparently inconsolable, left there alone, without the brother whose fate he'd volunteered to share.

Thurídur thought of her intelligent friend, a poet and deep thinker. She remembered them laughing, working together at sea, bringing in good catches, rowing hard before a storm, their talks of God and faith. Would that his sins be forgiven as he arrived at Heaven's door. A good man who had already suffered enough hell.

Once more, Thurídur had returned to Thorlákshöfn for the fishing season. The high promontory, with its broad view of the sea and anyone fishing, was where[7] people signaled to fishing boats in rough surf when to make an approach, just as they'd done for Farmer and Jón Rich in 1812. Family and friends of seafarers also climbed up to stand beside its cairn to watch their loved ones come in. Everyone took great care of the promontory cairn, because if it ever fell, it foretold of an impending shipwreck.

During the winter of 1840, the cairn fell. The people of Thorlákshöfn immediately restacked it, trying to save their fishing fleet from destiny.

Such attempts inevitably fail—destiny is never celebrated for its humanity.

The long winter season had nearly finished, the dark nights replaced by early April's light, the first Saturday of official summer under Iceland's traditional two-season year. Many boats were out fishing, including Thurídur's, now a six-oar owned by Thorleifur—the man she'd once employed as a favor.[8] Deputy Árni, the excellent captain with whom she'd competed when she'd first arrived ten years ago, was out in his large ten-oared boat. So was his brother Halldór, also on a ten-oar with a crew of fifteen. So were many others, including Jón Ólafsson—the man who had lived with Thurídur for a few weeks so many years ago when they were young, now a seasoned captain himself.[9]

They'd all gone out late, a gloomy morning despite the early dawn, the air thick and heavy. A stiff breeze blew from the south off the sea, creating some white caps but not strong enough to prevent them fishing, even though late in the season when they caught little.

As the day progressed, the wind increased; the swell rolling in across the ocean grew larger. About noon some boats returned to shore. Wind and waves continued to grow, and between half past one and three, all the boats were in—except four: those of Jón Ólafsson, Árni, Halldór, and Thurídur.

People on shore climbed up to the cairn to watch them come in. They paid particular attention to the dangerous, barely submerged rock Kúla at the cove's entrance. If the swell rose high enough to start breaking over it, they knew the seas had become too rough for the boats to make it in.

Thurídur came first. She clearly hadn't caught much, but she and her crew made good progress through the swell. Then as they reached the surf, they caught the crest of a single large wave, staying balanced and riding it all the way to the landing site. Deftly done. Thurídur, at sixty-three, continued as one of their very best captains.

The next boat was Jón Ólafsson's. He and his crew tried rowing east and from there into the cove to land. But there was too much surf, so they stopped, waiting. Finally, Jón Ólafsson saw the promontory signal of a break. They rowed like mad and made it safely ashore.

The swell began breaking over Kúla. Árni's boat now approached, deciding also to row in from the east. He too stopped, waiting for the signal of a break. It came, and with his strong crew beside him, they made it. Only one more boat out. His brother's.

Halldór, following Árni, came from the east. But he turned too soon and hit Kúla. As he and his crew tried to row away from the rock, a huge wave smashed over the boat, washing all the port-side oars overboard. The enormous waves now breaking over Kúla arched over the entire boat, crashing down on top of the crew and filling the boat until they sat on thwarts awash with water. The next wave washed away the rest of the oars and all the crew. Except one. In a boat full of water, the lone man began to float away from Kúla with no oars or any way to steer.

Árni and his crew had already pulled up his boat and taken off their sea clothes. But when people from the cairn ran down to report what had just happened, he ordered his crew to redress themselves immediately and prepare to go back out. As his deckhands, they were obliged to do as their captain ordered, no matter how foolhardy and regardless of danger. They pushed the boat to the water's edge, but by now the surf was so turbulent they couldn't even get it into the water. They stood together, helpless, waiting for a break.

As they waited, the elderly father of Árni and Halldór, wearing only his underclothes, hobbled down the bank toward them, holding his staff and led by a young man. He welcomed his son who'd come safely to shore.

"Once I get the chance, I'm going out again," Árni told him.[10]

"In the name of God," his father replied, "do not go back out in the face of obvious danger. This tragedy is bad enough as it is. There is no reason to add to it."

After saying this, he turned, allowing the young man to lead him back home, where he lay down on his bed.

Árni remained obstinately by his boat, still waiting for a break that never came. Finally, he had to give up and let his boat be pulled back up the shore. People rushed to help, relieved that he hadn't risked not only his own life but everyone else's on his crew. His father was right. They already had a great tragedy; Árni's action would have made it worse.

Those who stayed at the cairn saw the sea carry the boat with its single occupant west and then out toward the open sea. Because they knew where each crew member sat on each boat, they could speculate who he likely was, but they could never know for sure. When they could see him no more, they slowly walked down the hill. Fifteen men dead. Árni and Halldór's father never again rose from his bed and died two months later.

After this, Thurídur stopped being a captain. She felt the great strength one needed for this work beginning to fade; best to stop now before she brought tragedy on herself or her crew. She'd fished for fifty-two years and been a captain for twenty-four. In that time, she'd never lost a single crew member or damaged a boat under her care. She'd caught as much as the very best captains, even when she had a smaller boat and crew.

That year, Pastor Gudmundur Torfason wrote verses for all the captains of Thorlákshöfn, one for each captain. Except Thurídur. For her he wrote two. Here is one that has survived:

At her prow seas leap aside
as her fiery reins set the ride.
On the tail of this golden goddess
step few men even of prowess.[11]

28

WHAT IS HOME?

1841–1845

Giving up being a fishing captain—after having waited so many years to become one—was a hard decision. But it was time. More than time, as most captains stopped much earlier than Thurídur's sixty-three years. She decided she'd still fish as a deckhand for someone else for a few years, just as so many others did, not abandoning the sea work completely, still making fish-share income but leaving the responsibility in someone else's hands. As a deckhand she'd earn less, but she'd always done well regardless of crew position. Her work at the store and her guiding business would be quite adequate, for a few more years at least.

She'd fish where she could easily return between fishing days, she decided, from Álftanes (Swan Ness) near Reykjavík, just a few miles outside Hafnarfjördur. The major owner among the few boats fishing there was a woman, Thóra Jónsdóttir, prominent enough that her farm still bears her name, Thórukot. Thóra had become a widow when her husband, father, and brother all drowned at the same time.[1] The burden of such unthinkable grief did not destroy her. Instead she managed the farm and boat alone so well that she soon bought a second boat. Since this is the area where Thurídur chose to work, it could hardly have been for anyone else.

But no longer staying at the Thorlákshöfn fishing hut for several months each year left her staying in Hafnarfjördur much of the year—she would need a new place to live. When Ari graciously invited her to stay with them at the beautiful Ari's House, she readily accepted—as a temporary measure.[2] He had already done so much for her, she wouldn't impose on him for long. His large and boisterous family just kept getting bigger. Between María's midwifery, their own children, foster children—two of them now working for Ari at the store—and their various house servants, the house almost burst at its seams. But his thoughtful offer did give Thurídur breathing space to find something more suitable.

As she worked at the store greeting and chatting with customers, Thurídur reflected on this bustling town where she'd lived for six years. No fewer than thirty-one sailing schooners were now coming each year, 340 residents, many recent migrants from other parts of the country.[3] At the shop, gossip about the businessman Knudtzen was taking an increasingly intense tone as he bought more and more property, adding to the late Merchant Bjarni's house and shop the ownership of two more shops in Hafnarfjördur and part of a third in Reykjavík.[4] Knudtzen had also begun a project for a sulfur mine just outside Hafnarfjördur with none other than Jón Rich and Student from Eyrarbakki. He owned several trading ships. Thurídur heard notes of alarm from people talking in knots beside the store. The traders had grown tired of his aggressive behavior. Would he soon control everything?

So it came as not a complete surprise when in 1841 Thurídur, along with everyone else, learned that the other merchants had penned an open letter informing the public—and Knudtzen—that they'd managed to get a ruling passed stipulating that a merchant could own only one shop at a time. They'd see how he reacted to that.

With the help of her kind friends Ari and María, Thurídur soon found an excellent new place to live; how did she get so lucky, both with these friends and the housing?

Knudtzen's young manager, Peter Christian Petraeus, had moved into the late Merchant Bjarni's—now Knudtzen's—lovely timber house. This was really a homecoming for Peter, since he'd lived there as a teen when he'd worked as Merchant Bjarni's assistant.[5] He'd recently married Ingibjörg Níelsdóttir Olsen, who also knew the house well, as she'd grown up there too, living with Merchant Bjarni and his wife—not a mystery how the two got together. Ari and María were their good friends, even witnesses at their wedding.[6]

Just beginning their family, Peter and Ingibjörg had plenty of room, enough that Thurídur could rent space on their wide second story, a room with a wood floor and high beamed ceiling. Also, unlike in most houses, the room was dry and bright, with a large glass window. Since the house had a stove instead of the usual open fire, its air was also clear, not full of the choking smoke endemic in the stone-and-turf houses where she'd mostly lived.[7] Living space like a palace. In addition, Thurídur was saving money.

This all worked great until two years later when in 1844 Peter and his wife decided to move.[8] The insecurity of always living in someone else's space again reared its hoary head, but this time it didn't unsettle Thurídur. Instead, she finally managed to acquire a home of her own—triumph!

A square, two-story warehouse (*Skemman*) on the hill above Ari's House, her new home had an upstairs living space.[9] Its back of turf and stone was built into the hillside, but the front was timber with a glass window above the door. Wide, airy, and spacious, the loft living space came with an even larger glass window. A couple in their forties and their son stayed with her, and she even had a housekeeper, Hólmfrídur Sverrisen, who came in daily.

The space may have seemed simple to some in Hafnarfjördur, but Thurídur could hardly have been happier. She now had her own living space, better than most in Stokkseyri. Those last years in Stokkseyri District had been dark, with people intent on her destruction. But fate, and friendships, had led her to this new wonderful life she would never have experienced otherwise.

All along the Hafnarfjördur shore, people were abuzz, news arriving long before the 1844 spring postal ship even put down anchor. Among its passengers were the two surviving Kambur robbers, seemingly returned from the dead.

In 1839 a new king had ascended the throne in Denmark, King Christian VIII. While not as liberal as many had hoped, he had the previous year allowed reestablishment of the Icelandic Parliament, abolished since the Enlightenment reforms of 1800. Although still only a consultatory body to Danish rule, it was at least a Parliament.[10] He also reformed the Danish prison system, releasing a large number of prisoners—including, in 1844, Shank Jón Geirmundsson and Haflidi Kolbeinsson.[11] Why couldn't Jón Kolbeinsson have kept his despair at bay a few more years?

By the time Haflidi and Shank Jón stepped off the boat, they encountered a changed world. They'd been away fourteen years.

As the two men learned about various people they knew and loved, they also showed how they themselves had changed during those long years in prison. Considering he'd been sentenced to generally terrible conditions, Haflidi came out of the experience astonishingly well. While in prison, he'd somehow managed to get himself permission to tag along with the prison doctor, giving him assistance. From this, he learned medicine—a chance he'd never have got at home. Since doctors were in short supply in Iceland, doctoring quickly became Haflidi's new occupation.

He also returned to Iceland with a considerable sum of money, though he never flaunted it—he knew what trouble came of this! He said he'd learned this caution while in prison where inmates stole from each other. One could speculate he also knew well the dangers of envious neighbors.

Beyond his newfound medical knowledge, Haflidi also returned with, hidden in his pockets,[12] some potatoes, then unknown in this part of Iceland. He planted them in Stokkseyri near the seawall, protected from the wind. They grew well, and as people added them to their diet, the vitamin C they contained helped to prevent previously problematic scurvy.

He returned to the Big Lava farm, where he'd lived before, now held by his leaseholder little brother, Thorleifur. There Haflidi faced his wife having died and their child having grown into a teenager. At least he had a home.

Shank Jón Geirmundsson returned to Eyrarbakki, where the merchant store, now under new ownership, hired him to work outside for that first summer. There he quickly became infamous for not letting anyone touch anything. In the autumn, he went to live in Thorlákshöfn with his beloved daughter Sigga, now a married woman whom he hadn't seen since she was about ten. He hardly knew her anymore, but Johnsen had kept his word, and she'd grown to a healthy adult.

Shank Jón found that many people he loved had died. His ex-wife, whom he'd liberated to remarry on Johnsen's request, had passed away the previous year; even her child had died.[13] With a convoluted twist of emotion, he also learned that Johnsen, that man both so harsh and then so generous, had also recently died.[14] He'd fallen through the ice while attempting to cross a river and drowned, frozen in the saddle of his horse. People remembered that the horse, an excellent and usually compliant steed, had sensed this impending danger and had that morning refused to budge until Johnsen hit him several times.

Shank Jón's younger brother "Snap it Snorri" had also recently drowned while fishing in the south—and, it seemed, was apparently not quite ready to accept his abrupt demise.

On the evening he drowned, Thorleifur's wife saw what appeared to be Snorri standing in their doorway—even though Snorri had been staying in a fishing hut, not returning home each night.[15]

When Thorleifur arrived, she asked him to step to the side of the entrance, as Snorri had come in. Unlike his wife, Thorleifur knew Snorri was dead. Realizing that this had to be his ghost moving in, Thorleifur took a broom and swept him out. "If you can't stay outside, then get into the stable!" he shouted.

They never saw Snorri again, but for some time any horse they tried to stable besides their own would be outside in the morning, no matter how securely they fastened the door—unless Thorleifur's wife fastened it.

After waiting so many years to see his beloved daughter Sigga, Shank Jón found he didn't like Thorlákshöfn.[16] He had somehow saved an astonishing four hundred Danish state dollars during his years in Denmark, so he approached Gróa, the woman with whom he'd had the affair that broke up his first marriage. Her own husband having died, she now lived in the bustling community of Hafnarfjördur. When Shank Jón told her he could pay his own way as a lodger, Gróa quickly accepted and Shank Jón moved in, yet another familiar face for Thurídur in this growing town.

Shank Jón liked to sit at the front of the house entertaining adults and children alike with his fearsome stories of prison life in Denmark. That these horrific experiences could become engrossing tales reflected that he had finally found some tranquility—and perhaps even redemption.

In this passage of time, Thurídur watched her contemporaries die in increasing numbers, her school of swimming companions showing increasing gaps of empty blue sea. She learned of the recent deaths of Erlendur and, much too young, her misguided ex-husband, Jón Egilsson[17]—whom, despite his ill-conceived intimate blackmail, Thurídur remembered fondly; the other not so much. Now sixty-seven, she was older than either of them. Last year, she'd finally given up even deckhanding. Her work at sea had run as a continuous thread as everything else shifted and changed. Now that too had slid away.

Eventually she would have to retire from the store—what would she do then? In Hafnarfjördur, she'd found peace, stability, and acceptance, a place she wanted to remain. But without work, she'd be required to return to her home district Stokkseyri, a prospect she did not at all cherish. Was there any way to escape this?

In order to support herself and be able to stay in Hafnarfjördur, Thurídur decided to petition for a pension—again. She deserved it. CC (now Judge) Thórdur would not support her; that was clear. But what about this new Danish king, who'd released the Kambur robbers? He seemed to have more consideration for Icelanders than the last king. Perhaps he could be made aware of the achievements and dedication of one of his humble servants. Thurídur would write directly to him. She contacted Archdeacon Jakob, who readily agreed to write her a letter of support for this venture.

She had a clerk at the court office (*Kanselli*)[18] sponsor her and help her "write with rightful words and grace to look to the king's judgment."[19] She referred to a previous recent petition that Regional Governor Krieger[20] had promised he'd bring to the king's attention, but unfortunately, Krieger had "not been seen since then because the man laid down and died." Although she lamented that "this body which has given me such joy will now start to weaken," she explained that she had previously captained the boats of respectable men including Archdeacon Jakob and Student, who would testify to the care she'd taken of both her crews and their boats. The best pension, she suggested, would be what she'd been earning fishing, one hundred Danish state dollars a year. If the king could be pleased to have any pension or communication delivered to the Petraeus House in Hafnarfjördur, she would be grateful.

"[T]hrough the waves of the sea, I was more often the giver than the taker," she wrote. "Not for a single day that I have been a captain have I gone out without giving one or two fish to the poor with the permission of my crew members." Of her farming, she described the "field walls I repeatedly kept up at my expense, even though the sea tore them down every time I built them." She also noted her grief at losing her child, of her adoption of another, an invalid.

If this petition, with Archdeacon Jakob's accompanying support letter, was not sufficient, she wrote, could the authorities please "send me to Copenhagen myself to the king or to the highest authorities they can find. If I go on this venture, the authorities need to pay the cost of my travel. It would be best if I were allowed to wear male clothing because I have nothing else.

"What the Almighty pleases the authorities do now is under his advice and power.

"Thurídur Einarsdóttir"

As she waited for the response she hoped would come, she continued living in her comfortable warehouse home and working at the shop. The following May, a year after the Kambur robbers had returned, she watched in anticipation of the yearly arrival of the postal ship. It brought no word of her petition, but as it put down anchor, the waterfront erupted in even more curious chatter than usual. Gossip had it that this year among the passengers was a middle-aged woman who seemed to be German, and she'd arrived traveling alone.

29

A GUIDE FOR
ALL SEASONS

1845–1847

Ida Pfeiffer stood at the rail of the postal ship as it approached Hafnarfjördur harbor. Her first landing at this exotic land they called Iceland! It was mid-May in 1845, when it barely got dark, brilliant northern sunlight casting color vibrant and intense, the sky a bottomless blue.

The forty-eight-year-old Austrian was traveling alone, catching the cheapest rides she could. And now she was going to explore Iceland.[1] She'd come a long way to reach this point.

She remembered her childhood as idyllic, like Thurídur allowed to wear trousers, her father encouraging her to run around and build her strength, ensuring she got the same education as her brothers. But when she was nine he died, and her mother changed everything. No more wearing trousers; Ida was supposed to be a lady and play piano. She hated playing piano, going so far as to cut her fingers so she wouldn't be able to.

Ida was allowed a tutor. He introduced her to books about the world that became her escape, her passion and her dream—to explore for herself all these far-off lands. By the time she'd reached seventeen, the shared love of travel books between her and her tutor had blossomed to a mutual love of each other—but her mother quickly put a stop to that. Ida was to marry a man her mother deemed suitable to her status—preferably rich.

Unlike in many romantic novels, the young lovers never overcame parental dictate, and at twenty-two, Ida got married off to a man her mother found appropriate—also twenty-four years her senior and not a pleasant man. Ida had two sons with him, but overall, the marriage was an ugly example of how women too often fare in forced unions.

Through all this, Ida kept her dreams alive. It took her twenty years, but once her sons were grown, she managed to get a legal separation from her husband. Then he died. This left her impoverished but finally able to do what she wanted. Figuring that a trip to the Holy Land, thinly labeled a pilgrimage, would of her longed-for destinations appear the most acceptable for the middle-aged single woman she'd become, she learned from a priest the minimum he thought such a venture might cost, and then she managed to scrape together the funds. In many ways, it was a pilgrimage, one of her freedom.

When Ida returned from these travels, her friends encouraged her to publish her diaries. What a good idea!

Witty and observant, they became an instant best seller.[2] Ecstatic, she immediately used the money for her next adventure, this one to the Far North: Scandinavia, the Faeroe Islands, and exotic Iceland. This time she planned from the start to publish her accounts. She'd found a way to pay for her passion.

Carefully portioning out her limited funds and taking whatever vessel she could get, traveling on the same postal ship as everyone else, she'd arrived at Hafnarfjördur.

Thurídur watched the small crowd of Danish merchants gather around the woman who had just disembarked. Knudtzen immediately invited her to stay at his home—one of the four timber houses. Where else could such a lady stay?[3] Then Thurídur returned to her work while the female traveler wandered around town, drawing eyes wherever she went.

Ida's viewpoint was rather different. She found the timber houses, although "small" with "only five or six rooms on the ground floor," "quite European" inside; indeed, one could "fancy himself in some continental town, rather than in the distant and barren island of Iceland."[4]

After delighting in the otherworldly moss and lichen-covered lava formations of the area, she "betook" herself to the homes of the "peasants," stone-and-turf houses of a "more indigenous Icelandic appearance." In an inherent assumption of superiority reflecting the common European attitude toward the subjugated Icelanders as amoral savages, she just walked in, considering their homes open to her purview. There she encountered the dark passageways, the only furniture bedsteads with very little covering, and the smoldering open fire. "The visitor is at a loss to determine which of the two is the more obnoxious—the suffocating smoke in the passage or the poisoned air of the dwelling-room, rendered almost insufferable by the crowding together of so many persons."

Ida declared these homes "filthy," despicable hovels—which, to an eye unaccustomed to this kind of poverty, most of them were. She conceded that the dwellings of the very few "rich peasants" she encountered

in her Iceland travels "looked cleaner and more habitable, in propor-
tion to the superior wealth or sense of decency of the owners."

Down at the harbor, the female traveler had returned, and now
another commotion seemed to be brewing between her and the
Danish merchants including Knudtzen, who gathered around
her like bees drawn to a flower—if a somewhat problematic one.
Apparently she had decided, after her exploration of the area, that
she wished to move on; she'd seen enough of Hafnarfjördur. It was,
after all, a very small community. Even though it was five in the evening, she'd set off immediately for Reykjavík by horse. Alone. The
sun wouldn't set until midnight. Why shouldn't she go?

The Danish men attending her threw a fit. This would not do at all.

You don't understand what you are attempting, Knudtzen and
other merchants told her, most of whom would never make this trip
alone themselves. This is not Europe, there is no real road, you'll get
lost. You'll pass a chasm where you could easily fall and die. Sudden
snowstorms blow up often even in May.

Her plan was completely foolhardy. Everyone agreed. Would she
not prefer to wait and go by ship? By now a curious crowd had gathered. Thurídur and others at the merchant shop stopped to watch
these proceedings.

The dire warnings and objections did not in the slightest seem
to deter the female traveler. She would not wait, she informed the
men firmly. She intended to go—now, by horse, alone. "I comforted
[Knudtzen] with the assurance that I was a good horsewoman," she
wrote, "and could hardly have to encounter worse roads than those
with which I had had the honour to become acquainted in Syria." A

place, she noted tartly, she doubted any of the men standing around her had visited.

This sent the men into a frenzy. No, no, no! Why was this German [Austrian] woman being so obstinate? She could not go by herself. She had no clue about the terrain—she'd get lost and die, and it would be all their fault.

This called for serious consultation. Since they couldn't force her to stay, the only solution was to get her a guide. But not a man. A foreign, seemingly high-class woman going alone with a male guide was obviously unacceptable. That left one person—Thurídur.

Thurídur watched as Knudtzen approached her, knowing exactly what he was going to ask. Certainly, she would guide this woman to Reykjavík. Yes, she could do it now. It was a route she knew intimately and for her, even at sixty-eight and after she'd likely already been working at the shop for ten hours, comparatively easy money.

The two women set out. Ida rode a horse; Thurídur walked.

Ida was reportedly initially insulted by being assigned this slim older woman as her guide. But Knudtzen quickly disabused her of this opinion. If Thurídur and Ida had shared a common language, they likely would have found much to talk about. Instead, Ida wrote an account of their trip together, a marginally informed foreigner's perspective on both the terrain and Thurídur.

"In my guide," she wrote, "I made the acquaintance of a remarkable antiquity of Iceland, who is well worthy that I should devote a few words to her description. She is above seventy years of age [Thurídur was sixty-eight, although she and others thought she was seventy-one] but looks scarcely fifty; her head is surrounded by tresses of rich fair hair. She is dressed like a man; undertakes, in the capacity of messenger, the longest and most fatiguing journeys; rows a boat as skillfully as the most practiced fisherman; and fulfills all her missions quicker and more exactly than a man, for she does not keep up so good an understanding with the brandy-bottle. She marched on so sturdily before me, that I was obliged to incite my little horse to greater speed with my riding-whip."

The track at times was not easy, Ida wrote, being over piles of lava. They crossed a wide marshland that "shone with tender green," backed by "[s]everal chains of mountains, towering one above the other." Many of the small grass-and-moss hillocks dotting the land-scape she abruptly recognized as graves. "I could see over an area of at least thirty or forty miles, and yet could not descry a tree or a shrub, a bit of meadowland or a friendly village. Everything seemed dead."

"Heaps of lava, swamps, and turf-bogs surrounded me on all sides," she continued; "in all the vast expanse, not a spot was to be seen through which a plough could be driven." Of the chasm she noted, "Of the much-dreaded dizzy abysses I saw nothing." It is likely Thurídur took a divergent route that missed it. She also led Ida safely past all the marshes and lava stacks.

"The distance from Havenfiord [Hafnarfjördur] to Reikjavik [sic] is scarcely nine miles; but as I was unwilling to tire my good old guide, I took three hours to accomplish it." Meaning Thurídur walked an average of three miles an hour for nine miles over "diffi-cult" piles of lava and uneven track. Not a bad speed regardless of Ida's condescending opinion—while she rode a horse without once offering Thurídur a ride, regardless of their age difference (an offer Thurídur would have most assuredly refused).

At eight in the bright spring evening, they safely arrived in

Reykjavík, where Knudtzen had arranged comfortable lodgings for Ida. Thurídur presumably immediately turned around and walked the nine miles back home, pleased with the extra income. Ida, now securely housed at her destination, made no comment or expressed concern in her wonderfully detailed account for the well-being of her "antiquity" guide.

Although a tourist's presumption echoes throughout Ida's account, she—unlike most male adventurers—did learn through her travels, gradually becoming more aware and appreciative of difference, questioning European attitudes of superiority, coming to recognize that the peoples she met, although often poor, were her equals.[5]

In Hafnarfjördur, Thurídur received the heartfelt thanks of Knudtzen and the other Danish merchants. She'd saved the day—again.

Knudtzen soon recovered from Ida's visit, but otherwise his affairs had taken a downturn. The other merchants could breathe a sigh of relief, no longer having to concern themselves with his expanding operations. The sulfur mine venture came to nothing, and soon Knudtzen seemed to be so broke he had trouble paying his debts. In the end, he sold his Reykjavík shop, retaining only one in Hafnarfjördur—which was still one of the largest in Iceland. And he still had his ships. In Hafnarfjördur's continuing booming economy, he did just fine.[6]

Others did not.

On one of those bright May days of 1846, a European sailing ship arrived at Hafnarfjördur carrying some Danes infected with measles. They brought a stealthy silent virus no one saw coming.[7]

Iceland had a vaccination against smallpox—which Páll had declined to take at his peril. They had nothing against measles, no protection at all.[8] On padded feet, it quickly spread through Hafnarfjördur and from there to nearby Álftanes, where Thurídur had fished as a deckhand for a few years. Also located at Álftanes was Iceland's only school at the time, for upper-class boys headed for the clergy or further education in Copenhagen. When the boys returned to their homes in June, they took the infection with them, particularly to northwest Iceland.

Soon the infection had spread everywhere. People had no idea how long they were infectious, and most could not afford to stay away from work anyway, so they returned as soon as they began to feel better. By July the epidemic had spread along the entire south coast. Most susceptible to death were children under three—already at risk with the high infant mortality rate—people over fifty, and "drunkards," presumably those with underlying health conditions. In a desperate effort to slow the spread, farms in August halted the vital haying for three weeks and in some areas their September sheep roundup.

When the epidemic finally died down in December, it had killed about 2,000 people, or more than 3 percent of Iceland's population. It gave the year 1846 the highest mortality rate in Iceland's entire nineteenth century.

Thurídur did not catch the infection, but her house servant Hólmfrídur soon died of it. Many others also died that year, and although reasons for their deaths are not given, one can assume many of them died of measles. Ari's immediate family seemed to have got through unscathed, but both his parents, dear Gamlason— Thurídur's friend for forty-six years, her fellow deckhand who stood beside her when so many did not—and his wife, now both in their seventies, died.[9] A hard year.

Among those who died that year was Jón Snorrason.[10] One of his children was Gudmundur, husband of Thurídur's ex-sister-in-law, Margrét. Besides Gudmundur, Jón Snorrason also had two daughters, one of whom was the widow of Thurídur's former husband, Jón Egilsson—now with six living children. The second daughter was named Sigrídur.[11]

Jón Snorrason had been a respected boatbuilder. When as a teen he'd gone to old Brandur to see if he would teach him boatbuilding, Brandur had refused, suggesting instead that Jón Snorrason watch him, observe how he made his boats, and there he might learn something; after all, that is how Brandur himself had learned. And Jón Snorrason certainly had—all his boats bore the distinctive and innovative marks of a Brandur boat. From this, he had done very well. But in the inheritance, Gudmundur seemed to have gotten everything, the two daughters almost nothing, Sigrídur only a scrappy, tattered old mattress.

When Thurídur heard about this, she stepped in, traveling immediately to see Sigrídur. Women not receiving their inheritance was bad enough, but these women were also essentially her relatives. They deserved more inheritance than a mattress.

"Your brother Gudmundur is stealing a lot from you and your sister," Thurídur told her.

"That's something I can't do anything about," Sigrídur replied.

Thurídur gave her a half smile. "Well, I can teach you a way."

Sigrídur looked at her doubtfully. Gudmundur was a strong-minded man.

"You will not be alone," Thurídur reassured her. By now Thurídur knew her rights and the power of the law—knowledge and protection she wanted passed to other women. "Go to Archdeacon Jakob of Gaulverjabaer, and ask him to take your brother Gudmundur to court." She paused. "And you can tell Archdeacon Jakob that this is *my* advice."

Sigrídur followed Thurídur's suggestion. As a result, she and her sister inherited a farm—in addition, presumably, to the tattered old mattress.

Upon returning to Hafnarfjördur, Thurídur heard disturbing news. She'd expected this might happen at some point—her adopted daughter, Thórunn, now in her late thirties, had had a relapse stemming from the disabilities she'd had since childhood. After so many years of doing well working as a farmhand, she couldn't do it anymore.[12]

30

INTREPID TRAVELER

1847–1849

The only person who would step in to prevent Thórunn from becoming a pauper was Thurídur. It was her responsibility; she'd known this when she adopted her. Thórunn was now her daughter.

Because Thórunn had worked in one place for so long, that district was obliged to provide her with invalid pauper's relief.[1] But that would send her into who knew what bleak circumstances. Without a good place to live and medical help, she'd die. That, Thurídur vowed, was not going to happen.

She had an idea where Thórunn could go—if she could just somehow arrange it. On the higher land at the foot of the mountains, about thirty miles inland from Stokkseyri and in a different county, Thórdur Árnason had taken over as head pastor in 1845.[2] Trained and respected as an excellent doctor, he'd set up a medical facility at the church farm of Cloisterhills (*Klausturhólar*), where he and his wife, Vilborg Ingvarsdóttir, tended sick people. They asked a fee for their services, but everyone knew they also treated people regardless of their ability to pay. Perfect for Thórunn.

Having made up her mind, and now accustomed to venturing to places she'd never been, Thurídur traveled immediately to visit Pastor Thórdur to see if she could persuade him to take Thórunn—even though she had to admit Thórunn would be a long-term patient.

The area was lovely, gentle rolling hills nestled at the foot of steep mountainsides. Thurídur saw with approval that Pastor Thórdur, a man in his forties,[3] was already improving the church farms,[4] flattening the fields, digging an extensive system of drainage ditches, and building stone walls. Upon meeting the pastor and his intelligent wife, Vilborg, she found she liked them, cementing her choice of this as a good place for Thórunn.

Tall, wiry, and agile, Pastor Thórdur had dark eyebrows, lively blue eyes, a high forehead, curly hair, and a dark beard sporting the currently fashionable short sideburns. He was not classically handsome yet still attractive; his easygoing manner and ability to put people at ease were evident on this first meeting.

Thurídur was equally impressed with Vilborg, who could write "as well as educated men,"[5] known for her poetry, convincing logic, and wisdom.

Pastor Thórdur, clear-eyed on this commitment, considered Thurídur's request. Obviously neither Thórunn nor Thurídur could pay. Still, since Thórunn needed this care, the district where she'd worked would surely pay up. He nodded. Certainly, he'd do it.

A rush of gratitude and relief washed over Thurídur. Come any time, the pastor and Vilborg invited her. Visit your daughter, visit us.

And she did, making this a habitual pilgrimage during the summers as they all became close friends. Pastor Thórdur, temperate in his drinking, did have a temper, his periodic anger sometimes verging on rage.[6] But overall, he was delightful, artistic with a lovely singing voice, progressive; he also ensured a good education for his younger brother Jón who later became a librarian and well-known folklorist.[7]

Under the care of the pastor and his knowledgeable wife, Thórunn improved, not well enough to work, but gradually her health began to return. Thurídur had made the correct decision. Thórunn could hardly do better.

Thurídur stretched her back and sighed. Although she was seventy-one, she and everyone else thought she was seventy-four—and still working, far beyond the age of anyone else. "Young" Ari was now fifty-one, his wife María one year younger, most of their children grown adults.[8] They all knew Thurídur soon had to quit this job she'd held for fourteen years. But what would she do then?

Her petition to the king had come to nothing, no response at all. She didn't want to leave Hafnarfjördur, but without an income, she didn't have a choice. Her only option would be to return to her native Stokkseyri District, where she had kin and the district would have to take care of her if all else failed—not that she intended to become a pauper!

But what would this be like? Would she still face harassment and threats? Since Jón Rich was no longer deputy and reportedly in poor health, she could hope he would not have the influence or interest he once had. But what of the others, Gísli and those affected by the trials of 1828—would they still hate her? A full twenty years had passed since that dreadful time. Perhaps—hopefully—things had changed.

Having run out of options, she sadly packed up her belongings and said goodbye to Hafnarfjördur, left behind Ari and his large extended family, her cherished home, the bustling harbor and vibrant international community.

If she had to return to the community that had exiled her, she'd do it on her own terms. She'd had her own place in Hafnarfjördur for some time, and she liked it. Working steadily for years, she had savings. She'd use some of that to build herself a little cottage.

For this, she chose a space in the collection of cottages (*Skúmstaðahverfi*) in Eyrarbakki where she'd lived before at Gardbaer, near the sea and at the center of the community. She didn't own the land, but the cottage would be hers. There, for as long as her savings lasted, she could be in charge of her own home.[9]

While the cottage was being built, she stayed with friends at Óseyrarnes, west of Eyrarbakki and just east of the large Ölfusá River.[10] When it was finished, with a dig of humor and irony, she named the simple structure Main Street (*Aðalgata*). She'd spent many winter months living in fishing huts; the simplicity of this abode mattered little. But independence mattered a lot.

What a difference she found coming back! She'd been gone fourteen years, the same length of time as the surviving Kambur robbers had spent in Denmark, and like theirs, her experiences away had changed her perceptions of this place where she'd lived so much of her life. She noted that, unlike in Hafnarfjordur, fewer than ten small boats now fished from Stokkseyri and Eyrarbakki combined.[11] A few women still worked as deckhands, but not many. But then, there weren't many men fishing either.

She stood ready to face the demons that had inhabited this

community, human and social, but when she arrived, she found them scattered as on a spring wind. Time had softened previous resentment and grief, and she instead found herself treated with universal respect.

She also learned of disturbing happenings. For one thing, Móri had been on the rampage again. Shortly after New Year of 1846, people had found a man dead and badly beaten. In everyone's minds, Móri was the obvious murderer, into his third generation and not yet losing his malevolent hold—or perhaps a very human malevolent murderer sheltering behind a convenient culprit.[12]

Much more saddening was the news about Haflidi. It had happened two years ago.

The fishing season hadn't yet started—only six boats were fishing from Eyrarbakki anyway[13]—but because the catches had already been so good, various people jumped the official season and went out early. Magnús Jónsson of Eyrarbakki, hired on a larger boat in the south for the official season, was one of these, deciding that before he left he wanted to go out in his own small boat at Eyrarbakki. He needed a couple of others to go with him.

He'd previously worked for Thorleifur, so he went to his house early in the morning to see if he had two men he could spare for the day. Thorleifur had no one free and was about to shut the door when Haflidi, now fifty and overhearing the conversation, came bounding down from the loft still naked from his bed.

"Well," he said, "it's best I come with you now to see if I have lost my knack at the oars." The last time he'd worn sea clothes was when he'd been arrested.

As he was getting dressed, he told them about the great dream he'd had. "I was wading out to the sea through the surf," he said, "and it was so hot I could barely stand it. I think that's a sign for good fishing."

Misinterpreted dreams can be so dangerous.

Haflidi and Thorleifur's twenty-two-year-old half brother, Steingrímur Kolbeinsson,[14] went with him, as did another seventeen-year-old. One other boat joined them at sea.

The weather stayed fine the first half of the day, but then it rapidly changed. The wind came up and the seas whitened with froth, breakers growing in no time. The other boat headed to Thorlákshöfn, a course most now took when the surf got bad at Eyrarbakki and Stokkseyri. But Magnús headed straight into shore. A wave hit them, and they capsized. All five on the boat drowned.

Haflidi, after surviving the trials and imprisonment, returning home against all odds, and even becoming a prosperous doctor, had now drowned a mere two years later. His daughter inherited what everyone knew was a tidy sum of money—if she could find it.

When she'd previously asked Haflidi where he'd hidden his cash, he'd replied—cautious from his years in prison—that if he told her, she'd tell someone else and in no time the tale would spread everywhere, and then who knew who might want to steal it?

Shortly after his death, he did come to her in a dream to let her know, but as with so many dream messages from the departed, his meaning was cryptic. He said he'd hidden the money in a secret compartment. But where? In the gable of the house, in a wall, in a hidden section of a chest? No one could figure it out.

Thorleifur had still held out hope. The two brothers had previously made a pact that whoever died first would come back in some form to tell what the Other Side was like. Perhaps Haflidi would also reveal where he'd hidden his money. For two years Thorleifur waited, to no avail. Then recently, one night as he lay in that state between waking and sleep, Haflidi had finally appeared.

"It's not allowed," he said.

That's it. Apparently, that kind of privileged information was censored from the living. After this, Thorleifur couldn't sleep at all.[15]

Many of those involved with the trials of 1828 had now died or grown old. Although Jón Rich was still a power to be reckoned with for the many who leased from him, staying away from him at Eyrarbakki, Thurídur found that she had little to worry about. His farm buying[16] continued unabated as he bought the expansive East Stokkseyri holdings—the first holding he did not pay for entirely in cash—including the church properties and the Stokkseyri church itself. Since he never sold anything, he now owned twenty-four farms and twenty-six small holdings bought over fifty-five years, almost one a year.

Her friends had also aged, just as she had, the inevitable stream of life. Archdeacon Jakob, now seventy-eight, was finally retiring himself,[17] having an assistant take over his duties, although he still continued with settling disputes and court mediations. His beloved wife, Elín, had died the year before at seventy-nine, and after that he also gave up managing the church properties, passing that to his nephew Páll Ingimundarson. Without Elín, perhaps his role had lost its joy.[18]

During her years away, Thurídur had also changed, growing in experience and emotional strength, even as her physical body weakened with age. She'd lived an adventurous life most people could hardly imagine.

With Eyrarbakki's Danish influence, people there began calling her Captain as an honorific surname.[19] She continued to wear her signature trousers, tailcoat and short top hat, and for her own amusement she startled new acquaintances by telling them her name was Thormódur, a male name sounding similar to Thurídur, just to watch their growing confusion.[20]

More accustomed to and comfortable being around Iceland's elite, Thurídur became friends with the new county commissioner, Thórdur Gudmundsson,[21] a very different man from the one with the same first name who'd investigated and brought harsh judgment on the Kambur robbers and the local community.

In his late thirties, the new CC Thórdur G. was even better connected than his predecessor, his uncle in Parliament, his in-laws also politically well connected. He'd received a law degree in Copenhagen, married a woman of Danish descent, already served in a number of legal administrative positions and been a judge before he became Stokkseyri District's county commissioner. A good life with plenty of opportunities. Iceland was anything but equal.

But he seemed a decent sort, and actually lived nearby at Little Lava farm near Eyrarbakki. He also very much enjoyed Thurídur's company, inviting her over often, like so many others delighting in her intelligence and pithy wit. Once when she visited him, he asked her how she liked her coffee, still drunk mostly by the elite.

Thurídur, who'd become accustomed to drinking coffee among the wealthier residents of Hafnarfjördur, knew what she wanted as precisely as any modern-day gourmand. "Swift, steaming, short, and strong," she replied.[22]

Laughing, the county commissioner made sure she got exactly what she requested.

The next year, at the age of seventy-nine,[23] Jón Rich died from the respiratory illness he likely could have prevented. For Stokkseyri

District, it marked the end of an era, this man so clever yet problematic, who grew from seemingly inescapable poverty to become the richest person in South Iceland.

His legacy? For Thurídur, likely relief to have finally outlived him, his passing leaving one less malevolent shadow of those dark times. His death also directly affected some of those living on his properties. Gísli and Sesselja had to finally move from Kalastadir the year after he died.

When Jón Rich's wife passed away a few years later,[24] their three daughters all named Sigrídur inherited everything.[25] The oldest, said to have the bearing of a chieftain but also with a cold demeanor, and little respect for anyone but her own, had married one of Gamlason's sons—Ari's brother—and managed to keep her inherited riches the longest. The second daughter married a drunkard who mismanaged their farm, and their fortune from Jón Rich's closely guarded wealth dwindled rapidly. His favorite, the youngest, a well-liked and warm woman who'd married Deputy Adolf Petersen, lived a pleasant life spending her father's money.

Then Thurídur heard that Shank Jón Geirmundsson had died in Hafnarfjördur at fifty-nine, still telling stories, the only one of the Kambur robbers to have found a peaceful end.[26] This was truly the end of an era.

After exploring the countryside as a guide for the last decade or so, Thurídur now took up traveling for pleasure, spending each summer in the uplands at the foot of the mountains, warmer in summer than the coast, the air scented with wild thyme. As a concession to being in her seventies and because she enjoyed young company, she always took a boy as her companion. For two summers this companion was sometimes Geir Ívarsson, the grandson and foster child of the Sigrídur who'd inherited a farm instead of a tattered mattress thanks to Thurídur's intervention. These travels, Geir told his childhood friend Finnur Jónsson, opened his eyes to places he'd never seen.[27] Everywhere, he said, people welcomed him and Thurídur with open arms. Mostly he remembered Thurídur's kindness.

It was the same with another of Thurídur's boy companions, Thorsteinn. He recalled that his young pride soared when, upon being offered refreshment at houses where they stopped along their way, Thurídur would reply, "Not for me, my dear, but for the man who's with me."[28]

Visiting Thórunn, Pastor Thórdur, and Vilborg at Cloisterhills became a primary stop for Thurídur, and one year there she met Geir's then seven-year-old friend Finnur, who was also Vilborg's nephew, and there visiting with his older sister, Ragnhildur.[29]

Thurídur could tell Finnur was startled, even a bit frightened of her when he first met her—that happened fairly regularly, since most children had never seen a woman dressed in men's clothing before; indeed, most adults hadn't either. But she had a lot of time for children, and soon, with her hugs and warm attention, he relaxed and got used to her. She told him stories of adventures and intrigue to which he, and others, listened agape.

When she recounted the abuse she'd endured at the hands of people from Stokkseyri District, she could tell by the expression on the faces of her listeners that her eyes had started shooting their telltale sparks. The people might have died, but the memory of pain and anger remained.

One evening, she asked Ragnhildur to make a visored cap from some cloth she'd brought.

Of course, Ragnhildur replied.

Once she'd started sewing, Thurídur hovered at the girl's shoulder, instructing her exactly how to do it. Finally, Ragnhildur had had enough. She would make the cap as she saw best, she said, or she wouldn't make it at all.

Instead of being annoyed, Thurídur laughed. "Well, well," she replied, appreciating the girl's spirit. "Do as you like. You resemble your family, my girl."

Finnur later wrote about his meetings with Thurídur, reflecting how Vilborg, Pastor Thórdur, and others in his family deeply admired and cared for her for all the good she'd done for so many over the decades, regardless of how it had affected her own well-being.[30] "It was widely known," he wrote, "that Thurídur was happy to help anyone who had problems or was poor, those who were victims of bullying and in an unjust situation, whoever it was. She had such a rich sense of justice without discrimination. If she was unable to help by herself, then she arranged help for those who needed it."[31]

He felt some verses written by Icelandic poet Bjarni Thórarensen, written about Oddur Hjaltalín, also described Thurídur perfectly:

> *A king's heart he had,*
> *poor as a crofter*
> *from nurturing the poor himself.*
> *He built his own poverty*
> *ensuring others' good fortune.*[32]

In applying for compensation for Thórunn's care, Pastor Thórdur had hit a snag. The district deputy who made the final decision on this turned out to be...Árni Magnússon—the same captain of Thorlákshöfn whose brother had drowned and with whom Thurídur had had that rowing competition when she'd first started captaining there over fifteen years ago. Árni's wife also happened to be Johnsen's daughter, so when Johnsen drowned, Árni had taken over his farm near where Thórunn worked.[33]

Considered a generous, decent man and a strong leader, Árni was also as stubborn as stone; if he decided against something, he did not change his mind. Including covering Thórunn's care as a pauper. If Thórunn returned to the farm where she'd been a farmhand, the district would pay for her upkeep, on a pauper's minimal, debt-inducing stipend. But they would not repay her previous care at Cloisterhills nor for her continued stay there.

Pastor Thórdur took the case to court. And lost.

Thurídur refused to accept that decision. It meant Thórunn would no longer receive her needed care and that Pastor Thórdur, who'd taken her at Thurídur's request, was not going to be compensated for years of costs. This was unacceptable.

During her years in Hafnarfjördur, Thurídur had learned and grown. She now knew much more about the political legalities of Iceland than when Jón Rich had almost managed to crush her twenty years before. The confidence she had always shown at sea she could now exhibit in court.

She decided to appeal through legal action, grappling horns again with Árni, as a woman standing up directly against one of the area's most powerful men.

31

THE POWER OF A
SIMPLE SCRAWL

1850–1857

Just as with being at sea, Thurídur considered her strategies for the course of action she'd decided to take. She was not just calling to account in mediation court someone who had harassed her or others, or had not paid her. This time, she was mounting a case against a government official with the aim of getting the district to pay out funds it did not wish to expend. It was much bigger and more audacious than anything she'd ever done before, requiring real legal argument. She'd have to pay people to write legal documents and letters contending not only that Pastor Thórdur needed compensation but also that Thórunn was too ill to be moved.

"What I like the worst," she said, "is how Árni of Ármót is murdering my time."[1] But she was determined to win regardless of who she had to fight to do it: for Thórunn, for Pastor Thórdur, and because she knew it was the right thing to do.

In her endeavor, Thurídur was not helped by a growing scandal.

It seemed Pastor Thórdur had trouble keeping his penis in his pants.

First in about 1825, when Pastor Thórdur was twenty-two and still at divinity school, he was expelled because he'd got a servant girl pregnant.[2] After that, the new bishop taught him privately, so he was able to graduate with good marks. Eventually restored to favor within the church, Pastor Thórdur was allowed to become a pastor despite his transgression.

In 1841, while Pastor Thórdur was assistant pastor at Cloisterhills, a girl was born[3] whose official father was named as Nikulás Thórdarson. Rumors claimed, however, that the real father was Assistant Pastor Thórdur—knowledge strong enough that his name is penciled in as the real father in the margin of the official birth records.

This didn't cause too much of a ruckus, but a few years later, after Pastor Thórdur was made pastor, Guðrún Ingimundardóttir, the daughter of a local farmer and sister to a local district deputy,[4] gave birth to a child amid rumors that it was also Pastor Thórdur's.

Now the community rose in an uproar, everyone fighting, some supporting their pastor, others demanding that he be defrocked for this adultery.[5]

Thurídur reserved judgment and steadfastly stood by Pastor Thórdur. After all, he'd saved Thórunn's life. She knew herself the destructive power of community gossip. "One suspicious word in the Grímsnes [Cloisterhills area] case is worth more than ten children," she said.[6] Whether she knew of Pastor Thórdur's earlier activities is never mentioned.

Then Ámundi Einarsson, one of Pastor Thórdur's supporters, came forward to claim paternity. In court, Ámundi's daughter said she was sure Ámundi was not the father, but she couldn't prove this. Thurídur, testifying on Pastor Thórdur's behalf, also stuck to her exact knowledge, stating only that she knew Ámundi had never received any money from the pastor to claim paternity.

Then Jón of Búrfell farm, one of Pastor Thórdur's closest friends, turned against him—for not confiding in him, according to the documents, and for leaving him to learn of happenings through the rumor mill. Although this seems a bit dubious as a credible reason, the former friend united with another farmer named Hjörtur (not the same man as the Hjörtur of Kambur fame some years before) to mount a campaign against Pastor Thórdur. Vilborg believed her husband and defended him vigorously. Once when Pastor Thórdur and Búrfell Jón had agreed to a tentative reconciliation, Vilborg, disbelieving Búrfell Jón's intentions, tossed at him a verse:

> *The priest's cassock behind him flies*
> *but respectable men should know*
> *Jón and Hjörtur are low*
> *and will never let free of their lies.*[7]

That stopped any further reconciliation efforts. And although Ámundi's claim was enough to allow Pastor Thórdur to keep his frock, it only marginally settled his parishioners.[8]

None of this helped Thurídur in her case against Deputy Árni to get the pastor compensated and to keep Thórunn in his care. Many doubted that even she could win this one.

Summer passed, with Thurídur visiting her friends in the uplands, traveling from farm to farm. Autumn came amid the inevitable shortening of days. December brought bitter frost, preparations for a Christmas that was celebrated in too many households against a reality of too little food. And still Thurídur continued her legal battle against Deputy Árni. She refused to give up, but the case was taking its toll.

On one side, while the case dragged on, forty-year-old Thórunn stayed safely in Pastor Thórdur and Vilborg's care.[9] On the other, Thurídur's constant outlay to people writing the necessary official court documents had by now taken almost all her savings. She'd resorted to buying her goods from the shop on credit, a terrible position. If Deputy Árni hung on long enough, she'd be so destitute she'd have to give up. And he had a lot more resources than she did. If she could get even a modest pension, she could manage. Otherwise she was running out of options—except giving up the case, which she was not going to do. So, she asked for help—again—from her dear friend of now fifty years, Archdeacon Jakob.

Accordingly, in the quiet of a pre-Christmas afternoon, Archdeacon Jakob knocked at Thurídur's Main Street door, his step still firm at eighty-three, his sweet expression peaceful, his mind and sense of justice as sharp as ever. He'd brought paper and ink, ready to write. They'd petition the king again for Thurídur's richly deserved pension. They'd make this application even stronger than the last, submit a fuller account of her contributions, get better letters of support. She'd done so much for the district, the county, and for Iceland. How could the king refuse?

As Archdeacon Jakob dipped his quill in ink, Thurídur took a deep breath. Then she began to outline[10] the major events of her life, her fishing, her farm work, the chance of life she'd given to her adopted daughter, Thórunn, her years of service.

Most of this the archdeacon already knew. They'd grown

old together, the two of them, through more than most people's lifetimes—memories of such length they took seven closely written pages in Archdeacon Jakob's steady, elegant hand. In conclusion, Thurídur requested a small pension allowance, noting that the Eyrarbakki merchant had not refused her credit yet, but without some kind of stipend, she'd be unable to repay his generosity.

Archdeacon Jakob signed the account with her name and finished with a note that he'd penned this on Thurídur's behalf.

Perhaps this would move the authorities.

On Christmas Eve, Archdeacon Jakob sat alone in his own home, empty, echoing, festivities hollow without Elín. Once again, he dipped his quill in ink, this time for his own letter of support for Thurídur,[11] his words in Danish, the language of his intended readers. He explained that although Thurídur was entitled to welfare as an old-age pauper, living on the costs of her district was to her dishonorable, a humiliation she did not deserve and from which a government pension would free her. She had "in her precision been exceptional, from an early age good-hearted and unselfish in helping others, not sparing herself.... She has helped her neighbors in need, come to the aid of people when she had the ability and influence to do so." These were deeds to which several witnesses could attest.

As a second support letter, they decided to ask the coffee-drinking new CC Thórdur G., who they trusted would not undermine her petition as the previous county commissioner had.

CC Thórdur G. readily agreed. "To the King," he wrote in formal Danish, going bluntly to their highest authority.[12]

In Thurídur's voice—translated into Danish—he requested "in

deepest meekness" that His Royal Highness consider "it is rare that any man has, like myself, gone to sea for sixty-six[13] years and been captain for twenty-six winter seasons." Since, because of advancing age, Thurídur was no longer able to perform this strenuous work, the "widow"—seemingly the only respectable word for an older single woman—was very poor and humbly requested a small allowance.

The full application included both letters of support, Thurídur's seven-page personal history, and a list of boat owners and deckhands—friends, kin, their sons, who had all at some time worked for or hired Captain Thurídur. They would all attest to her excellence at sea.[14]

Glaringly obvious is who's missing from this list. Thurídur engaged numerous women on her boats and encouraged women to go to sea, some of them her longest-serving deckhands. Yet this list does not include a single one. Does this mean they knew the universally male officials and king would dismiss any female testimony of character as spurious?

They submitted the application. They waited. Again.

The winter passed. Not a word.[15]

By April, Thurídur sat in Main Street knowing she had nothing to eat. She pulled out a small scrap of paper she'd been keeping, dipped a quill into ink, and, with a rudimentary skill learned over a lifetime, requested that Merchant Gudmundur Thorgrímson, who'd taken over the diminished Eyrarbakki shop in 1847,[16] extend her more credit.

Merchant Gudmundur was a very different kind of Eyrarbakki shop manager than those Thurídur had known in the past. Beyond being good at his job, she felt a connection to him; he'd been born in Hafnarfjördur. He and his wife, Sylvia, both educated and brought up in Denmark, loved literature and music—Sylvia was a talented musician and singer. Together with Thorleifur—now the deputy his teenaged dream had foretold he would become—and the pastor who had taken over from Archdeacon Jakob, they even started a children's school.

Merchant Gudmundur and Thurídur had quickly become friends. He was unlikely to refuse her request, but she knew that without a pension, she had no way to repay him. Having to ask was humiliating. But she'd spent everything she had fighting for Thórunn.

"Highly Estimable Benefactor," she wrote. "May God reward your compassion where you have cared for me as a child in your arms. Now I seek your beneficence and forgive the audacity and help me of some sugar half a pound"—if she was going to keep fighting Deputy Árni, she needed more than sugar—"half a pot of brennivín, and two pounds barley bread. Ever forgive the presumption. Be always enveloped in God's mercy.

"Live well,

"Thurídur Einarsdóttir"

At the bottom of her request, surviving the passage of centuries, is a single notation in a different hand. "Yes," followed by Merchant Gudmundur's signature.[17]

Thurídur walked up the final hills of the uplands, her sturdy walking staff in hand. The evening's long shadows created a mosaic, etchings of brilliant, sunlit greens crisscrossed by shaded slopes where evening frost already glowed silver-blue. Beside her walked twelve-year-old

Magnús, a boy very different from the traveling companion of the same name whom she'd had to drag over that mountain pass a decade ago.[18] She'd brought the boy, one of her sister Salgerdur's grandsons, with her on her summer jaunts before. She liked his father, who'd been one of her many deckhands, a good one.

She was on her way to visit Deputy Einarsson's daughter Margrét, whom she'd known and liked since the girl's childhood. With her husband and children, Margrét had moved from Hafnarfjördur several years ago to this farm butted up against the feet of the mountains inland from Stokkseyri District. Thurídur now made summer visits to their home as often as she saw Pastor Thórdur and Vilborg. Together she and Margrét could reminisce about their lives in Stokkseyri District and in Hafnarfjördur, a special perspective they both shared.

As she and Magnús approached the homefield of the farm, Thurídur saw Margrét's oldest son, the teenaged Brynjúlfur, waiting for them. His eyes bright, he was almost bouncing in excitement.

Thurídur laughed quietly. She'd grown very fond of this clever boy. A shame Margrét and her husband couldn't afford to help him get some kind of education; with their seven living children, they were far too poor for that. Thurídur knew the boy might have had greater opportunities had they stayed in Hafnarfjördur. He was another one, just like Ari, not inclined to fishing. The boy also had some kind of physical weakness, not so much as Thórunn, but he wasn't strong, although in these last couple years he did seem to be getting better.

During her previous visits, Thurídur had noticed that instead of working outside, Brynjúlfur preferred to sit in their common room reading any book he could get his hands on. And writing or, as some said derisively, scribbling away in the dark.[19] She'd seen other farm children taunting him for his weakness and for his love of writing.[20] Such pursuits were reserved for the elite, most people thought, not an impoverished farmer's son like Brynjúlfur.

He was an unusual child, Thurídur had to agree. He was just different—as she was herself. Whatever other people's expectations might be, he seemed to have a talent for the things he loved. She knew her visits here were the highlight of the boy's summer, and she liked that. Perhaps he'd become a poet. Iceland could always do with more good poets—they certainly had enough bad ones, some so bad it broke the soul to hear them.

She waved to the boy as she and Magnús walked up the hill, and Brynjúlfur ran to greet them.

Thurídur sat on one of the beds in Margrét's common room, the slanted twilight filtering through a narrow gable window. Chores finished, the family members sat on various beds, knitting, carding wool, sharpening tools for the haying next month, everyone chatting, exchanging news and telling stories.

Salgerdur and her husband seem to be in bad straits, Thurídur told Margrét. One of their sons—not Magnús's father but their eldest—was being stingy when he could well afford to care for them.[21] Deputy Thorleifur...

She and Margrét smiled. "Deputy Thorleifur"—who ever thought they'd see this? He'd apparently written a letter to CC Thórdur G. demanding the son be forced to contribute before both parents became paupers dependent on his district's poor funds. Even people with children became paupers in their old age, it seemed, their children not caring enough to look after the parents who'd raised them.

As the evening wore on, Thurídur began entertaining them all with tales of her adventures at sea, funny lively accounts, the scary times of the Kambur robbery.

She looked over and saw that Brynjúlfur had pulled out some paper—however he'd managed to obtain that—and laid it on a stool beside him, writing with a handmade quill and ink. His letters weren't well formed—yet. She was sure he'd improve; he had the ambition to do it.

He looked up when he felt her eyes on him, and she smiled. She saw him flush in pleasure. He was taking notes on her stories, she realized, this mere boy with no formal education. Well, he was one of them; he knew the life—unlike any elite scholar; he certainly had a better chance of getting their stories right. Not a poet perhaps, but a writer recording a history. She nodded encouragingly. She certainly hoped he had the will to continue; that would be the only way any of what they knew and experienced would ever be told beyond their lifetimes.

The summer passed to fall, and amid the bright yellows of autumn grass and scarlet crowberry leaves, singing calls echoed up and down the near vertical mountainsides. It was 1853 and time for the annual roundup, collecting the sheep left to roam free in the mountains all summer, fat from eating fragrant herbs and highland grasses. Clambering up and down ravines and cliffsides, everyone who possibly could participated, including seventy-six-year-old Thurídur. Once collected, the sheep were sorted by their various owners' earmarks—marks that Gosi in his day had been so good at transforming to look just like his.

Eighty-year-old "Turk" Jón Thorsteinsson was out like everyone else. Generally reasonable except when he got drunk, he was unfortunately drinking now.[22] Seeing Thurídur in her trousers, he decided to start abusing her, his insults increasingly coarse.

What have you got under those trousers? he yelled at her. Are you "two-tooled" (*tvítóla*)? Meaning, did she have both a vagina and penis under her pants, at the time a very insulting taunt.

Even drunk, he should have known better. Thurídur was not about to let someone publicly abuse her. She retorted that he was welcome to look and promptly sued him.

Turk's case came before the mediation court that November, presided over by Archdeacon (ex, but still occasionally presiding) Jakob. Both men in their eighties and Thurídur not so far behind, the Archdeacon ordered Turk to apologize and ask Thurídur's forgiveness. Now very sober, Turk meekly did. Thurídur accepted this without demanding he pay any fine. His apology was sufficient; she had no interest in forcing an elderly man as impoverished as herself to expend funds he didn't have.

Thurídur had more pressing concerns with the ongoing case with Deputy Árni over her adopted daughter's care. It had dragged on over six years, the funds for Pastor Thórdur poignantly still not being compensated by the time of the recent death of his wife, Vilborg, at only fifty years old.[23] Thurídur tried not to let worry consume her; she'd spent everything she had on this case and more. If a decision didn't come soon, Pastor Thórdur would never be repaid for ten years of care, and her adopted daughter, the person for whom she'd taken responsibility, would become a pauper, likely soon to die. How could she endure that? Her only natural-born daughter had died before Thurídur; she would not let that happen to her Thórunn.

32

GUARDIAN ANGEL

1854–1860

In 1854, the court made a final decision—in Thurídur's favor. Against a powerful deputy and the district, she'd won.

No one had thought it could happen. Thurídur leaned her head against the wall. She'd done it. She'd ensured her daughter got the care she needed and fulfilled her promise to Pastor Thórdur. The district had to repay him the astonishing sum of 1,190 dried fish in compensation as well as 200 per year for Thórunn's continued upkeep.[1]

But—there was a small catch. During the long intervening years of the court case, Thórunn, under Vilborg and Pastor Thórdur's attentive care, had become so well they could no longer really argue she needed to remain there—an irony not lost on any of them.

So, despite the case outcome, Thórunn now returned to Deputy Árni's district. There, without her special care, her health quickly deteriorated, and already by the next year she was again too disabled to work. With this, she became a pauper dependent on Deputy Árni's district—what he'd agreed to fund in the first place.

But—a very big but—because Thurídur had won the court case, the district was now required to provide for Thórunn at a mandated level far above normal, ensuring she still got decent care,[2] long after Thurídur herself had died. By 1892, still alive at seventy-nine, Thórunn had cost Deputy Árni's district a whopping 1,600 króna.[3] He'd have done much better had he been equitable from the beginning.

Pastor Thórdur was now also financially set, but life in his parish did not improve. Although he'd avoided getting defrocked, farmers in his parish remained divided, groups of them refusing to even attend his services. Sides had become drawn on all kinds of issues, with Pastor Thórdur stuck in the middle. His former friend Búrfell Jón began fighting about "decency," demanding that men not be allowed to cut hay in only their underwear—a common practice for the hot and arduous labor (women never being considered for an equal dispensation)—although Búrfell Jón felt that, as a cooling technique, it would be quite acceptable for the men to wear no underwear at all under their trousers.[4]

So in 1855, Pastor Thórdur left, finding a position at Mosfell on the far side of Reykjavík near the sea, a full two days' journey away.[5] Sometimes, as Thurídur well knew, a change of scenery was a very good thing.

Only a few months later, in the bright of late summer, came a blow that Thurídur had known must come sometime. Just days before his eighty-fifth birthday, her dear, dear friend Archdeacon Jakob passed away, the man who'd first trusted her to be a winter captain.[6] She'd known him fifty-five years, ever since he'd come as a new pastor, and she'd worked for him as a young farmhand, when she'd left to move in with Jón Ólafsson and Jakob had said he would help her whenever he could. It was a promise he'd kept, even in the years just before he died, writing her the support letter and mediating on her behalf.

Was she devastated or at peace? Jakob lived a good life, had been prosperous, respected, and done good work. He'd surely now joined his Elín in Heaven. Death was inevitable. The yawning chasm of fearful dark existed for those who carried doubt—which Thurídur did not. Those left behind were the ones who knew the loss. Mortality is the blessing and curse of all living beings; grief at losing a long and cherished friendship is the privilege of those living long enough to grow old.

Thurídur stared at one of the hardest decisions of her life. She'd arrived at the age of eighty, still healthy, her eyes, hearing, and mind as sharp as ever. But she faced a harsh reality. By ensuring that her adopted daughter would never become an impoverished pauper, she had ensured that she herself would.[7] No one was going to award her a pension, not the king or anyone else. She deserved one for all her years of service for both her district and her country. A man who'd done half what she'd done would have received one years ago.

She pulled herself erect. She was impoverished because, against all odds, she'd fulfilled her responsibilities to her daughter and the man who'd helped her. If they had to pay her pension in the form of a pauper's stipend, so be it. She did not have to accept it with humiliation; she would stand tall, her head high knowing this and more was her due.

She went to CC Thórdur G. and Deputy Thorleifur—the

man she'd hired as a deckhand so many years ago when no one else would—to discuss the situation, these two men with authority in Stokkseyri District no longer foes but fond friends who admired her. She'd leave her independent Main Street cabin, which she wanted Ólöf, a female friend in need and of similar age to herself, to take over. Thurídur would not be auctioned off to the lowest bidder as was the usual practice.[8] Instead she'd move to live with her friends at the home of Gudmundur Steinsson at Eyrarbakki, a family of shipwrights and one of the boat owners for whom she'd captained. She'd often stayed with them before.[9]

Deputy Thorleifur agreed, as did CC Thórdur G. Unlike anyone else, Thurídur, even though a pauper, could choose where she wanted to live.[10] They all knew she deserved more.

Thurídur cast her sharp eyes over the sea as she walked between and around the houses of Eyrarbakki. No longer able to travel upcountry for the summers, she did this walk every day as the weather allowed. The physical boundaries of her world had decreased, but her engagement, curiosity, and keen observation—not to mention her wit and memory—remained the same.

She watched the grim toll of shipwrecks that still took the lives of so many; these had not changed, nor had the omens foretelling them.[11] When a shipwright building a doomed boat had thought he'd seen blood coming from a piece of driftwood, he considered not using it. But he was in a hurry, so he did. Then Merchant Gudmundur, Thurídur's generous shopkeeper friend, had had a vision while walking home the previous, very snowy New Year's Eve. Out to sea, he'd watched a ship appear to come ashore in an impossible way and then disappear. He could see all the crew clearly—except the captain, who didn't have a head. He told this vision only to his son, who later attested not only to the account but that, even though it was New Year's Eve, his father hadn't been at all drunk.

Then a deckhand of another boat dreamed he saw blood flowing out the door of the fishing hut facing his and into his own hut. Misinterpreting this to mean his own boat would sink, he fatefully changed to the other.

In the ensuing horrific spring wreck, the captain decided, unlike all the others, to row through the heavy surf to Stokkseyri instead of heading toward Thorlákshöfn. The boat flipped and thirteen men drowned, all washing to shore the same day, intact except the captain, who'd somehow lost his head.

Thurídur considered this wreck, one among so many she'd seen in her long lifetime. Yet even with this continuing tragedy, how the community had grown in these last few years she'd been living here! Almost double in size,[12] the number of local boats grown from almost nothing to 13 six-oared boats and an astonishing 39 two- and four-oared ones.[13] The increase in boats reflected the broadening of boat ownership to regular leasehold farmers instead of mostly the church and the landowning elite. Good to see. The small-time boat owners paid for access to the shore and a "poor fee," but with boat ownership, they could at least keep their fish instead of working for the profit of others.[14]

She noted how much each captain and deckhand caught each day, and the skill each showed in their seafaring. She observed new technologies: a fish trawl—a line with lots of hooks instead of a single or double.[15] Some boats were even using sails, not so much here but in the south generally. So much change. She smiled as she watched one small boy about six constantly hanging around the shore, as desperate to go fishing as she'd been at that age. She knew him, Jón Jónsson, Ingibjörg's grandson.[16]

Thurídur shook her head. The boy's father, another of Ingibjörg's children to pass away before she did, had died just after the child's birth. Sesselja and Gísli had fostered him—that couple, once friends who had caused Thurídur so much hardship and heartache, working in tandem with Jón Rich to crush her. Sesselja had lost so many of her own children, six of the eleven to whom she'd given birth, ongoing grief that eats anyone's soul.[17] Thurídur found that time had softened her anger and hurt. She felt no joy in Gísli and Sesslja's pain. Gísli had recently passed away himself—she'd now outlived even him. Sesselja was moving between her living children. At least they were looking after her.

As Thurídur walked through Eyrarbakki, her friend Ólöf, now staying at Main Street, rushed out to talk with her. The merchant house, which controlled the land of Main Street, was going to tear the cabin down.[18]

What? They had no reason to do this. But Thurídur immediately knew why—because they were afraid that if Ólöf stayed, they'd be obliged to take care of her. Their solution was to demolish her home, forcing her out and away from their responsibility.[19]

Thurídur, now in her eighties, would still not let such an injustice pass. She immediately dictated a letter to Merchant Gudmundur in protest. Was he this heartless? Surely not. He was after all her friend and had been consistently kind in giving her unrepaid credit.

"I am thankful to God for my good health," she wrote him, "that

I have been lucky in life" and that God had "not yet felled this fruit-less old tree." She'd often visited this Main Street cottage, which she felt confident was safe "under your protection and presence." But Ólöf, who had nowhere else to go, had reported that it was being demolished. "Who would choose this for their children when they had reached our age?" Thurídur asked rhetorically, pushing the merchant to reflect on how such a similar future action might impact his and his wife's own daughters. One may "cut the roof grass from gray hair and old bones," but in doing so, she wrote in powerful language, one must "consider the darkness of the grave."

"There is no correct religion that does not follow love," she reminded his conscience, the kind of religion he knew she had stead-fastly practiced herself.

"If I have offended anyone with these lines," she wrote, "I ask he give me the same forgiveness for my hand as the Savior promised the robbers on the cross, that they would be with Him in Paradise."

She did not sign this letter with her customary "Live well" but with good wishes that instead brought home the implications of Merchant Gudmundur's intended actions. "May God grant renewed life to your wife and children at their time of death. Thurídur."

Perhaps Merchant Gudmundur did not tear down the cottage. At least not that year.

Ingibjörg's grandson Jón Jónsson, the boy Thurídur had observed as he stood yearning to fish from the shore, fairly exploded with excitement. He was finally going to sea on his first winter fishing trip as a half share! He'd dreamed of this day as he'd listened to his foster mother, Sesselja, and grandmother Ingibjörg tell of their sea adventures with the great Captain Thurídur. Their stories he knew were true. You could trust them because, unlike the men, they weren't drunk when they told them. At seven years old, he was finally getting his chance.

By the day's end he almost burst in pride. He'd caught twelve fish!

You must give all these away, his Captain Páll told him. Our first catch we always give to poor older women in the community.[20]

Even though he was shy around the "very, very old" Thurídur because she "spoke loudly and with passion on whatever she was talking about," he was resolutely determined to give her half his first catch.

He did have a small problem—or a big one; the six fish were too heavy for him to carry. So he enlisted a larger friend—who coincidentally lived at the same previously dilapidated Símon's House hovel of Erlendur's half sister, Margrét, and later bought by Jón Rich—to carry them to the door of his Aunt Thórdís at their Gata leasehold where Thurídur was currently visiting, staying for a time at her beloved farm.

As Jón and his friend dragged the six fish through the door, Thurídur greeted him, wearing her signature tailcoat and short top hat—as well as trousers, of course. He got a bit scared just looking at her, but then she hugged him "with thankfulness and kindness such as I have never experienced before or since."

Thurídur started to look at the fish he'd brought, asking if he could show her the one he'd pulled up first.

He certainly could, as he'd marked it specially. His very first catch.

She examined it carefully, opening its mouth, and checking the wound from the hook. "You will have more fish biting on your hook, my boy," she told him. Then she hugged him again.

This time Jón felt on his face the wet of her tears.

She drew him inside and asked him about his trip, about the fishing. "I have no doubt," she said once he'd finished, "that your foster mother has taught you the Seaman's Prayer."

"Oh yes," Jón replied. "And my grandmother taught me the verse one must always say after the Seaman's Prayer."

"Of course, she did, blessed be," Thurídur replied, knowing she had taught the prayer so many years before to Ingibjörg. "Bring this prayer to Jesus."

"After you say this," she then instructed Jón, "you must always make the sign of the cross over yourself and the boat." She paused. "Come to me again the next time you return from the sea.

"Now, don't betray me," she reminded him as Jón turned to leave. "Meet me next time you come to land."

Three days later, in the evening after his next trip, Jón dutifully returned to Gata, this time having caught an impressive seventeen fish. His Aunt Thórdís told him Thurídur was in bed but he should come in anyway. He went to see her where she sat in bed in the family common room.

"You have caught the most of all the half-share deckhands," she immediately informed him as he walked in. "You caught seventeen fish, and next to you was Gísli of Rodgúll with eleven fish." From her bed and before they told her anything, she then listed all the half-share deckhands, ten in all, and exactly how many fish each had caught, all correct.

Neither Jón nor his Aunt Thórdís had any clue how Thurídur knew this.

Then Thurídur told him stories of the greatest seafarers. "From Stokkseyri there was Gísli, your foster father, and Jón Gamlason. In Thorlákshöfn were the brothers Árni and Halldór Magnússon, sons of Magnús Beinteinsson, who was also good. Jón Ólafsson..." These men, regardless of friendship, tussles, and betrayals over the decades, she named for their skill at sea without resentment or prejudice— except Jón Rich, whom she neglected to include; she'd directed his boat half the time anyway. She named not only the seamen but each man's forebears.

"It will be your future to be a captain," she then told Jón, "because in your Captain Páll you have as your role model one of the best. He is one of the best for coming in through the surf."

Indeed, Captain Páll was said to be a genius at getting through the Stokkseyri breakers. He was also one of the only captains who now refused to go to Thorlákshöfn when the seas got rough in Stokkseyri—the practice much changed now from when Thurídur with Jón Rich made the seemingly radical decision to go there in 1812. Páll always managed to brilliantly surf his boat safely in, regardless of the weather.[21] The only time anyone saw him deign to row to Thorlákshöfn was some years later for Jón's wedding.[22]

"But you must remember, my boy," Thurídur continued, "when you call your deckhands to row, you must always call them with these words: 'Dress in your sea clothes in the name of Jesus.'"

She showered Jón with more prayers and blessings, then brought out cake and candies. How did he get so lucky?

Jón later wrote that this was his great good fortune, far beyond mere candies, because from that day on, he had Thurídur's friendship. What she taught him became his fundamental "book" knowledge of the sea, rules and principles he forever followed.

"You can't tell me that all the prayers that Thurídur did had no meaning. I am sure it is quite the opposite, and I very much believe she was my guardian angel... You who might read this while I am alive or dead should not laugh at my superstition but rather mourn your own lack of faith. I wish that you could have, or will have, as warm blessings and prayers as I got because you will do well in life if you know how to use it. From this, I went as a half share and fished as much as the full deckhands."

Jón went on to become a captain, fishing safely for forty-six years. This he credited to Thurídur's knowledge and the protection of her blessings.

Despite everything, in her eighties and from her bed, Thurídur, with clever wisdom, shared her knowledge of an insightful lifetime to a next generation. She had the courage to retain compassion, the intelligence and strength to grow wisdom. This is the meaning of resilience.

33

THE SEA AT REST

1863

On November 13, 1863, the 87-year-old Thurídur came in at twilight after walking, lay down on her bed, and spoke with people for a while. Then all of a sudden, she started complaining of cramps in her stomach. The pain went away, but shortly afterward, a spasm wracked her body, so harsh it almost lifted her off the bed. A second, smaller spasm, followed by a third even smaller one.[1]

The household ran for the pastor, who lived just next door and acted as their doctor. He rushed over, but Thurídur showed no signs of life. They begged him to open her up, as was done for a heart attack.

No, he said, it was pointless. Thurídur had already passed.

Still, for a few days her body remained lukewarm under her left arm before it finally began to cool. After her November 20 funeral, they buried her, as a pauper having no funds, in an unmarked grave in the Stokkseyri church cemetery. The parish death records record her as "Pauper and Captain."[2]

AN AFTERWORD

It did not take long for any laudatory accolades accorded Thurídur during her lifetime to morph into something quite different. Histories are so often constructed to reflect current, preferred perceived realities, and as Iceland changed in the late 1800s, so did the interpretation of Thurídur's actions and life.[1]

During that time, gender roles in Iceland became less permeable, the model woman now a housewife.[2] Women working at sea who'd been previously applauded began to be diminished, their sea work demoted secondary. By the late 1800s, they were receiving open criticism as out of place and inappropriately masculine. With the advent of motorized vessels and dramatic changes to Iceland's fisheries, economy, and society in the early 1900s, women got pushed out of commercial fisheries altogether, the sea transformed into an exclusively male realm.

Ironically, had Thurídur been born fifty years later—even to the present—society would have been far less likely to permit the sea leadership and acclaim she achieved.

This change happened quickly after her death. In a sad commentary of changed attitudes, in the 1890s the pastor who had by then taken over Gaulverjabaer published an article using archival records to detail Thurídur's divorce and several of her court cases. Basically calling her "deficient old baggage," he strung together a series of pejoratives, including a word meaning a foolish person but literally a wether—a castrated sheep (*kerlingarsauðurinn*). He cast these court proceedings as examples of how Thurídur was not the outstanding person people thought she was but, rather, an attitude-ridden troublemaker (of course Thurídur did make trouble, whenever she saw others, or herself, unjustly treated, but this is not what he meant).[3]

Later historians followed in a similar vein, growing harsher as the decades slid into the mid-1900s. The historian Gudni Jónsson painstakingly edited Brynjúflur's work on Thurídur and the Kambur robbers, checking and correcting dates and relationships. Yet his opinions on Thurídur, about whom he wrote quite a bit, are rife with derogatory and inaccurate insinuations, also calling her a "hag" (*kerling*) and reinforcing the emerging trope of her as a woman who could not get along with men because of her work at sea.[4]

In one example of many, "[s]he was constantly warring with someone, often with little reason, making her unpopular among many... Her parting from her old captain Jón [Rich] was in such a way that he was against her ever since...three times she tried marriage, but each attempt was a total failure. Her hard temper and domineering ways caused all the men to choose to leave the relationship, rather than losing their freedom."[5]

Attitudes toward Thurídur did not improve through the 1900s.

An article published in the 1970s starts this way: "This hag (*kerling*) was an important woman, strongly built and hard-working, even though she was thin and her face angular and thin." Referring to her marriage to Jón Egilsson, this article continues, "Then finally she got married, she was then over forty and her groom was little more than twenty. Although the woman was then getting old, she had made a too hasty decision, this was a short kind of fun. That marriage lasted a short time although it may have been a fun kind of thing. Soon after they were married, some forward people from Stokkseyri began joking that this hag (*kerling*) would not allow her young husband full of energy to come into her bed. So it could hardly work out for the long run. In the end the husband went from their home after one year or so. After that captain Thurídur gave up on men, she had experienced that it was hard to get along with them inside the home even though she knew how to work with them alongside on a boat."[6]

Although insulting, these men would not have been writing about Thurídur at all had Brynjúlfur not written about her. Because yes, he did follow his dream of collecting accounts from Thurídur and others about her life, the robbery, and its aftermath. Thurídur "had a great way of telling stories," he wrote. "Talking with her was a lot of fun. From the first time to the last."[7]

It took him from his teens until his fifties to finish his oral compendium of knowledge, an ethnography of the most notable events of the lives of the neighbors and kin with whom he'd grown up, taken from their memories and personal experiences. With this, he almost single-handedly saved Thurídur's legacy. His account, published first as that series of newspaper articles in the early to mid-1890s, and later collected in the volume Dísa's mother copied for us, is the major reason so much detail, particularly of Thurídur's early life, exists at all. Without him, she would have been just another amazing woman about whom almost nothing is known.

In many ways, Thurídur's distinct and different self was more tolerated in Iceland's early nineteenth century than it was in the twentieth. A few women have written questioning these male attitudes about Thurídur, particularly Thórunn Magnúsdóttir, a direct descendant of Ingibjörg, who in the 1970s and 1980s wrote extensively about seawomen, including Thurídur.[8] Besides these exceptions, Thurídur isn't written about much at all. Among younger generations she is now virtually unknown.

In April 2021, soon after Iceland began allowing vaccinated United States visitors, I galloped over to meet up with my research assistant Sveinbjörg to collect details I needed to finish this book. First on our agenda was to see if we could retrace Thurídur's mountain trip and find the remains of the haunted shelter beside Ghost Pond where they'd stayed.

Equipped with old maps and accompanied by two Icelandic hiking friends, we headed out. The maps had Ghost Pond marked, so we drove gravel back roads getting as close as we could. High cloud stretched heavy after an early rain; above us whirred the golden plover and common snipe making its surreal clacking sound. Behind us loomed the dark lava mountainside that Thurídur and Magnús climbed; before us lay barren, bleak lava fields.

We could actually see Ghost Pond in the distance, but walking to it proved a problem. Snow had recently melted from these uplands and turned the lava ash into near quicksand. After trying to hop from tussock to tussock, we gave up and retreated.

Exploring further gravel roads, we approached Ghost Pond from the other side. There the lava surface ran in rippled striations, calcified remains of a molten current.

"There it is!" one of my eagle-eyed friends exclaimed.

We leaped from the car and scrambled across the moss and rocks to reach first the remains of a stone corral and then, on a drier rise of land, the circular stone foundation of the shelter, maybe ten feet by ten, a corridor entrance covered with moss and lichen but easily discernible. Beside it stood an old sign in Icelandic; someone at some time had wished to commemorate this travelers' shelter as a special place. The sign's weathered wooden post tilted to one side in the manner of an untended gravestone.

The sign, amazingly still legible, informed us that in 1844, only about five years after Thurídur stayed there, the shelter had been moved closer to the mountains, this one abandoned because of its relentless hauntings. One unhappy visitor from that time—who at least wasn't alone and seemingly had links to divine intervention—wrote a verse of his experience that has disturbing echoes of Grímur's:

> On a bench sitting inside
> we rested enjoying the night.
> Then the door latch rattled aside
> we leapt to our feet in fright
> a monster appeared
> coming at me from Hell.
> But its fire and coals disappeared
> when I blessed it farewell.[9]

The poem echoed in my head as I stared into the tiny enclosure.

Around us, lava stretched for miles. The place could hardly have looked more desolate. I would not want to spend the night there.

We then drove up the mountainside on a gravel road still spotted with snow, figuring out where Magnús had gone wrong and how Thurídur had got them to what even now is the closest possible building they could have found. The distance they walked was at least twenty miles.

"They should make this way into a Thurídur's Path," one of my friends suggested. From the ridge we could see for miles, in the far distance the sea.

Then we climbed out of the biting wind back into the car and drove to the nearest town for a hot cup of coffee. Modern life does have its perks.

Sveinbjörg and I walked up to the pleasant house by the sea. We'd come to see Geiri, his great-great-grandparents the family of the Eyrarbakki shipwrights with whom Thurídur spent her final years—at the same house where he himself grew up. Of anyone, he knows the most of Thurídur and her life. Among other things, he is confident he knows almost precisely where Thurídur would have been buried in the church graveyard. Hale and hearty, he invited us into his sunny living room.

We talked about Móri, who remained a presence in the Stokkseyri area until the 1980s—which is about nine generations. In his later years, Móri became downright protective of the family he haunted, making people's cars die if they neglected to pick up hitchhiking descendants. Keeping up with the times, he also loved cars, particularly trucks. Often people driving through the area at night on their way to Reykjavík would suddenly acquire a new passenger, Móri getting a ride into town.[10]

"I encountered Móri," Geiri told us once we had chatted for some time. "I was always terrified of the dark, and one time in the late 1960s or early 1970s, I had visited my parents and was slowly driving away, just past Kalastadir. It was a fairly new car, one with four doors. I heard the back door on the passenger side open, shut, and then felt a strong presence in the back seat. Someone was there. I drove the few miles toward Eyrarbakki, then the door opened again, shut, and the presence was gone. It was Móri catching a ride. And after that I was never scared of the dark again."

Over time, Móri became harder to see, his legs beginning to disappear as though floating. But even though no one sees Móri anymore, his presence endures in a Stokkseyri Ghost Museum dedicated almost entirely to him—a bit tattered these days, as was Móri himself, I suppose. Only now people are paying money to let him scare them.

Stokkseyri is off Iceland's major Ring Road and has never been used as a backdrop for some famous movie or television series such as *Game of Thrones*; it is not touted as a major destination to set mouths agape with the stark beauty of sheer cliffs dropping directly to the sea or glaciers that cascade in mammoth frozen waterfalls. Even today, it gets comparatively few tourists; its major draws besides the tranquility of its quiet beauty are a local lobster restaurant and Móri's ghost museum.

There Sveinbjörg and I met up with Stokkseyri resident Tóti, who, in the manner of a savant, can list from his expansive memory the name of every farm in the region, its inhabitants dating back centuries and various details of their lives. No one commercially fishes out of Stokkseyri or Eyrarbakki these days—far too dangerous and unsuited for today's larger motorized vessels—but Tóti, who's gone out all his life, knows the skerries and channels in the manner of the captains of Thurídur's time.

We walked along the shore as he pointed out where Thurídur often took out her boat at Mouse Passage, where the fishing huts stood, where they pulled up the boats. We walked from farm to farm, seeing how close together most of them were. With him, we saw a living landscape, its history embedded in every rock, ditch, or horizon.

We walked across the meadows and rocky shore to a flat stone slab known to locals as Thurídur's Stone (Þuríðarhella). Captains often pulled their boats up onto designated, relatively flat slabs, roping the boats to a heavy rock with a hole in it. One end of Thurídur's Stone has a basin-like indentation, today crumbling and covered with lichen. Here Thurídur and her crew washed their fish in its clean rainwater. I splashed my hands in the cold water, watching droplets fall from my fingers. Here Thurídur also held her hands two centuries ago.

Sveinbjörg and I stood in the bright sun at the edge of Stokkseyri. The place was deserted. There had just been a COVID-19 outbreak at the local elementary school, and in response, the health authorities had quarantined the entire school, the staff, and most of their families.

We wandered the empty streets. This community is growing; for the first time since I've been coming here, new houses are being built on the interior meadows for recent arrivals from Reykjavík, an hour's commuting distance in good weather (which all winter it is not), finding respite from the capital district's increasingly unaffordable housing. These newcomers bring vitality but have little connection to or interest in the area's past. Knowledge like Tóti's and Geiri's will not last many years more.

We spoke of Thórdís Markúsdóttir, the powerful woman accused of witchcraft and after whom Thurídur named her daughter. Over the intervening centuries, the witchcraft claim about Thórdís has only grown, supplemented by numerous stories; nicknamed Stokkseyrar-Dísa, she is now presented as a witch in other areas of Iceland to titillate tourists and Icelanders alike, serving to effectively erase her legacy as a woman who became one of the most powerful ship and land owners of Iceland's seventeenth century. We mused over how cruelly history so often treats powerful women.

"Let me show you the reconstructed fishing hut of Thurídur," I told Sveinbjörg. "It was pretty dilapidated last time I was here."

As we walked the streets to the reconstructed fishing hut, that place I had first found out about Thurídur, a sudden shout rang out. Children spilled from houses, immediately running across the grass. They must have all received their negative COVID test results and been released. We looked at each other and laughed.

And there before us was Thurídur's fishing hut, its sod roof that distinctive yellow of vegetation newly emerged from snow. The hut and surrounding stone wall seemed in much better repair than I'd remembered, beside it a large sign in both Icelandic and English. Reading it, I abruptly realized that this structure had been placed on the site of Thurídur's beloved Gata. I looked around, this grassy green land set between the houses taking on an increased meaning.

I bent my head to go inside and saw a sturdy latch, a new door carefully reconstructed in the style of Iceland's nineteenth century. Inside, the peaked ceiling, now wood lined, was much higher than I'd remembered; small lights went on automatically as I entered, so I could actually see interior details. Wooden beds, also modeled after the originals, flanked facing walls, and a glass window let in light above the door—a nice touch, although the hut would never have had a glass window originally. It seemed almost pleasant.

I could spend a night or two here, I thought. A warmth suffused my body. Someone who knew a great deal about the old construction methods and these original huts had spent considerable time and effort restoring this hut dedicated to Captain Thurídur, nurturing this testament to the community's remarkable ancestor. It didn't feel like a cave at all anymore.

Others may have forgotten Captain Thurídur, but someone here in Stokkseyri and Eyrarbakki still cared. That caring is where our strength lies.

ACKNOWLEDGMENTS

People often say it takes a village to raise a child. Well, this book took an entire town. All responsibility for the content and any errors are of course my own, but this book never could have been completed without the incredible collaboration and contributions of others.

I am very grateful for funding support from: National Geographic Society for initial fieldwork; a Snorri Sturluson Icelandic Fellowship from the Árni Magnússon Institute for Icelandic Studies for archival research; the Stefánsson Arctic Institute; and the NordForsk-funded Nordic Centre of Excellence project Arctic Climate Predictions: Pathways to Resilient, Sustainable Societies (ARCPATH).

Thank you to my wonderful agent Amy Bishop, who encouraged and supported me through the book's proposal, writing, and publication. At Sourcebooks, I was lucky enough to have excellent editor Erin McClary who guided me to make this a much better book. Also thanks so much to production editors Emily Proano and Sarah Otterness, art director Jillian Rahn, design lead Hannah Strassburger, template lead Laura Boren, cover design Ploy Siripant and marketing director Liz Kelsch—you are all stars! Thank you to Bob Moore who expertly created the initial maps.

This book would never have happened without the collaboration and inspiration of my dear friend Ágústa Flosadóttir; I feel both lucky and grateful for her friendship. I am also honored that people from the Stokkseyri and Eyrarbakki area encouraged me--a foreigner--from the onset many years ago to write a book on 'their' Thurídur. Kristján Geir Arnþórsson and Herborg "Heba" Auðunsdóttir believed in me and this project over so many years, their generosity of spirit means more than I can express. Siggeir "Geiri" Ingólfsson, a lifelong scholar of Thurídur, welcomed my interest when we first met decades ago, selflessly sharing the knowledge and materials he'd gathered through a lifetime of study—I write this with great sadness as in the final phases of this book's publication, he passed away, never able to hold in his hands this book to which he contributed so much. Þórður "Tóti" Guðmundsson has likewise tirelessly shared his knowledge of the Stokkseyri area fishing and farming history that I could have learned nowhere else. Elfar Guðni Þórdarson and Helga Jónasdóttir let me join their lively afternoon coffees where I learned so much both from them and the others who gathered there. Lýður Pálsson of the Húsið Eyrarbakki Museum was always ready with help (and a welcome cup of coffee) from his extensive knowledge, no matter how many times I came by with more questions (often); he also photocopied and gave me invaluable unpublished papers on the Kambur robbers from his father, historian Páll Lýðsson's collection.

In Hafnarfjörður, my exploration of Thurídur's life there was greatly enriched by the participation of Byggðasafn Hafnarfjarðar

Museum curator Rósa Karen Borgþórsdóttir; her enthusiasm, knowledge, and ability to weave together tiny pieces of informaiton gave me courage to keep looking, sure we would together find more about this fairly unknown period of Thurídur's life. Arndís Þórðardóttir of the Hafnarfjörður library also provided much appreciated help in sleuthing out obscure sources.

In Thorlákshöfn, thank you to Sigurður Jónsson who shared his extensive historical knowledge of that harbor, and to Nanna Rögnvaldardóttir for researching the history of geographical landmarks.

None of this project would have been possible without the ongoing hospitality of people, now dear friends, who welcomed me into their homes, sometimes for months. These include: in Reykjavík, Ágústa Flosadóttir and John Lyons, Sigurlaug Gunnlaugsdóttir and Gylfi Pall Hersir, and Arna Garðarsdóttir; in Stokkseyri, Kristján Geir Arnþórsson and Herborg "Heba" Auðunsdóttir and Tinna Ýrr Jóhannsdóttir; and in Grundarfjörður, Sunna Njálsdóttir and Olga Aðalsteinsdóttir.

I am so grateful to everyone at the National Archives of Iceland, particularly Helga Bjarnadóttir and Unnar Ingvarsson, who searched and pulled out box after box of old documents, generously giving their time over the weeks and weeks of research we conducted there. My research assistant Guðlaug Bergsveinsdóttir was beside me throughout these weeks, her eyes much sharper than mine, scanning document after dusty document for any name or clue that might indicate that it was something valuable to us. I could not have done this research without her. The actual reading of these old often crumbling documents in their handwritten nineteenth-century Icelandic and Danish was another matter, and this could have never been accomplished without the skilled participation of Ágústa Flosadóttir, Katie Parsons, Már Jónsson, Ólafur Arnar Sveinsson, and Emil Gunnlaugsson. Thank you all so much.

At the National and University Library of Iceland, I would particularly like to thank Bjarki Sveinbjörnsson and, in the Manuscripts Division, Gunnar Marel Hinriksson. I am also grateful to Gunnar Marel and Þóra Lilja Sigurðardóttir for sharing with me their extensive research into the life of Thórdís Markúsdóttir collected through seventeenth century Alþingi records and other documents. In Selfoss, Þorsteinn Tryggvi Másson of the Héraðsskjalasafn Árnesinga (Regional Archives), and Bjarni Harðarson provided invaluable assistance.

So many details of this book were only possible through the knowledge and expertise of others. Thank you to scholars Már Jónsson, Aðalheiður Guðmundsdóttir, and Hrefna Friðriksdóttir for providing information about early Icelandic laws regarding women and trousers, and about the usage of hymnals, also Össur Skarphéðinsson for sharing his knowledge of Grímur ice skating across Lake Þingvellir. Thank you also to Pétur Gunnarsson for sharing his family knowledge and research in the Grímsnes area, and to Hildur Hákonardóttir for sharing her extensive historical knowledge of Árnessýsla. A deep thanks also to Níels Einarsson of Akureyri who has given much appreciated support and encouragement throughout this long project.

My assorted research assistants over the years literally made the research for this book possible as we combed library shelves and archives together. In addition to Guðlaug and Emil motioned above, they include Gunnhildur Jónasdóttir, Þóra Lilja Sigurðardóttir and Ólafur Ingi Guðmundsson. During the last year and a half of research and writing, constrained by the enforced isolation of the coronavirus pandemic when I was unable (except a few short trips) to even come to Iceland, Sveinbjörg Smáradóttir became an invaluable companion, virtually at my side searching for details, discussing ideas, correcting errors, putting in the long hours that allowed this book to come to completion.

In the United States, thank you to Dan Mandeville and John Bolcer of University of Washington libraries for their archival reference advice, Chris Thornton for his encouragement, James Willson for his alpine insights, and Lorri Hagman whose earlier guidance on organizing a book project also helped me so much with this one.

Some gracious people read earlier drafts of portions or all of this book, making valuable comments and corrections. They include Ágústa Flosadóttir, Kristján Geir Arnþórsson, Lýður Pálsson, Gunnar Marel Hinriksson, Rósa Karen Borgþórsdóttir, Inga Fanney Egilsdóttir, Bobbi Ballas, James Willson, and Kathy Cosley.

As always, my deep gratitude continues to Colin Robinson, whose selfless bone marrow donation is the reason I remain alive to even attempt this project. My love to James, who with humor and equanimity gave encouragement and support through the years this book took, through my long periods away in Iceland, my often-obsessive concentration, and my various moments of despair. Thanks to the baristas of our local coffee shop, Broadcast and Temple Pastries, who provided a vital cheerful human contact when I went there each afternoon for a break and takeout cup of coffee (my entire social life for many months). And finally, grudging appreciation to our cat Mister who constantly reminded me I needed to take a break from the computer when he wanted food, wanted out, wanted...something...

READING GROUP GUIDE

1. What made Thurídur such an effective leader, particularly compared to her male counterparts?

2. Thurídur garnered her fair share of enemies throughout her life. Why do you think that was?

3. Thurídur grew to understand and show deep compassion, even for those who wronged her. Do you know someone in your life who has this ability or who consistently helps others?

4. What do you think drove Thurídur to foster her sister's daughter when Thurídur could barely support herself? And why do you think both of Thurídur's siblings were so unwilling or unable to care for their elderly mother? What might this suggest about differing attitudes toward self, survival, and ambition?

5. Why do you think Thurídur continued to sue on behalf of others and encourage others—especially women—to sue their wrongdoers even though doing so gained her so many enemies?

6. When CC Thórdur and Johnsen began interrogating community members about any petty theft they may have witnessed, friends and neighbors began to turn on each other—a witch hunt of sorts. The author writes, "In such inequality, simple thievery counted as a survival tactic." Do you think the act of thievery is ever justified?

7. Although Iceland is currently heralded for its strides toward gender equality, power structures during Thurídur's time, in both gender and society as a whole, were very different. How might the impact of a single person's actions shift through history? How might their actions have implications today?

8. There are several cases throughout the book where people neglected to care for their elderly parents. Do you think elder care is still an issue in today's society? How does the treatment of the elderly in the United States compare to that in other countries?

9. At one point, Poet Jón Kolbeinsson says, "No one is without faith. Everyone believes in something, but no one believes everything." Do you agree or disagree with this statement?

10. History is full of instances where men received credit for a woman's achievements—Thurídur included. Can you think of any such cases of this happening? Have you ever been involved in such a situation?

11. The measles epidemic of 1846 decimated Iceland, and there are clear parallels between it and the novel coronavirus pandemic that began in 2020. Discuss the similarities and the differences. Do you think we've learned anything since then?

A CONVERSATION
WITH THE AUTHOR

How did you first come across the story of Thurídur? What compelled you to write about her?

The account I give in the preface of first encountering Thurídur on a trip to Iceland, followed by long winter nights typing my Icelandic housemate's translations into my laptop, are accurate. But—this was all twenty years ago. Why did this book take so long?

At that time, I was working mostly in Brazil, on the other side of the planet from Iceland; even so, my interest in Iceland and Thurídur continued to grow. About twelve years ago, I began going to Iceland on short research trips. Opportunities opened up, and it seemed a direction I should explore. Eventually I completely redirected my research interests to Iceland, with a particular focus on gender, fisheries, and fishing communities. I also realized that I loved writing narrative nonfiction. Only after publishing a successful book on Icelandic seawomen in general, which briefly includes Thurídur, did I begin to feel qualified to write this current book. Encountering Thurídur changed my life, and for that I am deeply grateful. Even more strongly now than I felt when I first learned of her, I know Thurídur's story needs to be known.

What challenges did you face while researching and writing about Thurídur?

The biggest hurdle was that almost all the sources were written in nineteenth-century Icelandic, some of them by hand in faded ink on yellowed crumbling documents, which was only possible to overcome through the help of my team of excellent research assistants and various Icelandic scholars. Also, the breadth of detailed historical information necessary to make the society in which Thurídur lived understandable to modern readers created vast areas for potential errors that took continual rechecking to try to avoid. This story also includes details about the lives of people whose descendants, and neighbors of descendants, will not only read the book but are sure to discuss it at length; this makes the bar for accuracy very high.

Did you learn anything about Thurídur or Iceland while doing your research that surprised you?

I learned that Thurídur was even more amazing than I understood from first reading and hearing about her. Her skill at sea is fairly undisputed, but her fights on behalf of justice, even in the face of threat and dire consequence, have either never before been uncovered or were effectively erased after she died. I marvel at her clear-sighted intelligence, her compassion, and an insight that went beyond her era, her courage a testament to any time or place.

Iceland is known for its passion and dedication to storytelling and literature. Do you think that played a role in your ability to research and write this book?

The passion and dedication to literature and storytelling among Icelanders is a major reason anything was recorded about Thurídur at all. The tradition of people exchanging stories remembered through generations and writing biographies and other detailed accounts of their daily lives and that of their neighbors made the depth and insights of this book possible. Thurídur herself was known as an excellent storyteller, and her voice is a vital one at the heart of what Brynjúlfur recorded in his invaluable book of her life and the events surrounding the notorious Kambur robbery.

When one is writing historical narrative nonfiction, it can be difficult to fill in the gaps of a story. How did you go about making a cohesive narrative based on what you discovered?

My research assistants and I did exhaustive research on Icelandic daily life of Thurídur's time, combing libraries and archives for obscure old books, legal documents, and letters for clues. Every incident, law, or occurrence of her life and the lives of those close to her, we investigated to ferret out the meanings behind seemingly simple or disjointed statements and interactions. We explored national and international events of the times as they might relate to her life; we researched folklore and folk customs to better understand people's actions and reasons for their reactions. We studied fishing and farming practices, the physical homes of people in that area, the boats, the land, and coastline from which they fished. We also walked the land, talked with local people who have unrecorded historical knowledge, working to understand and, as much as possible, feel what it was like to live in this place and time.

To create a cohesive narrative from this disparate material, I first outlined the initial chapters, then reread all our research findings— which I had already organized in various databases by source, genealogies, and relevant subject categories—dumping slices of that material into files corresponding to the outlined chapters. Once this was done, I read it all again, looking for emerging connections and insights. Then, putting all this aside, I began on a blank document, writing solely from my head. The resulting initial draft I went over to correct details and mark emerging areas that needed additional research. Then I started at the beginning and rewrote it again...and again...and again...

What was your routine and process like while writing *Woman, Captain, Rebel*?

I wrote this book during the novel coronavirus pandemic, when near solitude became commonplace even for those who are not reclusive writers. I was thankful for this project, as the concentration of writing itself became my nearest companion, my daily stability.

For me, scheduled routine is critical with any self-directed project such as writing. I get up early, before six, go for a morning walk or run, have breakfast, read the morning newspaper, make a cup of tea or coffee, and then turn on the computer, ready to begin work by eight. I have a standing desk and force myself to take a short break at least every hour (this is hard!), stop for lunch, and walk to a local coffee shop for a breath of fresh air in the afternoon. In this way, I find I can write for about six hours before my brain revolts, a distinct moment. I factor in time for yoga twice a week, qigong, and once a week for a hike, kayak, or backcountry ski depending upon the season. These periods of meaningful exercise are vital for me to keep my body functioning and also just to refill my creative coffers.

Do you read more fiction or nonfiction? What books have you read recently that you've loved?

I read both. For research of course, I read masses of nonfiction. For relaxation I would say I read both about equally. For nonfiction, I lean mostly toward narrative nonfiction, as I love reading a good writer's incisive or poetic prose, often more evident in the writing of narrative nonfiction and fiction.

I recently finished reading Colin Tóibín's *The Magician*, a historical fictional account of the life of the German writer Thomas Mann. Mann's *The Magic Mountain* deeply influenced me in high school (even though I am sure I understood only a small portion of it), so I was intrigued to read of his life. This impressively researched book brought so much more, using the foil of an incredible life to illuminate from an intimate German perspective both World Wars, an often chilling reflection of our world today. A captivating, powerful, and beautifully written book. I loved it.

NOTES

A PREFACE OF DISCOVERY

1   "The single exception." There are mentions of a few other female fishing captains in Iceland's eighteenth and nineteenth centuries, but almost nothing is recorded of them. Margaret Willson 2016.

2   On Iceland's nineteenth-century housing conditions, see Sigurður Gylfi Magnússon 2010:48–51.

HELL RESURRECTED: A PROLOGUE

1   "The sun fades away," Sigurður Nordal, ed. 1980.

2   In general, descriptions of the eruption, Jón Steingrímsson 2002; Jón Steingrímsson 1998; E. L. Jackson 1982:42–50; Ian R. Stone et al. 2005–2007:223–234.

3   "black haze of sand," Jón Steingrímsson 1998:25.

4   "requiring a boat to cross," Vefsafn.is n.d.

5   On this apparent miracle, see Jón Steingrímsson 1998:49; 2002:48–51.

6   Description of the sun and moon, Jón Steingrímsson 1998:27.

7   Ash like petrified seal's hair, Jón Steingrímsson 1998:27.

8   Description of the effects on the sheep, Jón Steingrímsson 1998:76–77.

9   "The water...raw." Jón Steingrímsson 1998:41.

10 On the resulting famine from the eruption, Daniel Vasey 1991; E. L. Jackson 1982:42–50; Þorvaldur Þórðarson and Stephen Self 2003:159–171.

11 "it is illegal," Icelandic General Penal Code, no. 221/1940.

12 In general of the creation of the ghost Móri, Jón Árnason 1862, 1:187. For the nine-generations curse, Páll Lýðsson n.d.
There is some disagreement about whether the man who turned away the boy was Thurídur's father Einar Eiríksson or his father (Guðni Jónsson 1940, 1:91). Nearly all the sources and all oral history related to Thurídur state it was her father, the ghost is never mentioned before this incident, and also this timing makes sense since people were starving. So I am going with that assessment for this book.
A *móri* in Icelandic is a kind of specter. This one's name has changed over the centuries depending upon which farm he attached himself to, changing from "Skerflóðsmóri" to "Selsmóri" and later to "Kampholtsmóri." For simplicity's sake and to make the text more readable for non-Icelandic speakers, I have just used Móri throughout when referring to him.

CHAPTER ONE: DARING TO BE DIFFERENT

1 In general for Thurídur's family and her first fishing trip, Brynjúlfur Jónsson 1954:1–4.

2 That Thurídur's family ate seaweed, Thurídur's autobiography, Skúli Helgason 1988, 2:311.

3 "those with boats mostly survived," Guðni Jónsson 1957, 11:10–11.

4 "'precocious,'" Brynjúlfur Jónsson 1954:2.

5 "up to twelve hours," Lúðvík Kristjánsson 1982, 2:462; Þórunn Magnúsdóttir 1979.

6 "sea clothing, usually made from the skin of sheep," see Lúðvík Kristjánsson 3, 1983:39–46.

7 "Everyone wore a skin," Lúðvík Kristjánsson 1982, 3:29–66; Þórunn Magnúsdóttir 1984:34–35, 50.

8 "Without sea clothes," Skúli Helgason 1988, 2:199.

9 "daughter they'd named Salgerdur," Íslendingabók (Iceland Genealogy Database).

10 "Most babies seemed to die," For centuries, Iceland had the highest infant mortality rate in Europe—for infants not expected to live, emergency "short baptisms" became disturbingly frequent. See Ólöf Garðarsdóttir 2002:20, 51.

11 "a few women who wore trousers," Þórunn Magnúsdóttir 1979; Margaret Willson 2016.

12 "no one had much heat," see Sigurður Gylfi Magnússon 2010:46–60.

13 "'Delicate,'" Brynjúlfur Jónsson 1954:3.

14 "Pulled up high on the bank," Lúðvík Kristjánsson 1982, 2:116–118.

15 "Most in pretty bad," Lúðvík Kristjánsson 1982, 2:116; Þórunn Magnúsdóttir 1979:82.

16 "Some were just," Guðni Jónsson 1960, 1:178.

17 On Iceland's historical reasons for employing women at sea, see Margaret Willson 2016.

18 "'Almighty merciful...,'" Lúðvík Kristjánsson 1982, 2:215.

19 "No one went to sea," Lúðvík Kristjánsson 1982, 2: 211–222.

20 Description of the Stokkseyri shore, thank you to Stokkseyri residents Þórður "Tóti" Guðmundsson, Elvar Guðni Þórdarsson and Helga Jónasdóttir for sharing their knowledge of this coast and local historic fishing practices. We also visited the area and consulted old maps for accuracy in these descriptions.

21   "letting the boat drift," Lúðvík Kristjánsson 1982, 2:193; 1982, 3:240.

22   "baited it with lugworm," Lúðvík Kristjánsson 1985, 4:81–85.

23   "'soon as her,'" and all other quotes relating to Thurídur in this section, Brynjúlfur Jónsson 1954:3.

24   "father had been fined," Guðni Jónsson in preface of Brynjúlfur Jónsson 1954:XII.

25   "Leprosy," Embætti Landlæknis 2014; Jón Gunnlaugsson 1982:92–95.

26   "When Thurídur was fourteen," Íslendingabók (Iceland Genealogy Database).

27   "it killed him," Thurídur's autobiography, Skúli Helgason 1988, 2:311. She mentions that her father died of leprosy (*spítelskur*). Also see Björn Bjarnason 1910:48–65, 141–151, 229.

28   "tiny landowning elite," Guðný Hallgrímsdóttir 2019:5.

29   "at least three cows," Guðný Hallgrímsdóttir 2019:5.

30   In general on the farmhand contracting system and paupers, Gísli Gunnarsson 1983:13–29; Gísli Á. Gunnlaugsson 1993:341.

31   In general on Bjarni and Thurídur sustaining their family, Brynjúlfur Jónsson 1954:4–10.

32   "'luckier fisherman,'" Brynjúlfur Jónsson 1954:4.

33   "Bjarni quickly raised," Guðni Jónsson 1994:70–71; Brynjúlfur Jónsson 1954:4.

34   "'it was considered,'" Brynjúlfur Jónsson 1954:4.

35   "'Calm and reticent,'" and all other quotes in this paragraph, Brynjúlfur Jónsson 1954:2.

36   "'peculiar and different,'" and all other quotes in these two paragraphs, Brynjúlfur Jónsson 1954:2–4.

37   In general for Jón Rich, his birth and youth, Brynjúlfur Jónsson 1954:4–7; Jón Gíslason appendix in Brynjúlfur Jónsson 1954:217–219.

38   "first child," Jón Gíslason appendix in Brynjúlfur Jónsson 1954:217.

39   "Dr. Bjarni Pálsson," Dr. Bjarni Pálsson, Iceland's first Director of Health, served 1760–1779. Known for caring for his patients, he fought for the opening of a special hospital for patients with leprosy. Embætti Landlæknis 2014; Jón Gunnlaugsson 2014.

40   "'if she became pregnant,'" Jón Gíslason appendix in Brynjúlfur Jónsson 1954:217.

41   "'little pleased,'" and the following account of Jón Rich, including quotes, Brynjúlfur Jónsson 1954:4–7.

42   "two pennies for every one," and rest on Jón Rich in this section, including quote, Brynjúlfur Jónsson 1954:4–7; Jón Gíslason appendix in Brynjúlfur Jónsson 1954:217–219.

43   "red wood log," Brynjúlfur Jónsson 1954:4–7.

CHAPTER TWO: WHAT PRICE SURVIVAL?

1   "'agreed with each,'" Brynjúlfur Jónsson 1954:16.

2   "To curb the impoverished," Gísli Gunnarsson 1983:14, 16, 23.

3   "three possible scenarios," Bergsveinn Skúlason 1984:7–31; Guðný Hallgrímsdóttir 2019:56–57.

4   "Marriage...would by law," Erla Hulda Halldórsdóttir and Guðrún Dís Jónatansdóttir, eds. 1998:142; Erla Hulda Halldórsdóttir 1997:60.

5   "The status difference," Jónas Jónasson 2010 (1934):296.

6   "Living together outside," Sigríður Ingibjörg Ingadóttir 1993:55–62; Anna Agnarsdóttir 2008:31–33.

7   "Europeans, placidly ignorant," see Sumarliði R. Ísleifsson 2015:65–88; Sigríður Ingibjörg Ingadóttir 1993:55–62.

8   "So, in about 1786," There is some difference of opinion on these events. According to Brynjúlfur Jónsson 1954, Gudlaug married Thorvaldur, who then killed himself because of a lack of hay, although in the 1801 Iceland census (Manntal) Gudlaug is listed as a once-married widow. Íslendingabók (Iceland Genealogy Database) also indicates that he is her father's brother. Guðni Jónsson (1952:360–361) discounts the suicide, claiming the uncle lived in the shelter of Gudlaug and Jón Rich into his old age. However, in no other text is this later care or even Thorvaldur's later existence mentioned, and given Jón Rich's personality and later relationship with his mother, it seems very unlikely. The suicide sounds much more plausible; otherwise they would not have moved. So for this account, I am sticking with the suicide as recounted by Brynjúlfur Jónsson, but that Thorvaldur was an uncle as in the census and genealogy data.

9   "Cash outlay," No records we could find gave any clue on how he managed this seemingly unattainable feat.

10   "on December 3, 1793," Guðni Jónsson 1952:59–60, 359.

11   "the fabled 'demon pants,'" Jón Árnason 1862, 1:428–429, and 3:1955 (1862):595.

12   "'daringly,'" Brynjúlfur Jónsson 1954:6.

13   "While everyone slept," in general, account of the Great Flood, Brynjúlfur Jónsson 1954:7–9; Vigfús Guðmundsson 1945, 1:40; Lýður Björnsson 2006; Gísli Viggósson, Jónas Elíasson, and Sigurður Sigurðarson 2016.

14   "Many people let," Brynjúlfur Jónsson 1954:8.

15   "'Let's get our,'" Brynjúlfur Jónsson 1954:8.

16   "Eyrarbakki had a levy," Vigfús Guðmundsson 1945, 1:39–40; Vigfús Guðmundsson 1945, 2:73–75.

17   "decimated Eyrarbakki's," Vigfús Guðmundsson 1945, 1:40.

18   "'awaited his death,'" Brynjúlfur Jónsson 1954:8.

19   "In Stokkseyri District," Vigfús Guðmundsson 1945, 1:41.

20   "invalid old man" Brynjúlfur Jónsson 1954:8.

21   "of the twenty-four boats," The numbers of boats lost during the Great Flood in the Stokkseyri area vary somewhat between various accounts, presumably because of a variance in what the writers are considering the borders. Whatever the exact number, it was most of them.

22   "When Jón Rich heard," in general, including quoted conversation, Brynjúlfur Jónsson 1954:9–10.

23   "The winter fishing season," Lúðvík Kristjánsson 1982, 2:378.

24   "'I lack brawn,'" Brynjúlfur Jónsson 1954:9. The exact quote of Thurídur's tart reply in
      verse to Jón Rich in Icelandic was "*Brestur-dug, en ekki hug.*"

25   "Fishing contracts were taken," Lúðvík Kristjánsson 1983, 3:118.

26   "'Let's let it go,'" Brynjúlfur Jónsson 1954:9.

CHAPTER THREE: UNCERTAIN TERRITORY

1   "'I would prefer,'" and this section, including quoted conversation, Brynjúlfur Jónsson
     1954:9.

2   On Margrét and the marriage, Brynjúlfur Jónsson 1954:12.

3   "'I'm just as happy,'" Brynjúlfur Jónsson 1954:8.

4   "'hard...domineering,'" Brynjúlfur Jónsson 1954:12.

5   "Men on the farms," Anna Sigurðardóttir 1985:390–394.

6   "Seawomen enjoyed a status," Lúðvík Kristjánsson 1983:57–59; Anna Sigurðardóttir
     1985:390–394.

7   In general on Móri and the other two ghosts, Jón Árnason 1862, 1:361–362, 359, 378;
     Guðni Jónsson 1940, 1:91–97.

8   "'Móri has many a dance,'" Guðni Jónsson 1958:410. The full verse in Icelandic:
     Móri hefur mikinn dans
     mest í norðanroki
     það er smalaseppi hans
     Sæmundar í Foki.

9   "Ghosts were an ever-present," Jónas Jónasson 2010 (1934):420–433.

10   "She chewed his," Jón Árnason 1862, 1:361.

11   "crossing the narrow," Guðni Jónsson 1944, 5:89–90.

12   "'Cloister' (*Klaustur*) Jón Magnússon," Jón Árnason 1862, 1:361–362.

13   "'See beyond his nose,'" Icelandic Online Dictionary n.d.

14   In general on Pastor Jakob Árnason, Páll Eggert Ólason et al., 1948:5.

15   In general, on Magnús Stephensen and the Icelandic Enlightenment, W. M. Senner,
      2000:411–430; Þórunn Valdimarsdóttir and Pétur Pétursson 2000:17–23; Michael Fell
      1999:191–203.

16   "'morass of intellectual and spiritual sloth,'" Michael Fell 1999:194.

17   "published a new hymnal," Baldur Andrésson 2008; Michael Fell 1999:191–203;
      Sigurður Líndal, ed. 2006:328; W. M. Senner 200:411–430.
      Magnús aimed to adapt the Icelandic religious rituals in accordance with Denmark's
      and emphasized that the hymnals were not correctly written and/or translated. The old
      "standardized" and season-related hymnals, he stipulated, should not be sung during
      services anymore, the priest instead choosing hymns related to what he was preaching.
      Magnús Stephensen also altered famous authors' hymnal texts without asking them first.
      Sigurður Líndal, ed. 2006:328.

CHAPTER FOUR: COMPROMISES OF HONOR

1   In general, on the hymnal account at the church, Brynjúlfur Jónsson 1954:12–15.

2   "'shameful and disgusting,'" Guðni Jónsson 1961, 2:110.

3   "Infamously quick temper," Brynjúlfur Jónsson 1954:13–15.

4   "a modest stone-and-turf," Jónas Jónasson 2010 (1934):346–352.

5   "Many men brought," Jónas Jónasson 2010 (1934):359.

6   "Jón Rich and Gudrídur," Guðni Jónsson 1957, 11:36.

7   "'Come on those who,'" Guðni Jónsson 1960, 1:110.

8   "Pastors had," Jónas Jónasson 2010 (1934):380–381.

9   "and won," Brynjúlfur Jónsson 1954:15; Jón Pálsson 1945:7–18.

10   "Clerical postings," Hjalti Hugason 2018:178.

11   "many parsons filled that role," Jónas Jónasson 2010 (1934):312.

12   Pastor Jakob married Elín in 1797

13   "'sweet man...peaceful nature,'" Brynjúlfur Jónsson 1954:12.

14   "Pastor Jakob also seemed," Guðjón Ólafsson 2009.

15   "Steward Jón," Brynjúlfur Jónsson 1954:12.

16   "'more than others,'" Brynjúlfur Jónsson 1954:3.

17   "distraught," Brynjúlfur Jónsson 1954:16.

18   "Pastor Jakob...always found," E. Þórðarson, ed. 1857:33.

19   "'There you will have,'" and rest of the conversation between Pastor Jakob and Thurídur, Brynjúlfur Jónsson 1954:16.

20   For this section on Jón Ólafsson, Brynjúlfur Jónsson 1954:16.

21   "'evidence'"..."'feckless,'" Brynjúlfur Jónsson 1954:16.

22   "Once Helga had given," see Gísli Á. Gunnlaugsson and Loftur Guttormsson 1994:251–268.

23   "Older people," see Gísli Á. Gunnlaugsson and Loftur Guttormsson 1994:251–268.

24   "'I have no better advice,'" Brynjúlfur Jónsson 1854:17.

CHAPTER FIVE: DARK SHADOWS AMID JOY

1   "'able, reliable,'" and the rest of this introduction to Erlendur, Brynjúlfur Jónsson 1954:17.

2   On the spring fishing season, Lúðvík Kristjánsson 1982, 2:378.

3   "Erlendur's two elder," and in general for this section on Margrét and Thórdur including quotes, Jón Ólafsson appendix in Brynjúlfur Jónsson 1954:220–221.

4   In general, on Thurídur's pregnancy, Brynjúlfur Jónsson 1954:17–18.

5   "meant immediate precautions," Jónas Jónasson 2010 (1934):259–260.

6   "Thurídur wasn't much different," Margaret Willson 2016.

7   "'worn-out teeth,'" Bergsveinn Skúlason 1984:33–35.

8   "Luckier women," Jónas Jónasson 2010 (1934):261.

9   "rocking crib," Jónas Jónasson 2010 (1934):267–269.

10   In general, about Þórdís Markúsdóttir, Árni Óla 1954:205–209; Jón Espólín 1821:3; Þormóður Torfason's letter journal, n.d.; Jón Halldórsson 1922:592–670; "Fitjaannáll" 1922:112–113; Unnar Stefánsson 1988:104. Thank you to Gunnar Marel Hinriksson (a descendant of Thórdís's father's brother) of the Manuscripts Division of the Iceland National and University Library, and Þóra Lilja Sigurðursdóttir for sharing their extensive research on Þórdís Markúsdóttir.

11   On the witchcraft case of Thórdís, see Már Jónsson 2021, 2:334.

12   The last year a person was burned for witchcraft in Iceland was 1683 (see Páll Sigurðsson 1971:60), but the last burning, for blasphemy, was in 1685, see Már Jónsson 2021, 1:41.

13   "just about to expel her," Björk Ingimundardóttir 2001:140–151.

14   "Stokkseyri was a busy," Guðni Jónsson 1960, 1:179.

15   On the labor and rent system (kvaðir) that forced people to go to sea for little or no personal pay, see Óskar Guðlaugsson 2017:27–35.

16   In general, on the fishing huts, Guðni Jónsson 1948, 7:108; Guðni Jónsson 1960, 1:212–213; Skúli Helgason 1988, 2:57–67; Lúðvík Kristjánsson 1982, 2:409.

17   "'lagsmaður'," Skúli Helgason 1988, 2:188.

18   "play chess with the Pope,'" Guðrún Kvaran 2008.

19   "'leaked like sieves,'" Skúli Helgason 1988, 2:64.

20   "rats only came," Skúli Helgason 1988, 2:65–66.

21   "The fishing hut life," Guðni Jónsson 1960:215–216; Skúli Helgason 1988, 2:196–197.

22   In general, this section on Thurídur's role and relationship with Jón Rich, Brynjúlfur Jónsson 1954:9–10.

23   "'persistent at sea,'" Brynjúlfur Jónsson 1954:10.

24   "'very clear-sighted,'" Brynjúlfur Jónsson 1954:10.

25   "'gregarious,'" "'entertaining,'" Brynjúlfur Jónsson 1954:10.

26   Jón Gamlason description, Jón Gíslason appendix in Brynjúlfur Jónsson 1954:222.

27   "Kristján," Brynjúlfur Jónsson 1954:18–20.

28   "Danish manager," Brynjúlfur Jónsson 1954:22; Lýður Pálsson 2014:10–23.

29   Niels Lambersen, The Danish merchant of Eyrarbakki was generally called just Lambersen, omitting his first name, but because the name is so similar to that of his son, I have taken the liberty to use his first name of Niels generally for this book to reduce reader confusion between Niels and his son.

30   "Denmark decided a trade monopoly," Gísli Gunnarsson 1987:50–65. On the punishment for Icelanders' trading with others besides Danish merchants, see Gunnar Karlsson 2000:141–142. Although Denmark's official Trade Monopoly of Iceland ended in 1787, the period after that (called fríhöndlun) still stipulated Icelanders had to trade only with Danish merchants, but it allowed them to choose which merchant instead of one being assigned to them.

31   "The House," Lýður Pálsson 2014:10–23.

32   "unreliable...lazy,'" Vigfús Guðmundsson 1945, 1:318–321, 323.

CHAPTER SIX: IN THE PALE DEEP OF SWANS

1 In general, on Margrét and Thórdur, Jón Gíslason appendix in Brynjúlfur Jónsson 1954:221; Brynjúlfur Jónsson 1954:18.

2 In general, for this section on Thurídur and Erlendur, Brynjúlfur Jónsson 1954:17–18.

3 "'I cannot swear,'" and following quoted conversation, Brynjúlfur Jónsson 1954:18.

4 In general, for Thurídur moving to Rocky Brook, Brynjúlfur Jónsson 1954:20; The farmer's name at Grjótlækur (Rocky Brook) was Sturlungur Jónsson (Guðni Jónsson 1952:257–258).

5 "'lucky hauls,'" Lúðvík Kristjánsson 1982, 3:303, 305–310.

6 "Cows, like fish," Michael Fell appendix in Jón Steingrímsson 1999:324.

7 In general, for Erlendur's later life, Brynjúlfur Jónsson 1954:18.

8 "He never contributed," Thurídur's autobiography in Skúli Helgason 1988, 2:311.

9 "Margrét continued," Jón Gíslason appendix in Brynjúlfur Jónsson 1954:221.

10 "The next residents," Brynjúlfur Jónsson 1954:18–19.

11 "divorce," on Icelanders' right to divorce, Þórunn Valdimarsdóttir and Pétur Pétursson 2000:183.

12 "she took him," Bækur sáttanefnda. Árnessýsla VI Gaulverjabær, I. Sáttabók (Mediation Court) 1807–1856. June 25, 1820, Sigríður Hannesdóttir vs Jón the Elder Gamalíelsson.

13 "A superb farmer," Guðni Jónsson 1952:227–228.

14 On Jón Rich's becoming a deputy (*hreppstjóri*) and the deputy role, Guðni Jónsson 1957, 11:11.

15 "in later years," an example of these accounts in her handwriting, Sýslumadurinn í Árnessýslu BA 23 Innsend bréf. 1844.

16 "three daughters," Guðni Jónsson 1957, 11:11.

17 On Thórdís's death, Brynjúlfur Jónsson 1954:20.

18 "the ominous raven," Jónas Jónasson 2010 (1934):299.

19 "No grief touched," Thurídur's autobiography in Skúli Helgason 1988, 2:312.

20 "'When will God,'" all quotes and in general for this section, Brynjúlfur Jónsson 1954:21–22.

21 "There is an Icelandic," Jónas Jónasson 2010 (1934):300.

22 "a parson arrived," and including verse, Guðni Jónsson, footnote in Brynjúlfur Jónsson 1954:22. The poem in Icelandic:

Eitt fórst skip á Eyrarbakka, ýtar greina,
Fjórir menn þar fengu bana,
Fölir djúpt í landi svana.

23 In general, on Thurídur, Jón Einarsson's family and neighbors, Brynjúlfur Jónsson 1954:20.

24 Description of Jón Einarsson, Guðni Jónsson 1957, 11:18.

25 Deputy Jón Einarsson's second wife was Sesselja Ámundsdóttir, who at thirty was one year younger than Thurídur.

26 The husband at Brattsholt was ex-deputy Jón Ingimundarson. He retired as deputy in 1803 to be replaced by Jón Rich.

27   In general, on Helga's death, Brynjúlfur Jónsson 1954:20–21; Jón Gíslason appendix in
      Brynjúlfur Jónsson 1954:221. On Jón Einarsson's son's drowning, Guðni Jónsson 1960:255.

CHAPTER SEVEN: NAKED WIND

1   "charity that relieved," Jónas Jónasson, 2010 (1934):301.

2   "his own foster parents," Bjarni Guðmundsson 1879:128.

3   "huge amount of work," Guðni Jónsson 1960, 1:138–140, 147–150; Jónas Jónasson
      2010 (1934):34–39.

4   In general, on spring farm work, Jónas Jónasson, 2010 (1934):56–60; Guðni Jónsson
      1960, 1:141.

5   "end of spring fishing season," Guðni Jónsson 1960, 1:214.

6   In general, for this sea adventure, Brynjúlfur Jónsson 1954:32–33; Jón Gíslason appen-
      dix in Brynjúlfur Jónsson 1954:222–223; Thurídur's autobiography in Skúli Helgason
      1988, 2:311.
      There is some difference of opinion on the exact date of this tragic incident, Thurídur,
      Brynjúlfur, and Jón Gíslason all placing it as Feb. 6, 1815. But Guðni Jónsson, after
      doing extensive checking, determined that the actual date was Feb. 25, 1812. There was
      another wreck in 1815, and the two were often conflated. After looking through archi-
      val and published material relating to the wrecks, I agree with Guðni's assessment, which
      he included in a footnote in Brynjúlfur Jónsson 1954:221.

7   "five women," Sigurður Þorsteinsson 1939:10.

8   "'Only hope to live,'" Jón Gíslason appendix in Brynjúlfur Jónsson 1954:222.

9   "four hours' row," Brynjúlfur Jónsson 1954:32; Guðrún Kvaran 2007.
      The distance is described as "four weeks of sea" (*fjórar vikur sjávar*) from Stokkseyri.
      One week of sea was approximately one hour's row, or 7.5–9 kilometers.

10   Description of Thorlákshöfn geography and landing areas, Eiríkur Einarsson 1968.
      Thank you also to Sigurður Jónsson of Thorlákshöfn for sharing with us his knowledge
      of the geography before the area was changed to create its current harbor.

11   "where he both directed," Skúli Helgason 1988, 3:17–18.

12   "'Saints of our Father,'" this and the following conversation in this paragraph, Brynjúlfur
      Jónsson 1954:31.

CHAPTER EIGHT: RECKONINGS

1   "rose to a promontory," Eiríkur Einarsson 1968; Lúðvík Kristjánsson 1983, 3:185;
      Guðni Jónsson 1949, 7:109.

2   "system of signals," Skúli Helgason 1988, 2:51.

3   "'Stay the hell,'" Jón Gíslason appendix in Brynjúlfur Jónsson 1954:223. The Icelandic is
      "*Jafnt og helvíti í hellunefið!*" Thank you to Nanna Rögnvaldardóttir for finding the old
      reference that explained the geographical significance of his shout.

4   "'Shut all your traps!'" Brynjúlfur Jónsson 1954:33.

5   "'rowed for their,'" Thurídur's autobiography in Skúli Helgason 1988, 2:311.

6   "'By the grace,'" Thurídur's autobiography in Skúli Helgason 1988, 2:311.

7   The river she crossed is the Baugstaðarós River.

8   "'It occurred to her,'" and all quotes in this paragraph, Brynjúlfur Jónsson 1954:33.

9   "'At that point,'" Thurídur's autobiography in Skúli Helgason 1988, 2:311.

10   On Salgerdur and Thórunn, Brynjúlfur Jónsson 1854:40.

11   "Thórunn, a three-year-old girl," Thurídur's autobiography in Skúli Helgason 1988, 2:311.

12   "She could foster," Thurídur's autobiography in Skúli Helgason 1988, 2:311.

13   "Fostering was," Gísli Á. Gunnlaugsson 1996:11–33.

14   "As late as," Gísli Á. Gunnlaugsson 1993:341–358.

15   On Salgerdur's dislike of Thurídur for taking the child, Thurídur's autobiography in Skúli Helgason 1988, 2:312.

16   In general for this seafaring account, Thurídur's autobiography in Skúli Helgason 1988, 2:311.

17   "except Sundays," Jónas Jónasson 2010 (1934):362.

18   They were fishing at Bakkasjór.

19   On the description of the Stokkseyri and Eyrarbakki shores, Thank you to Stokkseyri resident Þórður "Tóti" Guðmundsson for demonstrating exactly how the boats entered the Eyrarbakki channels. We additionally consulted old maps of the area.

20   "only one boat," Guðni Jónsson 1960, 1:222–223.

21   "an ebb tide," Lúðvík Kristjánsson 1982, 3:159–160.

22   "'weaker,'" Thurídur's autobiography in Skúli Helgason 1988, 2:311–312.

23   All quotes in this seafaring section are from Thurídur's autobiography in Skúli Helgason 1988, 2:311–312.

24   "authorities issued an award," Guðni Jónsson 1957, 11:14.

25   "excellent captain," Brynjúlfur Jónsson 1954:10.

CHAPTER NINE: BETRAYAL IS A MANY-COLORED CLOAK

1   In general for this section on the cow, Thurídur's conversation with Pastor Jakob, including all quotes, Brynjúlfur Jónsson 1954:34–37; Skúli Helgason 1988, 2; Guðni Jónsson 1960, 1:36–42.

2   "Little Thórunn seemed," Thurídur's autobiography in Skúli Helgason 1988, 2:311.

3   On Jón Rich's reputed stinginess, see Jón Gíslason appendix in Brynjúlfur Jónsson 1954:218; Guðni Jónsson 1957, 11:35.

4   On Thurídur's expressing anger through her sparking blue eyes, Finnur Jónsson 1945:131; Þórunn Magnúsdóttir 1979.

5   "one and a half shares," Þórunn Magnúsdóttir 1984:51.

CHAPTER TEN: COMMANDING TURBULENCE

1 "She quickly cleaned," Guðni Jónsson 1960, 1:79.

2 "including Ingibjörg," Þórunn Magnúsdóttir 1979.

3 "the customary shot," Lúðvík Kristjánsson 1985, 4:277–278.

4 "Stunningly handsome," Brynjúlfur Jónsson, supplementory document nr. 22–23 (CC Þórður Sveinbjarnarson's assessment of Sigurður Gottsvinsson) 1954:254–256. Written Jan. 22, 1830, by Þórður Sveinbjarnarson.

5 In general for the accounts of "Gosi" Gottsvin Jónsson and his family, Brynjúlfur Jónsson 1954:42–88; "'I'm fine, man alive!'" Brynjúlfur Jónsson 1954:57.

6 "'Bring the cask here,'" and the rest of this account with the boy stealing, Brynjúlfur Jónsson 1954:61.

7 "real father," Brynjúlfur Jónsson 1954:46; Guðni Jónsson 1942, 3:64.

8 "'I hope such good,'" and the following account including quotes, Brynjúlfur Jónsson 1954:35–37.

9 On Sigrídur's involvement in writing the verses, Guðni Jónsson 1949, 8:107; Guðni Jónsson 1952.

10 "brought vibrancy and validity to the retention," Soffía Laufey Guðmundsdóttir and Laufey Guðnadóttir 2001.

11 On farmers memorizing and writing stories, diaries, and verse, see Sigurður Gylfi Magnússon 2010:147–166.

12 For those interested in the Icelandic Sagas, an excellent discussion of them and good translations can be found in Jane Smiley, ed. 2001.

13 "'níðkveðlingar,'" Brynjúlfur Jónsson 1954:36.

14 On the insulting verses, Brynjúlfur Jónsson 1954:36–37; Lúðvík Kristjánsson 1985, 4:268–269; Þórunn Magnúsdóttir 1979.

15 "'Jón Egilsson,'" verse, in Brynjúlfur Jónsson 1954:36. In Icelandic:

Hreint ónýtur halurinn Jón
Í há-andófi situr,
en Eyjólfur skúmur eins og flón
ekki er haldinn vitur.

16 Although the insulting verses were supposedly forgotten, people certainly remembered them well enough that they got recorded for us to read two hundred years later.

CHAPTER ELEVEN: INTIMATE BLACKMAIL

1 "skippering a six-oared spring boat owned by Student," Thurídur's list of boat owners for whom she worked, Sýslumaðurinn í Árnessýlu BA-28 Innsend bref; Thurídur's autobiography in Skúli Helgason 1988, 2:313.

2 "'on overfriendly terms,'" Brynjúlfur Jónsson 1954:23.

3 In general, this section on Student and the child, Brynjúlfur Jónsson 1954:22–27.

4 "'Take this with you,'" and rest of account, Brynjúlfur Jónsson 1954:27.

5   "Stína was fined," Lýður Pálsson 2014:18.

6   For information on Jörgen Jörgensen and the attempted takeover of Iceland, see Gunnar Karlsson 2000:195–198; Knut Gjerset 1924:356; Lýður Pálsson 2014:18.

7   "hired as his assistant clerk," Manntal á Íslandi (Iceland Census) Árnessýsla 1816.

8   In general, the paragraphs on the Kolbeinsson brothers, Brynjúlfur Jónsson 1954:99–102.

9   Haflidi's physical description, Brynjúlfur Jónsson, supplementary documents no. 29 (CC Þórður Sveinbjarnarson's assessment of Haflidi Kolbeinsson) 1954:259. Written Feb. 17, 1830, by Þórður Sveinbjarnarson.

10 In general, on Haflidi Kolbeinsson, Brynjúlfur Jónsson 1954:27–30, 100–101; Lýður Pálsson n.d.

11 Jón Kolbeinsson's physical description, Brynjúlfur Jónsson, supplementary document no. 25 (CC Þórður Sveinbjarnarson's assessment of Jón Kolbeinsson) 1954:257. Written Feb. 17, 1830, by Þórður Sveinbjarnarson.

12 "'diplomatic,'" Brynjúlfur Jónsson 1954:100.

13 "Poet Jón," Jón Kolbeinsson did not, in any source, have the nickname Poet Jón, but as he was often referred to as a very good poet, I am taking the liberty to use it as a nickname to distinguish him from the other Jóns.

14 All quotes in this chapter on Thorleifur Kolbeinsson, Brynjúlfur Jónsson 1954:103; Lýður Pálsson n.d.

15 On Thorleifur's dreams, Brynjúlfur Jónsson 1954:103; Lýður Pálsson n.d.

16 "'heralded his brother's betrothal,'" Lýður Pálsson. n.d.

17 This Mouse Passage trip in general, Jón Gíslason, as told to him by one of Thuríður's deckhands. Jón Gíslason appendix in Brynjúlfur Jónsson 1954:226; Guðni Jónsson 1954, 10:25.

18 On the geography of Mouse Passage, Thank you to Þórður "Tóri" Guðmundsson of Stokkseyri for showing us Mouse Passage and demonstrating how the boats used it to get to the fishing grounds.

19 "'silferð,'" Lúðvík Kristjánsson 1980, 1:189–191; "Sílferð," in Snara, 2021, snara.is.

20 "'Thuríður sees,'" In the winter of 1826–1827, Eiríkur Snorrason at Hólar put together verses about all the captains of Stokkseyri. This one about Thuríður has survived. Guðni Jónsson's preface in Brynjúlfur Jónsson 1954: xviii. The verse in Icelandic:
    Þuríður snarast þóftu á mar
    Þýtur svar: "Menn æri"
    Stýrir hjarar. Strönd har
    strikað vara særi.

21 In general, on Ingibjörg, Brynjúlfur Jónsson 1954:37; Guðni Jónsson footnote on that same page.

22 The house servant was Guðfinna Þorsteinsdóttir, twenty-one years old. Manntal á Íslandi (Iceland Census) Árnessýsla 1816.

23 Sections on Jón Egilsson in general, Brynjúlfur Jónsson 1954:38–39.

24 "Many men married much," Már Jónsson 1990, 19:106–114.

25   "By law, it was his." Erla Hulda Halldórsdóttir and Guðrún Dís Jónatansdóttir, eds. 1998:144.

CHAPTER TWELVE: CHOICES OF CONSEQUENCE

1   "a contract that if broken," Lúðvík Kristjánsson 1983, 3:117–118.

2   In general, on Jón Egilsson and Thurídur's breakup, Brynjúlfur Jónsson 1954:38–39.

3   "could now leave," Brynjúlfur Jónsson 1954:38.

4   "she decided to hire," Brynjúlfur Jónsson 1954:41.

5   This section in general on Snorri, including quote, Brynjúlfur Jónsson 1954:40. The quote in Icelandic is *"Með skyndi nú, Snorri!"*

6   Pastor Jakob became archdeacon June 15, 1819, Guðni Jónsson 1961, 2:104–105.

7   "'subservient and simple,'" Brynjúlfur Jónsson, supplementary document nr. 7 (testimonies by clergy) 1954:243.

8   "'chiseled from a strong mind,'" Guðni Jónsson, Thurídur's biography in Brynjúlfur Jónsson 1954:xi.

9   "twenty-seven-year-old Jón," Íslendingabók (Iceland Geneology Database).

10   In general, this section on Jón Geirmundsson and Halla, including quotes, Brynjúlfur Jónsson 1954:89–93.

11   "'walking it to its hide'" (*ganga sér til húðar*), Gunnar Sveinsson and Kristleifur Þorsteinsson 1971, 2:150–151.

12   "horse eating was considered deplorable," Gunnar Sveinsson 1962:14–44.

13   "who'd never learned to write," Brynjúlfur Jónsson 1954:89–93.

14   "twenty-five-year-old Halla," Íslendingabók (Iceland Genealogy Database).

15   "'Hateful rages,'" Brynjúlfur Jónsson 1954:93. In Icelandic:
Heiftin geisar hart um torg
herðir kölski ganginn:
Skankaveldis brunnin borg,
Buðlng hennar fanginn.

16   "the serving woman...moved," Brynjúlfur Jónsson 1954:93.

17   "Thurídur decided...to formally adopt," Brynjúlfur Jónsson 1954:40; Þórunn Magnúsdóttir 1979.

18   Description of Móri in general, Brynjúlfur Jónsson 1954:19; Jón Árnason, ed. 1862, 1:378; Páll Lýðsson n.d.

19   "his new specialty," Jón Pálsson 1946:140.

20   In general, on Jón Rich's stinginess, Guðni Jónsson 1960, 1:78.

21   "'Those who have,'" Guðni Jónsson 1954, 10:25.

22   New Year's Eve account in general, Guðni Jónsson 1957, 11:32–33.

23   "days around that time," Guðjón Ólafsson 2009:122–123. Specific weather indication days included Christmas Eve and the thirteenth day after Christmas.

24   "'The weather was bad,'" Guðni Jónsson 1957, 11:32.

25 Coffin account in general, Guðni Jónsson 1957, 11:25–26.

26 "'He was aggressive in life,'" Guðni Jónsson 1957, 11:25–26. The verse in Icelandic:

Ágengur var hann,
Meðan hjá ýtum dvaldi
Þar um verk hans vitna,
enda liggur hann nú
lífs andvani
stolnum undir steini.
Jón Thorarensen.

27 In general, this section on Kristófer and Ingunn, Brynjúlfur Jónsson 1954:29–30, 40–41.

28 In general, on Thurídur's move, Brynjúlfur Jónsson 1954:41.

29 "'short of daring,'" Brynjúlfur Jónsson 1954:41.

CHAPTER THIRTEEN: THE BITTER BITE OF REGRET

1 In general, on Thurídur working at Ingunn's farm, Brynjúlfur Jónsson 1954:40–41.

2 "Most people," Skúli Helgason 1988, 2:312.

3 On Haflidi's return to Ingunn's, Brynjúlfur Jónsson 1954:102.

4 In general, Jón Geirmundsson's moving to Stéttir and his second marriage, Brynjúlfur Jónsson 1954:40, 93–94.

5 "now married to Student," Brynjúlfur Jónsson 1954:40–41.

6 In general, on Sigga, Brynjúlfur Jónsson 1954:93–94.

7 On bones and shells being used as toys, Jónas Jónasson, 2010 (1934):271.

8 "'varied,'" Brynjúlfur Jónsson, supplementary document nr. 7 (testimonies by various clergy) 1954:242.

9 On Jón Einarsson, his death, and his wife's remarriage, Brynjúlfur Jónsson 1954:13–15, 105–106; Guðni Jónsson 1961, 2:110.

10 In general, on the case with Ólafur, Bækur sáttanefnda. Árnessýsla VI Gaulverjabær, I. Sáttabók (Mediation Court) 1807–1856. Jan. 12, 1824. Þuríður Einarsdóttir vs Ólafur Jónsson. Unfortunately, the archival court documents do not state Ólafur's exact words.

11 "hit him," Brynjúlfur Jónsson 1954:93.

12 "Sigrídur had taken her lout," Bækur sáttanefnda. Árnessýsla VI Gaulverjabær, I. Sáttabók (Mediation Court) 1807–1856. June 25, 1820, Sigríður Hannesdóttir vs Jón the Elder Gamalíelsson.

13 "Kristján Jónsson," Bækur sáttanefnda. Árnessýsla VI Gaulverjabær, I. Sáttabók (Mediation Court) 1807–1856. Jan. 16, 1822, Kristján Jónsson vs Margrét Guðnadóttir.

14 "wanted the farm for themselves," Jón Gíslason appendix in Brynjúlfur Jónsson 1954:224. The owner who took over Grímsfjós farm was Guðmundur of Lágafell.

15 In general, on Sesselja and Gísli, Guðni Jónsson 1960, 1:256; Guðni Jónsson 1952:286–287. Gísli's father, who drowned in 1812, was Þorgils Gíslason of Kalastöðum, Guðni Jónsson, 1960, 1:256.

16   "she was getting remarried," Jón Gíslason appendix in Brynjúlfur Jónsson 1954:225.

17   On Gísli's confrontations with people, and his descriptions, Guðni Jónsson 1952:286.

18   On Thórunn's becoming a farmhand, Þórunn Magnúsdóttir 1979.

19   "Salgerdur's husband," Brynjúlfur Jónsson 1954:41; Jón Gíslason appendix in Brynjúlfur
       Jónsson 1954:225.

20   On Icelandic and European divorce law, Þórunn Valdimarsdóttir and Pétur Pétursson
       2000:183; Brynja Björnsdóttir 2016. The new marriage law, set in Denmark 1824,
       stated that if people didn't like being together and both husband and wife wanted to
       separate after having been married for at least three years, after having failed to settle
       with a priest's assistance, and shown decent behavior, they were allowed to divorce.

21   In general, Thurídur's separation from Jón Egilsson, Bækur sáttanefnda. Árnessýsla VI
       Gaulverjabær, I. Sáttabók (Mediation Court) 1807–1856. bls. 52–53, May 25, 1825,
       Þuríður Einarsdóttir vs Jón Egilsson.

22   In general, on Thurídur's suit with Gísli Ólafsson, Bækur sáttanefnda. Árnessýsla VI
       Gaulverjabær, I. Sáttabók (Mediation Court) 1807–1856. bl. 53, May 27, 1825, Þuríður
       Einarsdóttir vs Gísli Ólafsson.

23   On fishing contracts, Lúðvík Kristjánsson 1982, 3:118.

24   "She decided to hire," Brynjúlfur Jónsson 1954:102.

25   "his actions," in general on this account of Sigurdur, Brynjúlfur Jónsson 1954:80.

26   On Sigurdur's marriage, Brynjúlfur Jónsson 1954:80–81.

27   Thurídur's account on Sigurdur as deckhand, including quote, Brynjúlfur Jónsson
       1954:102, 114.

28   On Sigurdur's stepson, Brynjúlfur Jónsson 1954:126.

29   "'touch of evil,'" Brynjúlfur Jónsson 1954:102, 114.

CHAPTER FOURTEEN: STRANGE HAPPENINGS

1   This section on Thuridur's moving from her sister's, Brynjúlfur Jónsson 1954:41.

2   "very few managed," Guðni Jónsson 1953:373–378.

3   "lesser person," Finnur Magnússon 1989:140–156.

4   Account of Jón Rich's "advice," including quote, Guðni Jónsson 1957, 11:18; Jón
       Gíslason appendix in Brynjúlfur Jónsson 1954:226.

5   On Niels, Lýður Pálsson 2014:20–21.

6   On Lambert, Lýður Pálsson 2014:16.

7   On Lambert and the store conditions, Lýður Pálsson 2014:19; Vigfús Guðmundsson
       1945, 1:326–328.

8   On the summer store activities, Lýður Pálsson 2014:19.

9   On the administrative roles and power, Lýður Björnsson 2006, 7:16–22, 27–28.

10   Early life of Thórdur Sveinbjörnsson, Lýður Pálsson n.d.

11   In general, on Jón Rich and the County Commissioner Thórdur, Guðni Jónsson 1957,
       11:25.

12   "'I do not delete,'" Jón Gíslason appendix in Brynjúlfur Jónsson 1954:218.

13   Description of Hjörtur, Brynjúlfur Jónsson 1954:105–106.

14   "'It would be a good,'" Brynjúlfur Jónsson 1954:105–106.

15   Account of Sigríður's visit, Þórður Jónsson appendix in Brynjúlfur Jónsson 1954:232–233.

16   Account of the robbery, including quotes, Brynjúlfur Jónsson 1954:107–110, 134–140.

CHAPTER FIFTEEN: MALICE IS A MANY-HEADED HYDRA

1   In general, for events with CC Thórdur, Johnsen, and others regarding the follow-up of the robbery, including quoted conversations, Brynjúlfur Jónsson 1954:111–119.

2   On attitudes about the fishing communities by Iceland's elite, Finnur Magnússon 1989:145.

3   Descriptions of CC Thórdur and Johnsen, Lýður Pálsson n.d.; on CC Thórdur, Páll Eggert Ólasson 1952, 5:113; on Johnsen, Páll Eggert Ólasson 1940, 3:195–196.

4   "'corrupt spirit'" and rest of paragraph, including all quotes, Guðni Jónsson in his preface in Brynúlfur Jónsson 1954:v.

5   On tarring fishing boats, Lúðvík Kristjánsson 1982, 2:240–242.

6   On seawomen wearing trousers, Þórunn Magnúsdóttir 1979; Margaret Willson 2016.

7   "could be divorced," When Bróka-Auður from the Icelandic saga *Laxdælasaga* wore trousers, the only "penalty" was the same as for men who wore women's clothing—which was that the spouse could demand a divorce, if they chose. Jane Smiley, ed. 2001:333–335.

8   Laws on women wearing trousers, In *Grágás* (collection of laws from the Icelandic Commonwealth period), a clause states that men found guilty of wearing women's clothes and vice versa were punished by fjörbaugsgarður, having to leave Iceland within three summers and stay away for three years before they could return. The clauses in *Grágás* are in two places in Konungsbók. *Grágás* was abolished in 1271 with Járnsíða and Jónsbók in 1281. After that, prohibitions of cross-dressing did not apply, regardless of convention. *Grágás* 1852, 2 Article 155·47 and Article 254:203. Fjörbaugsgarður is explained in Jakob Benediktsson 1974, 1:184–185.

CHAPTER SIXTEEN: A RISING SCENT OF MURDER

1   In general, for this chapter of CC Thórdur's interrogations, including quotes, Brynjúlfur Jónsson 1954:111–125.

2   "The merchant shops encouraged," Lúðvík Geirsson 1994:172–173.

3   "'Ah, that is no doubt,'" and following conversation, Brynjúlfur Jónsson 1954:116.

4   "'Why are you so downcast?'" and following conversation, Brynjúlfur Jónsson 1954:117.

5   "'Have you learned anything?'" and following conversation, Brynjúlfur Jónsson 1954:118.

6   This section on Thurídur's meeting with Sigurdur, Brynjúlfur Jónsson 1954:119, 124.

7   "'Not Jón Sturlaugsson,'" and following conversation, Brynjúlfur Jónsson 1954:119.

8   "This oath before God," Jónas Kristjánsson 1982:79–85.

CHAPTER SEVENTEEN: DO ANGELS STEAL?

1   On CC Thórdur's arrests, Brynjúlfur Jónsson 1954:120–121.

2   "The accused were generally held," Einar Arnórsson 1919:54.

3   On Haflidi's asking for a job, including quotes, Brynjúlfur Jónsson 1954:122–123.

4   This section about Jón Kobeinsson's buying butter, Brynjúlfur Jónsson 1954:124–125.

5   "'Things have gone so far,'" Brynjúlfur Jónsson 1954:124–125.

6   Thurídur comforting Sigga, Brynjúlfur Jónsson 1954:122.

7   Thurídur's conversation with Jón Kolbeinsson, including quotes, Brynjúlfur Jónsson 1954:122–123.

8   "'Yet they say God,'" This is a Biblical reference to Ahab's decision to attack Syria, a decision cemented by a lying prophet sent by God. In the New King James version of the Bible: "So he said, 'I will go out and be a lying spirit in the mouth of all his prophets.' And the Lord said, 'You shall persuade him and also prevail; go out and do so.'" 1 Kings 22:22.

9   On CC Thórdur's opinion of Stefán Pálsson, Lýður Pálsson n.d. Stefán was a district deputy 1825–1830.

10   "'but there is some weakness,'" and rest of quotes, Lýður Pálsson n.d.

11   "Godly power of oaths," Páll Sigurðsson 1978:120–144.

CHAPTER EIGHTEEN: HOW DOES ONE KNOW GOD?

1   This section on Thurídur's meeting with Shank Jón, Brynjúlfur Jónsson 1954:131–132.

2   "these clothes gave," Lúðvík Kristjánsson 1983, 3:66.

3   On fishing not being done on Sundays, Lúðvík Kristjánsson 1983, 3:121.

4   Milk as a rescue for starvation, Jónas Jónasson 2010 (1934):46–52.

5   In general, on details of the robbery from these investigations, Brynjúlfur Jónsson 1954:132–153.

6   "'Even if it were a crime,'" Brynjúlfur Jónsson 1954:136.

7   "'If you go, I will go,'" and following conversation, Brynjúlfur Jónsson 1954:136.

8   "After Sigurdur had heard," and following conversation, including quotes, Brynjúlfur Jónsson 1954:138–139.

9   "the heavy specter of giving a false," and following testimony in this section, Brynjúlfur Jónsson 1954:139.

10   "had dug it up," Brynjúlfur Jónsson 1954:141.

11   "CC Thórdur allowed," Brynjúlfur Jónsson 1954:142.

12   On Thorleifur's dream, Brynjúlfur Jónsson 1954:146–147.

13 "'It became popular,'" Þórður Sveinbjarnarson 1916:55.

14 "an official license," Thurídur later wrote several official requests to the government in which she listed her accomplishments. She mentions having other awards but never receiving this license. Nor does anyone else, and we were unable to find any record in the archives of even a request for such a license being made. Since it seems it was not illegal in the first place, this is not really a surprise.

CHAPTER NINETEEN: IN THE BELLY OF THE BEAST

1 In general, on the expanded investigations, Brynjúlfur Jónsson 1954:148–160.

2 "even old women," Brynjúlfur Jónsson 1954:155. The sixty-nine-year-old Helga of Hamrar was called for further interrogation.

3 "In July, CC Thórdur received," Þórður Sveinbjarnarson, 1916:53.

4 "'Surrounded by robbers,'" and rest of paragraph, including all quotes, Þórður Sveinbjarnarson 1916:53.

5 "steadfastly defended him," Brynjúlfur Jónsson 1954:149.

6 "'I am blowing away the filthy spirits,'" Brynjúlfur Jónsson 1954:155.

7 On Gosi's arrest and torture, Brynjúlfur Jónsson 1954:148–152.

8 In general, on the judgments and outcomes, Bynjúlfur Jónsson 1954:159–165.

9 The murder case of Agnes and Friðrik in the north of Iceland, Einar Arnórsson 1931, 3:399–400; Eggert Þór Bernharðsson 2013:33–41.

10 "'flock,'" and rest of paragraph, including all quotes, Þórður Sveinbjarnarson 1916:53–56.

11 On the end of the investigations, Brynjúlfur Jónsson 1954:159–165.

12 "Because Archdeacon Jakob," Brynjúlfur Jónsson 1954:175.

13 "Now he began," and the following court case, Bækur sáttanefnda. Árnessýsla VI Gaulverjabær, I. Sáttabók (Mediation Court) 1807–1856. bl. 56. July 10, 1827, Þurídur Einarsdóttir vs Jón Jónsson.

14 "required captain's salary," Lúðvík Kristjánsson 1985, 4:187–191.

15 "clear law," Margaret Willson 2016:38–40.

CHAPTER TWENTY: THE DEVILS ARE DANCING

1 The accounts of Valdi's vision, Guðni Jónsson 1960, 1:258–259.

2 The story of the young man who came by the hut looking for work was told to me by Siggeir "Geiri" Ingólfsson of Eyrarbakki, a local scholar of Thurídur, who first heard it from his grandmother's sister when he was twelve (growing up in the house where Thurídur spent her final years). He told me the account twice over a ten-year period, and both times it was, word for word, exactly the same. I have taken the liberty of breaking the story into two parts to fit the chapter's storyline.

3 The account of the Apr. 8 wreck, Guðni Jónsson 1960, 1:258–259.

4   On the May 5 wreck, Guðni Jónsson 1960, 1:259.

5   "began a migration," Guðni Jónsson 1961, 1:179. There were fourteen and a half (half meaning half ownership) boats in 1833, with the lowest number in 1846.

6   "she approached," Brynjúlfur Jónsson 1954:40–41; Jón Gíslason appendix in Brynjúlfur Jónsson 1954:225.

7   On Jón Egilsson's later life, Brynjúlfur Jónsson 1954:39; Jón Gíslason appendix in Brynjúlfur Jónsson 1954:231.

8   On divorce in nineteenth-century Iceland, Ólöf Garðarsdóttir and Brynja Björnsdóttir 2018:91–111.

9   On Thurídur and Jón Egilsson's divorce, Bækur sáttanefnda. Árnessýsla VI Gaulverjabær, I. Sáttabók (Mediation Court) 1807–1856. 27, bls 57–58. June 6, 1828, Þuríður Einarsdóttir vs Jón Egilsson; Jón Steingrímsson appendix (1891) in Brynjúlfur Jónsson 1954:230–232.

10 "He did, and according to accounts," Brynjúlfur Jónsson 1954:38–39.

11 In general on this growing conflict and outcome, An account of this was recorded by Gísli and Sesselja's son Jón Gíslason (appendix in Brynjúlfur Jónsson 1954:224–226). Only three years old at the time these events occurred, he had a skewed understanding reflecting mostly what his parents told him. Guðni Jónsson (1940) later transcribed four original handwritten county documents concerning the suspected hay theft but in his article retained Jón Gíslason's version of the conflict and events, conflating the two issues. We found additional county documents and diary entries that revealed the actual events were dramatically different from these earlier interpretations. Thank you to historian Már Jónsson, who generously transcribed several of the most difficult handwritten documents.

12 His full name was Gísli Pétursson. I am using only the patronymic to avoid confusion in the text. Mar. 27, 1829, letter, transcribed in Guðni Jónsson 1940, 7:258.

13 Letter from Jón Rich to CC Thórdur, Mar. 14, 1829, transcribed in Guðni Jónsson 1940, 7:258.

14 "'punish those,'" Mar. 14, 1829, letter, transcribed in Guðni Jónsson 1940, 7: 258.

15 "the men...required report," Mar. 24, 1829, letter, transcribed in Guðni Jónsson 1940, 7:258.

16 "desperate letter," Mar. 27, 1829 letter, transcribed in Guðni Jónsson 1940, 7:258.

17 "received a letter," Bréfabók Árnessýslu, June 13, 1829, nr. 219.

18 "'What is my crime?'" and other details of Thurídur's circumstances, letter Þuríður to CC Þórður Sveinbjarnarson, Sýslumadurinn í Árnessýslu, July 25, 1829, Nr. 235; Bréfabók Árnessýslu, July 25, 1829, nr. 218.

19 "In response," letter from CC Þórður Sveinbjarnarson to district deputies (hreppstjóra), Sýslumadurinn í Árnessýslu Nr. 426, Innsend bréf, Aug. 17, 1829.

20 "Gísli had no intention," Bréfabók Arnessýsla, Aug. 23, Sept. 2, 1829, nr. 260.

21 "decided to do nothing," Bréfabók Arnessýsla, Sept. (date unreadable), 1829, nr. 219, 235.

22 On Gísli and Jón Rich's kin relations, Gísli's brother, Gudmundur Thorgilsson, was married to Málfrídur Kolbeinsdóttir, Brynjúlfur Jónsson 1954:33; Jón Gíslason appendix in Brynjúlfur Jónsson 1954:223, 225.

23 On Jón Rich's actions, Jón Gíslasson appendix in Brynjúlfur Jónsson 1954:224–226; Guðni Jónsson 1954, 10:20.

CHAPTER TWENTY-ONE: STAND PROUD, MAN ALIVE!

1 "'I rarely have,'" and rest on the expanded interrogations in north Iceland, Eggert Þór Bernharðsson 2013:33.

2 On the three convicted of murder, Einar Arnórsson 1931, 3:399–400.

3 On the beheading of the accused in north Iceland, Einar Arnórsson 1931, 3:399–400.

4 The details of these judgments, Brynjúlfur Jónsson 1954:160–165.

5 "petitioning the authorities," Brynjúlfur Jónsson 1954:160–165.

6 "'sassy' daughter," Brynjúlfur Jónsson supplementary document nr. 7, testimonies by clergy on various local inhabitants, comment by Archdeacon Jakob 1954:244.

7 "he declared he would take," Brynjúlfur Jónsson 1954:165–166.

8 "'An old man becomes a child,'" Brynjúlfur Jónsson 1954:165.

9 On this account of Sigurdur and the transport to Denmark, Brynjúlfur Jónsson 1954:172–174; supplementary document nr. 21 (CC Þórður Sveinbjarnarson assessment of Sigurður Gottsvinsson) Brynjúlfur Jónsson 1954:253–254.

10 On CC Thórdur's later life, Lýður Pálsson n.d.; Þórður Sveinbjarnarson 1916:63–64, 100–101.

11 On the boat Thurídur was skippering being smashed up, Thurídur's autobiography in Skúli Helgason 1988, 2:311–313.

12 On Thurídur's captaining for Student and his actions, Thuridur lists Student Sívertsen and the farmer Magnús Beinteinsson of Thorlákshöfn as the owners of the boats on which she captained there, Thurídur's autobiography in Skúli Helgason 1988, 2:313; Guðni Jónsson 1962, 2:81–94; Thurídur's list of deckhands and boatowners, in Árnessýsla BA-28 Innsend bréf.

13 "Fishing, on the decline," Guðni Jónsson 1960, 1:179. For some years after 1833 only fourteen boats fished out of Stokkseyri. The boats also grew smaller, with almost no ten-oared boats, until about 1853.

14 "CC Thórdur wasn't going to press," CC Thórdur wrote in his diary that since Gísli would not leave peacefully, he would not pursue it further. Bréfabók Árnessýsla, Aug. 23, 1829, nr. 260.

15 Thurídur's application letter, penned by Student, Rentukammer 1928-B20/0011 B20—Bréfadagbók 16 1828–1830. Jan. 24, 1830.

16 Archdeacon Jakob's support letter, Rentukammer1928-B20/0011 B20—Bréfadagbók 16 1828–1830, Feb. 9, 1830; Þórunn Magnúsdóttir 1979.

17 CC Thórdur's "support" letter, Rentukammer 1928-B20/0011 B20—Bréfadagbók 16 1828–1830, Feb. 15, 1830.

CHAPTER TWENTY-TWO: ESTABLISHING ESCAPES

1 "allowing bigger boats," Guðni Jónsson 1960, 1:179; Skúli Helgason 1988, 2:58.

2 "Seaman's Prayer," Lúðvík Krisjánsson 1883, 3:211–222.

3 In general, on the competition between Thurídur and Árni, including quotes, Skúli Helgason 1988, 3:87–88.

4 They went to Vogarsjór outside of Selvogur, by Hlíðavatn lake. Skúli Helgason 1988, 3:87–88.

5 They were at Hafnarnes peninsula. Skúli Helgason 1988, 3:87–88.

6 "'In a storm's fierce,'" Guðni Jónsson 1942, 3:38. Shortly after 1830 some verses were composed about the captains of Thorlákshöfn. The author is unknown, and most of the verses are lost, but these on Thurídur have survived. In Icelandic:

Alvön stríði í stórri ergi
stefnis hýðir úlf á mar,
frú Þuríður hrædist hvergi
hljes óblíðu sviptingar.

Undirgefnir eftir vonum
augum stefna á meykóng sinn,
hafa svefn, en vaka í vomum
víra gefn og hópurinn.

7 Decision from Regional Governor (*stiftamtmaður*) Kriegar, Rentukammer 1928-B20/0011 B20—Bréfadagbók 16 1828–1830, Feb. 27, 1830.

8 "'making the ground more fertile,'" Lúðvík Kristjánsson 1983, 3:209–210.

9 "Sigrídur received," Guðni Jónsson 1952:227.

10 Description of Gardbær and that Thurídur stayed there, Thurídur's autobiography in Skúli Helgason 1988, 2:311–313; Brynjúlfur Jónsson 1954:175.

11 "working independently," Anna Sigurðardóttir 1985:386.

12 "scything hay," Thurídur's autobiography in Skúli Helgason 1988, 2:311–313.

13 Women's pay for scything hay, Margaret Willson 2016:38–40; Guðný Hallgrímsdóttir 2019:6.

CHAPTER TWENTY-THREE: FURY UNBOUND

1 On Ingibjörg's children, Þórunn Magnúsdóttir 1979:30–33.

2 "respected midwife and herbalist," Icelandic Roots, 2021.

3 On Ari's hiring Thurídur, Thurídur's list of deckhands and boatowners, Sýslumadurinn í Árnessýslu BA-28 Innsend bréf; Skúli Helgason 1988, 2:313.

4 "who had drowned," Brynjúlfur Jónsson 1854:32–33; Guðni Jónsson 1960, 1:255–256.

5 Páll's marriage application, Bækur sáttanefnda. Árnessýsla VI Gaulverjabær, I. Sáttabók (Mediation Court) 1807–1856. Aug. 16, 1815.

6 Gudrún's divorce application, Bækur sáttanefnda. Árnessýsla VI Gaulverjabær, I.

Sáttabók (Mediation Court) 1807–1856. May 2, 1825, Guðrún Jónsdóttir vs Páll Hafliðason.

7   "'not a good man,'" and rest of description, Brynjúlfur Jónsson 1954:176–177.

8   "one of the many," Brynjúlfur Jónsson 1954:107, 134.

9   In general, for the rest of this account of Páll and Gudrún, Brynúlfur Jónsson 1954:176–177.

10   "'thief'" and other quotes in this paragraph, Brynjúlfur Jónsson 1954:176–177.

11   "This she promptly did," Brynjúlfur Jónsson 1954:176–177.

12   "and the law," See Sigurður Gylfi Magnússon 1997: 144. According to the law on mandatory discipline in households since 1746 (Húsagatilskipun), the "master" of the house had almost unlimited power over those who lived there and should discipline them as "needed." But attacking in anger was not the right way to do it—at least not to children.

13   "regardless of how he treated her," See Sigurður Gylfi Magnússon 1997:144; Guðný Hallgrímsdóttir 2019:61.

14   The settlement of Páll and Gudrún's suit, Bækur sáttanefnda. Árnessýsla VI Gaulverjabær, I. Sáttabók (Mediation Court) 1807–1856. bls. 65. Nov. 26, 1831, Guðrún Jónsdóttir vs Páll Hafliðason.

15   "The ruling on that," Bækur sáttanefnda. Árnessýsla VI Gaulverjabær, I. Sáttabók (Mediation Court) 1807–1856. bls. 65. Dec. 5, 1831, Þuríður Einarsdóttir vs Páll Hafliðason.

16   "This time," Bækur sáttanefnda. Árnessýsla VI Gaulverjabær, I. Sáttabók (Mediation Court) 1807–1856. bls. 65. Dec. 9, 1831, Þuríður Einarsdóttir vs Páll Hafliðason and Vilborg Bjarnadóttir. Vilborg Bjarnadóttir lived at Einarshofn farm.

17   "she'd said her words," Bækur sáttanefnda. Árnessýsla VI Gaulverjabær, I. Sáttabók 1807–1856. bls. 66. Jan. 23, 1832, Þuríður Einarsdóttir vs Vilborg Bjarnadóttir.

18   "inevitable court case," Bækur sáttanefnda. Árnessýsla VI Gaulverjabær, I. Sáttabók 1807–1856. bls. 67–68. July 23, 1833, Þuríður Einarsdóttir vs Páll Hafliðason.

19   The exact value of a silver specia is unclear. Each Danish state dollar was equal to twenty-seven grams of silver. Specia were much more valuable than state dollars because they always kept their value. However, the specia was not used much in trading between commoners but more as a stock or for gifts. Gísli Gunnarsson 2000.

20   "He did not take her up," Bækur sáttanefnda. Árnessýsla VI Gaulverjabær, I. Sáttabók 1807–1856. bls. 67–68. July 23, 1833, and Aug. 25, 1833, Þuríður Einarsdóttir vs Páll Hafliðason; Jón Steingrímsson appendix (1891) in Brynjúlfur Jónsson 1954:232.

21   Johnsen's taking care of Jón Geirmundsson, Brynjúlfur Jónsson 1954:191.

22   On Jón Geirmundsson's wife, Brynjúlfur Jónsson 1954:181–182.

23   "Jón Rich bought" and other farm transactions, Guðni Jónsson 1952:96.

24   On Sigurdur's time in prison, Ármann Kristinsson's appendix in Brynjúlfur Jónsson 1954:234–237. In winter 1952–1953, law students at the University of Iceland did a program on the Kambur robbery, encouraging Ármann Kristinsson to look at original source material in Copenhagen to find the records relating to Sigurdur. The account taken here is from his findings. Sigurdur was the last Icelander to be executed

in Copenhagen—after this, Icelanders executed their criminals themselves. Gunnar Karlsson 2004.

25   The account of the gunshot, Thurídur's autobiography in Skúli Helgason 1988, 2:312.

26   On Ari Jónsson and his offer, Brynjúlfur Jónsson 1954:177.

CHAPTER TWENTY-FOUR: IS PEACE POSSIBLE?

1   In general, for Thurídur's time in Hafnarfjördur, Brynjúlfur Jónsson 1954:176–181.

2   In general, on Hafnarfjördur, including numbers of residents in 1835, Sigurður Skúlason 1933:332, 375–395; Lúðvík Geirsson 1994:141–185. Thank you to curator Rósa Karen Borgþórsdóttir of Hafnarfjördur Byggðastafn (Museum) for her extensive research, collaboration, and knowledge, which added considerably to these chapters on Hafnarfjördur.

3   "been a trading hub," Lúðvík Geirsson 1994:32.

4   "daughter of...Bjarni; nephew of...Brandur," Sigríður Bjarnadóttir lived in Hafnarfjördur from at least 1835, Manntal á Íslands (Iceland Census) Gullbringusýsla 1835, 1840, 1845. Brandur's nephew living there was called Gísli Pétursson á Óseyri, Guðni Jónsson 1962, 2:192.

5   That one of the timber houses was Ari's, Manntal á Íslands (Iceland Census) Gullbringusýsla 1835.

6   The description of Ari's house, from Magnús Jónsson of Bær at the beginning of the twentieth century. Gísli Sigurðsson in Íris Krisjánsdóttir manuscripts n.d.

7   On Ari's household, Manntal á Íslands (Iceland Census) Gullbringusýsla 1835; Sigurður Skúlason 1933:300; Lúðvík Geirsson 1994:155; Gunnar Hall 1958.

8   On María and Ari's foster children, Marta Valgerður Jónsdóttir 1975:6–7; Helgar-Tíminn 1984:10–11.

9   Thurídur lodgings, Manntal á Íslands (Iceland Census) Gullbringusýsla 1835, 1840. At Skúmsstaðir, she lived as a lodger in the home of Phillipus Þorkelsson (age fifty-nine) and his wife, Guðrún Teitsdóttir (age fifty-eight). She is noted as "housewoman, captain, living off her own work" ("húskona, formaður, lifir af sínu").

10   That other women worked in the shops, Lúðvík Geirsson 1994:177.

11   The women unloading the ships, Anna Sigurðardóttir 1985:403–404.

12   On the description of the work and store, Lúðvík Geirsson 1994:168–169, 175–177; Brynjúlfur Jónsson 1954:177–178.

13   In general, description of Ari, Sigurður Skúlason 1933:300; Gunnar Hall 1958.

14   On the culture around alcohol sales and on the store description, Lúðvík Geirsson 1994:172–173, 175–176.

15   "'corn brennivín' or 'human-shit brennivín,'" Matthías Johannessen and Páll Ísólfsson 1961:22–23.

16   About Thurídur's working in the store, Brynjúlfur Jónsson 1954:177–178.

CHAPTER TWENTY-FIVE: ASCENDING MOUNTAINS

1   On Knudtzen and the other merchants, Ásgeir Guðmundsson 1983–1984; Sigurður Skúlason 1933:268–269, 286.

2   "official store manager," Lúðvík Geirsson 1994:358.

3   On Bjarni Sívertsen and his life, Lúðvík Geirsson 1994:9, 95, 111–135; Sigurður Skúlason 1933:253–278.

4   That Thurídur visited Margrét, who was then living in Hafnarfjördur, Brynjúlfur Jónsson 1954:210.

5   Details of Thurídur's working as a messenger, her autobiography in Skúli Helgasson 1988, 2:311–314.

6   "had the unsavory nickname," Brynjúlfur Jónsson 1954:178.

7   "haunted shelter," Although the name of this hut and its exact location are not in Brynúlfur's account, given the direction they were headed, the routes of the time, and the names given in the account, it is the only route they would have traversed and the only possible place they could have stayed. Descriptions of the route are from Brynjúlfur Jónsson 1954:178–180 and personal exploration of the area.

8   Grímur account, Sigurður Nordal and Þorbergur Þórðarson 1993:239–242.

9   "ice skating," Össur Skarphéðinsson 1997–1998.

10   In general, on the mountain trip, Brynjúlfur Jónsson 1954:178–180.

11   "walking staffs," Þorsteinn Einarsson 2000.

12   "'We'd be wiser to turn back,'" The Brynúlfur Jónsson account does not give this as a quote but does record without quotes exactly what Thurídur said in an account that could have come from no one but her. Therefore, I have taken the liberty to put it in quotes for the sake of the narrative. Brynjúlfur Jónsson 1954:178–180.

CHAPTER TWENTY-SIX: FATE LISTENS TO NO ONE

1   In general, on the mountain trip, Brynjúlfur Jónsson 1954:178–180.

2   In general, on Gríndavik account, Thurídur's autobiography in Skúli Helgason 1988, 2:311–314.

3   Account of Ingibjörg and the seal, Þórunn Magnúsdóttir 1984:39–40.

4   "Many Icelanders considered," For a discussion on Icelandic attitudes about seals, see Níels Einarsson 2011:35–48.

5   "'We have eaten,'" Margaret Willson 2016:64–67. The seawoman's name was Rósamunda Sigmundsdóttir. See Bergsveinn Skúlason 1976:170–180.

6   Letter regarding Salgerdur and Kristján's daughter, Sýslumaðurinn í Árnessýslu BA-28 Innsend bréf. Jan. 24, 1840.

7   "she'd hired," Thurídur's list of deckhands, Sýslumaðurinn í Árnessýslu BA-28 Innsend bréf.

8   On Móri, Jón Árnason 1862; Páll Lýðsson n.d.

9   Thurídur's letter to Archdeacon Jakob, Sýslumaðurinn í Árnessýslu BA 28 innsend bréf,

Nov. 13, 1839. Thank you to Ágústa Flosadóttir and Katie Parsons in the transcription and translation of this difficult-to-read letter.

10   On Gudrún's later life, Brynjúlfur Jónsson 1954:175–176; Þórunn Magnúsdóttir 1979.

11   Páll and Gudrún's divorce was Feb. 3, 1837, Brynjúlfur Jónsson 1954:177; Þórunn Magnúsdóttir 1979.

12   On this theft case against Páll Haflidason, Páll Lýðsson n.d.

13   On CC Thórdur's later life, Lýður Pálsson n.d.

14   On Páll's death, Brynjúlfur Jónsson 1954:177. He died Jan. 15, 1840, Íslendingabók (Iceland Genealogy Database).

CHAPTER TWENTY-SEVEN: FIERY REINS OF THE SEA

1   On Jón Rich's health and retirement, Guðni Jónsson 1952:361–362; 1957, 11:18.

2   Jón Rich bought Gata, July 11, 1836, Guðni Jónsson 1958:237.

3   Lambert and the auction, Lýður Pálsson 2014.

4   In general, on Thorleifur, Lýður Pálsson n.d.

5   Snorri's working for Thorleifur, Brynjúlfur Jónsson 1954:90.

6   On Jón Kolbeinsson's death, Brynjúlfur Jónsson 1954:193 and footnote by Guðni Jónsson; preface by Guðni Jónsson, same page, in Brynjúlfur Jónsson 1954: viii.

7   In general, on the wreck of 1840, Guðni Jónsson 1948, 7:108.

8   On Thurídur's captaining Thorleifur's boat, Guðni Jónsson 1948, 7:108. That the boat was likely Thorleifur's is also in part from calculating the timing and from her list of boat owners for whom she worked as captain, Sýslumaðurinn í Árnessýslu BA-28 Innsend bréf.

9   On Jón Ólafsson, Guðni Jónsson 1948, 7:108.

10   "'Once I get the chance,'" Guðni Jónsson 1948, 7:108. The original account gives his words as spoken but does not put them in quotes. I am taking the liberty of doing this for the readability of the narrative.

11   "'At her prow,'" Guðni Jónsson preface in Brynjúlfur Jónsson 1954: xix. In Icelandic:
    Stökkur láin fleyi frá,
    er fírug snýr á tauminn,
    virðar knáir vellagná,
    verða fáir sporði á.

CHAPTER TWENTY-EIGHT: WHAT IS HOME?

1   The information on Thóra Jónsdóttir, Hannes Davíðsson 1984:4.

2   That Thurídur lived with Ari and his family for a year, Manntal á Íslandi (Iceland Census) Gullbringusýsla 1844.

3   In 1840, Hafnarfjördur's population was 317, in 1850 it was 334. Sigurður Skúlason, 1933:375. The number of ships is from 1843 to 1850, Sigurður Skúlason 1933:332.

4   On Knudtzen and the other merchants, Lúðvík Geirsson 1994:143–149; Sigurður Skúlason 1933:286–269.

5   Information on Peter Christian Petraeus, Sigurður Skúlason 1933:268–269.

6   On Peter and his wife, Prestþjónustubók Garðaprestakalls 1816–1862:177. They got married in 1838. Thank you to curator Rósa Karen Borgþórsdóttir of the Hafnarfjörður Byggðasafn (Museum) for providing this information.

7   On Thurídur's staying at the Petraeus house, There is no record of where in this house Thurídur stayed, but since it is still standing, I was able to explore it with curator Rósa Karen Borgþórsdóttir. The ground floor was clearly rooms for the immediate family; their servants and any lodgers such as Thurídur would have stayed in one of the three upstairs rooms, all of which fit the description here. She almost certainly shared her room with others.

8   That the Petraeus family and Thurídur left the house, Manntal á Íslandi (Iceland Census) Gullbringusýsla 1844.

9   The details of the warehouse (Skemman), Thurídur's home, is from the son of the couple who lived there with her Ólafur Böðvarsson, from a manuscript by Gísli Sigurðsson n.d.

10 On the reestablishment of the Icelandic Parliament, Þórunn Valdimarsdóttir and Pétur Pétursson 2000:17–23; Michael Fell 1999:191–203.

11 In general, on the return of the two Kambur robbers and their experiences in prison, Brynjúlfur Jónsson 1954:193.

12 On Haflidi and the potatoes, Hildur Hákonardóttir 2008:190.

13 "her child had died," Brynjúlfur Jónsson 1954:181–182.

14 Account of Johnsen's death, Brynjúlfur Jónsson 1954:190–193.

15 In general, on Thorleifur Kolbeinsson and Snorri, Lýður Pálsson n.d.; Brynjúlfur Jónsson 1954:90.

16 In general, on Jón Geirmundsson's later life, Brynjúlfur Jónsson 1954:198.

17 The dates of both Erlendur's and Jón Egilsson's deaths, Íslendingabók (Iceland Genealogy Database).

18 "had a clerk," She asked the kammerráð/kammerherra, a title of men who worked in the rentukammer (Treasury Department, Danish). Icelandic Encyclopedia Online 2011.

19 On Thurídur's petition letter, dated May 25, 1844, including all quotes, transcribed in Guðni Jónsson 1962, 2:81–91.

20 "Regional Governor Krieger," There is no copy of this earlier petition in the archives, but since she refers to it as fairly recent, it seems she did write another one for which there is no local record. This could indicate that the Regional Governor—whom, considering the Danish merchants she came to know, she very likely met while working in Hafnarfjörður—may have actually sent it out of Iceland. One can speculate that had he not died, perhaps with his support she might have received a pension. Or not, of course.

CHAPTER TWENTY-NINE: A GUIDE FOR ALL SEASONS

1   In general, on Ida Pfeiffer's life, John van Wyhe 2019.

2 Ida's book of these first travels was translated into English, Ida Pfeiffer and H. W. Dulcken 2012 (1852).

3 The Hafnarfjördur perspective on Ida's visit, Brynjúlfur Jónsson 1954:180.

4 Description and all of Ida's quoted perceptions, Ida Pfeiffer 2007 (1853):41–46.

5 On Ida's later travels, Ida Pfeiffer 2018 (1855, 1856).

6 In general, on Knudtzen, Lúðvík Geirsson 1994:142–152.

7 On the measles epidemic, Sandra Gunnarsdóttir, Haraldur Briem, and Magnús Gottfreðsson 2014; Sandra Gunnarsdóttir 2013.

8 Icelanders started vaccinating against measles in 1966. Sandra Gunnarsdóttir, Haraldur Briem and Magnús Gottfreðsson 2014.

9 Jón Gamlason died Dec. 11, 1846. His wife died June 6, 1846, in Hafnarfjördur. Icelandic Roots 2021.

10 Jón Snorrason died July 13, 1846. Íslendingabók (Iceland Genealogy Database).

11 In general, on this account of the Jón Snorrason inheritance and Thurídur, Finnur Jónsson 1945:130–131.

12 In general, this section on Thórunn being unable to continue working, Brynjúlfur Jónsson 1954:209. She had worked in Hraungerði District.

CHAPTER THIRTY: INTREPID TRAVELER

1 On the pauper payment for invalid farmworkers, Gils Guðmundsson 1992:21–24.

2 Details of Pastor Thórdur's life, Finnur Jónsson 1945:68–69, 108–110; Páll Eggert Ólason 1952, 5:309–310. Thank you to Pétur Gunnarsson for pointing out this source.

3 "in his forties," Íslendingabók (Iceland Genealogy Database). Pastor Thórdur was born Nov. 21, 1803.

4 Description of Pastor Thórdur, Finnur Jónsson 1945:107–115.

5 "'as well as educated men,'" Guðni Jónsson 1942, 3:38; Finnur Jónsson 1945:108.

6 That Pastor Thórdur got angry and on educating his brother, Finnur Jónsson 1945:68–69.

7 Pastor Thórdur's brother, Jón Árnason, collected dozens of accounts about Móri, including several included in this book.

8 "Ari was now fifty-one," Manntal á Íslandi (Iceland Census) Gullbringusýsla 1848.

9 On the cottage Thurídur had built, Brynjúlfur Jónsson 1954:180.

10 Location of Óseyrarnes and that Thurídur stayed there, Guðni Jónsson preface of Brynjúlfur Jónsson 1954: xvi.

11 "fewer than ten," Guðni Jónsson 1960, 1:179.

12 In general on Móri, Jón Árnason, ed. 1862:361–62, 378; Guðni Jónsson 1940, 1: 91–93.

13 "only six boats were fishing," Guðni Jónsson 1960–1961:179.

14 On Thorleifur and Haflidi's younger brother, Brynjúlfur Jónsson 1954:98. The brother, Steingrímur, was born in 1824 and died in 1846. Íslendingabók (Iceland Genealogy Database).

15 The account of Haflidi's drowning and related accounts, Brynjúlfur Jónsson

1954:195–198. As for Haflidi's money, no one found it for decades, long after everyone in this book was already dead. He'd brought a chest back with him from Denmark, which people had searched for a secret compartment but found nothing. It later got auctioned off, moved from person to person until finally, in about 1890, with its lock and hinges broken and its detailed Danish painting worn away, a farmer decided to chop it up for firewood. And there emerged the secret compartment containing two hundred Danish state dollars sewn into cloth to keep it from jingling. Only after much sleuthing did the farmer figure out its origin.

16 Details on Jón Rich's farms, Guðni Jónsson 1957, 11:28–31.

17 Details on Jakob's retirement, farm, and other management, Bjarni Guðmundsson 1879:131.

18 "Elín at seventy-nine," Íslendingabók (Iceland Genealogy Database). Elín died May 14, 1847.

19 "honorific family surname," Brynjúlfur Jónsson 1954:181 (footnote).

20 "Thormódur," Brynjúlfur Jónsson 1954:176.

21 In general, on CC Thórdur Gudmundsson, Páll Eggert Ólafsson 1952, 5:97.

22 "'Swift, steaming, short, and strong,'" Guðni Jónsson 1942, 3:38–39. In Icelandic: "*heitt, fljótt, sterkt, lítið.*"

23 "In 1849," Íslendingabók (Iceland Genealogy Database). Jón Rich died Aug. 17, 1849.

24 "Jón Rich's wife," Íslendingabók (Iceland Genealogy Database). Gudrídur died Jan. 22, 1854, at eighty-three years old.

25 On Jón Rich's daughters, Guðni Jónsson 1957, 11:37; Brynjúlfur Jónsson 1954:199.

26 On Shank Jón Geirmundsson's death, Brynjúlfur Jónsson 1954:198. Date corrected by editor Guðni Jónsson in footnote to Aug. 31, 1851 at 59.

27 Geir's account, including quotes, Finnur Jónsson 1945:131.

28 Account of Thorsteinn, including quotes, Guðni Jónsson 1942, 3:38–39. The boy's name was Þorsteinn Símonarson from Gamla-Hraun.

29 In general on this account with Finnur and his sister, including quotes, Finnur Jónsson 1945:130–131.

30 "Finnur later wrote," Finnur Jónsson 1945:131.

31 "'It was widely known,'" Finnur Jónsson 1945:131.

32 "'A king's heart,'" poem by Bjarni Thorarensen in Eining 1955:11. The entire poem in Icelandic:

Konungs hafði hann hjarta
með kotungsefnum,
á líkn við játæka
fátækt sína ól,
öðrum varð hann gæfa
ei sér sjálfum
og hjálpaði sjúkur
til heilsu öðrum.

33 In general, on the case with Deputy Árni, Brynjúlfur Jónsson 1954:209.

CHAPTER THIRTY-ONE: THE POWER OF A SIMPLE SCRAWL

1   "'murdering my time,'" Finnur Jónsson 1945:109.

2   Details of Pastor Thórdur's life, Finnur Jónsson 1945:107–110; Páll Eggert Ólason 1952, 5:87. On Jón Þórðarsson, Pastor Thórdur's child conceived in the Bishop's School at Bessastaðir, Páll Eggert Ólason 1950, 3:309–310.

3   "a girl was born," including some of the fight details, Páll Eggert Ólasson 1952, 5:87–89. The reference indicated for this source is Dómabók Árnesýslu (book of judgments) 1840–1851, v, 19. Thank you to Pétur Gunnarsson for pointing out this source.

4   "the daughter of," Guðni Jónsson 1942, 3:86–87; Finnur Jónsson 1945:110–111. Her brother was Deputy Einar of Kaldadarnes. The farm where she lived was Nordurkot.

5   "others demanded," Guðni Jónsson 1942, 3:86–87.

6   "'One suspicious word,'" Guðni Jónsson 1942, 3:38.

7   "'The priest's cassock,'" Finnur Jónsson 1945:112. The verse in Icelandic:

    Blaktir á Þórði buran svört
    en bragnar mega trúa,
    um Búrfells-Jón og Brúar-Hjört
    þeir bila seint að ljúga.

    Thank you to Kristján Geir Arnþórsson of Stokkseyri for his help in translating this verse.

8   Some of the Pastor Thórdur fight details, Páll Eggert Ólasson 1952, 5:87–89; Finnur Jónsson 1945:107–115. The dates, Manntal á Íslandi (Iceland Census) Árnessýsla 1850; Thurídur's testimony is in Dómabók Árnessýslu (book of judgments) 1840–1851. bls. 190/367.

9   "Thórunn...stayed safely," Manntal á Íslandi (Iceland Census) Árnessýsla 1850.

10 Thurídur's petition letter, transcribed in Skúli Helgason 1988, 2:310–313; Guðni Jónsson 1962, 2:81–94. The letter is dated Dec. 20, 1852.

11 Archdeacon Jakob's letter, transcribed in Skúli Helgason 1988:310–313; Guðni Jónsson 1962, 2:81–94. The letter is dated Dec. 24, 1852.

12 On CC Thórdur G.'s letter, including quotes, Bréfabók Árnessýslu, nr. 1174, Jan. 6, 1853.

13 "sixty-six years," I get "only" fifty-five years from 1788 to 1843, but perhaps Thurídur is referring to seasonal years set to the fishing cycles.

14 "a list of boat owners," Thurídur's list of deckhands and boat owners, Sýslumaðurinn í Árnessýslu BA-28 Innsend bref.

15 On this pension application, Since we found all these documents in the Iceland National Archives, it is clear no official ever sent them to Denmark, let alone the king.

16 In general, on Merchant Gudmundur Thorgrímsson, Lýður Pálsson 2014:24–38.

17 Thurídur's request for supplies, transcribed in Skúli Helgason 1988, 2:312; Guðni Jónsson 1962, 2:81–94. The request is dated Apr. 18, 1853. Thank you to Siggeir Ingólfsson for sharing a copy of the original request.

18 On Magnús Kristjánsson's visit, Brynjúlfur Jónsson 1954:210; 1957:105–106.

19 "scribbling away," Brynjúlfur Jónsson 1914:404–405.

20 "other farm children taunting him," Valdimar Briem 1915:1–9.

21 Letter from Thorleifur Kolbeinsson, Sýslumadurinn í Árnessýslu BA-29 Innsend bréf, Sept. 28, 1854.

22 On Thurídur's suit with "Turk," Brynjúlfur Jónsson 1954:208; Bækur sáttanefnda. Árnessýsla VI Gaulverjabær, 1. Sáttabók 1807–1856. Nov. 21, 1853, Þuríður Einarsdóttir vs Jón Þorsteinsson.

23 On Vilborg's death, Mar. 1853, Íslendingabók (Iceland Genealogy Database).

CHAPTER THIRTY-TWO: GUARDIAN ANGEL

1 "sum of 1,190," Brynjúlfur Jónsson 1954:209.

2 "Thórunn now returned," Brynjúlfur Jónsson 1954:208–210; On Thórunn's living location, Manntal á Íslandi (Iceland Census) Árnessýsla 1855.

3 "1,600 króna," Brynjúlfur Jónsson 1954:209 (footnote).

4 On the conflict between farmers, Finnur Jónsson 1945:110–115; Guðni Jónsson 1942, 3:38, 86–87.

5 On Pastor Thórdur's move to Mosfell, Páll Eggert Ólason 1952, 5:309–310.

6 On Archdeacon Jakob's death, Jakob Árnason's obituary, E. Þórðarsson ed. 1857:32. He died Aug. 19, 1855, Íslendingabók (Iceland Genealogy Database).

7 On this case leaving Thurídur destitute, Brynjúlfur Jónsson 1954:210.

8 "as was the usual practice," See Ólöf Garðarsdóttir 2016:5–20.

9 "She'd move," Manntal á Íslandi (Iceland Census) Árnessýsla 1840, 1860; Thurídur's list of deckhands and boat owners, Sýslumaðurinn í Árnessýslu BA-28 Innsend bréf.

10 "Thurídur...could choose," Brynjúlfur Jónsson 1954:210.

11 Account of this wreck and the omens, Guðni Jónsson 1960, 1:262–263. The wreck occurred Mar. 20, 1862.

12 "Almost double in size," Lýður Pálsson 2014:25–26.

13 "The number of local boats," Guðni Jónsson 1960, 1:179.

14 On the broadening of boat access, Þórunn Magnúsdóttir 1979.

15 "a fish trawl," Guðni Jónsson 1960, 1:197–200.

16 "Jón Jónsson," Sigurður Þorsteinsson 1939:10–13.

17 On Sesselja's children dying, Icelandic Roots 2021. Thank you to Sunna Njálsdóttir for finding this information.

18 In general, on Thurídur's letter to Merchant Gudmundur Thorgrímson, including quotes, A copy of this 1862 letter was shared with me by Siggeir Ingólfsson from his private collection. Although I did not get it from National Archives of Iceland, the original will be located there in the Sýslumaðurinn í Árnessýslu.

19 "they'd be obliged," Thank you to Lýður Pálsson of the Húsið Eyrarbakka Museum for this informed insight. See also Gísli Gunnarsson 1983:20.

20 The account of Jón Jónsson and Thurídur, including quotes, Sigurður Þorsteinsson 1939:11–13.

21   On Jón's captain Páll, Sigurður Þorsteinsson 1939:13.

22   On Páll's going to Jón's wedding, Sigurður Þorsteinsson 1939:13 (footnote).

CHAPTER THIRTY-THREE: THE SEA AT REST

1   The account of Thurídur's death, Brynjúlfur Jónsson 1954:210.

2   On Thurídur's funeral and burial, Brynjúlfur Jónsson 1954: 211; Prestþjónustubók Stokkseyrarprestakalls (Stokkseyri parish death records) 1857–1882:133. Thank you to Siggeir Ingólfsson for sharing his research into these records and to Þorsteinn Tryggvi Másson of the Héraðsskjalasafn Árnesinga (Regional Archives) for his kind assistance.

AN AFTERWORD

1   For a discussion on Iceland's changing attitudes toward women working at sea in the late 1800s and early 1900s, see Margaret Willson 2016.

2   For a discussion on the changing attitudes toward a woman's acceptable role, see Erla Hulda Halldórsdóttir 1997.

3   On this interpretation of Thurídur's court cases, Jón Steingrímsson appendix (1891), in Brynjúlfur Jónsson 1954:230–232.

4   Guðni's attitudes about Thurídur are apparent in much of his writings about her. For an example, see his Preface of Brynjúlfur Jónsson 1954: v–x.

5   "'she was constantly,'" Guðni Jónsson's biography of Thurídur in Brynjúlfur Jónsson 1954: xvii.

6   "'This hag,'" and rest of quote, *Húsið, sem flestir skoða*, 1972:339–341.

7   "'had a great way,'" Brynjúlfur Jónsson 1954:210.

8   On women writers who have questioned twentieth-century attitudes about Thurídur, see Erla Hulda Halldórsdóttir 1997A; Margaret Willson 2016; Þórunn Magnúsdóttir 1979, 1984.

9   "'On a bench,'" This verse is by Sigurður Breiðfjörd Ferlir 2007. In Icelandic:

Inni á bálki einum þar
undum lengi nætur.
Við hurðarloku hringlað var
hrukkum þá á fætur.
Leit ég eina ófreskju
á mig hélt 'ún rynni.
Hvarf í eld og eimyrju
undir kveðju minni.

10   In general, on Móri, Jón Árnason I, 1862; Einar Ól. Sveinsson 1940; Páll Lýðsson n.d.

REFERENCES CITED

In this bibliography, I have listed references for Icelandic authors as first name first, followed by their patronymic, as is the Icelandic convention. Other names I have listed as surname first, followed by first name, as is non-Icelandic English-language convention.

PUBLISHED WORKS

Alþingi. "Þórður Guðmundsson, Æviágrip," 2016. https://www. althingi.is/altext/cv/is/?nfaerslunr=621.

Anna Agnarsdóttir. "Aldahvörf og umbrotatímar." In *Saga Íslands*, edited by Sigurður Líndal and Pétur Hrafn Árnason, IX:5–151. Reykjavík: Hið íslenzka bókmenntafélag, 2008.

Anna Sigurðardóttir, *Vinna kvenna á Íslandi í 1100 ár*. Reykjavík: Kvennasögusafn Íslands. 1985: 390–394.

Ármann Kristinsson. "Endalok Sigurðar Gottsvinssonar." In *Sagan af Þuríði formanni og Kambránsmönnum*, 234–37. Reykjavík: Menningar-og fræðslusamband Alþýðu, 1954.

Árni Daníel Júlíusson. *Landbúnaðarsaga Íslands*. Vol. 1. Reykjavík: Skrudda, 2013.

Árni Daníel Júlíusson, Jón Ólafur Ísberg, and Helgi Skúli Kjartansson, eds. *Íslenskur söguatlas. Frá öndverðu til 18. aldar*. Vol. 1. Reykjavík: Almenna bókafélagið, 1989.

Árni Óla, "Stokkseyrar Dísa," *Morgunblaðið* 84, no. 12 (1954): 205–209.

Ásgeir Guðmundsson. *Saga Hafnarfjarðar 1908–1983*. Vol. 2. Saga Hafnarfjarðar, 1908–1983. Skuggsjá, 1983.

Baldur Andrésson. "Aldamótabókin 1801." In *Tónlistarsaga Reykjavíkur: með inngangi um sögu sönglífs í landinu frá því land byggðist*, 2008. http://www.musik.is/Baldur/TsagaRvk/1000–1800/til1800_8.html.

Bergsveinn Skúlason. *Þarablöð: Þættir frá Breiðafirði*. Reykjavík: Víkurútgáfan, 1984.

Bjarni Thorarensen in "Bækur Menningarsjóðs 1954." *Eining*, 1955.

Björk Ingimundardóttir. "Sett úr af sakramentinu." In *Kvennaslóðir. Rit til heiðurs Sigríði Th. Erlendsdóttur sagnfræðingi*, edited by Anna Agnarsdóttir, 140–151. Reykjavík: Kvennasögusafn Íslands, 2001.

Björn Bjarnason, ed. *Skírnir: Ný tíðindi hins Íslenzka bókmentafélags*. Vol. 84. Reykjavík: Hið íslenzka bókmenntafélag, 1910.

Björn Magnússon Ólsen. "Um kaffi." *Tímarit hins íslenzka Bókmenntafélags*, Jan. 1, 1896.

Björn Þorsteinsson and Guðrún Ása Grímsdóttir. "Enska öldin." In *Saga Íslands*, edited by Sigurður Líndal, V:5–12. Reykjavík: Hið íslenzka bókmenntafélag, 1990.

Brynja Björnsdóttir. "Ég vil heldur skilja við þann sem ég elska heldur en að lifa í ósamlyndi alla ævi. skilnaðarlöggjöf, umfang og ástæður hjónaskilnaða á íslandi 1873–1926." Master's, University of Iceland, 2016. http://hdl.handle.net/1946/23586.

Brynjúlfur Jónsson. *Sagan af Þuríði formanni og Kambránsmönnum*, edited by Guðni Jónsson. Reykjavík: Menningar-og fræðslusamband Alþýðu, 1954.

—. "Æfisaga mín." *Skírnir* 88, no. 1 (1914): 404–14.

—. *Íslenzkir Sagnaþættir.* Vol. 1–2. Reykjavík: Menningar-og fræðslusamband Alþýðu, 1957.

—. *Dulrænar smásögur,* edited by Guðni Jónsson ed. 2nd ed. Vol. 1–2. Menningar-og fræðslusamband alþýðu, 1955.

Eggert Þór Bernharðsson. "Friðrik, Agnes, Sigríður og Natan." *Saga* 51, no. 2 (2013): 9–55.

Einar Arnórsson. *Meðferð opinberra mála. Fylgirit með árbók Háskóla Íslands háskólaárið 1918–1919.* Reykjavík: Háskóli Íslands, 1919.

Einar Arnórsson, ed. *Landsyfirrjettardómar og hæstarjettardómar í íslenzkum málum 1802–1873.* Vol. 3. Reykjavík: Sögufélag, 1931.

Einar Ól. Sveinsson. *Um íslenzkar þjóðsögur.* Reykjavík: Sjóður Margrétar Lehmann-Filhés, 1940.

Eiríkur Einarsson. "Þorlákshöfn." Örnefnastofnun, 1968. http://nafnid. arnastofnun.is/media/uploads/8700%20Árnessýsla/8717%20 Ölfushreppur/PDF/Þorlákshöfn.%20Eir%C3%ADkur%20 Einarsson%20(merkt).pdf.

Embætti Landlæknis. "Sagan," 2014. https://www.landlaeknir.is/um-embaettid/saga/.

Erla Hulda Halldórsdóttir. *Að vera sjálfstæð: ímyndir, veruleiki og frelsishugmyndir kvenna á 19. öld.* Reykjavík: Tímarit Sögufélags, 1997. https://timarit.is/gegnir/000517357.

—. "Hugleiðingar un Þuríði formann og viðhorf til kvenna." *Húsgangur: Innanhússblað Landsbókasafns Íslands,* Oct. 1997A. Kvennasögusafn Íslands. KSS 16. Úrklippusafn Kvennasögusafns. Einkaskjalasafn.

Erla Hulda Halldórsdóttir and Guðrún Dís Jónatansdóttir, eds. *Ártöl og áfangar í sögu íslenskra kvenna.* Reykjavík: Kvennasögusafn Íslands, 1998.

E. Þórðarson. *Útfararminning Jakobs Árnasonar prests í Gaulverjabæ og prófasts í Árnesþingi. Með ágripi af sögu hans.* Reykjavík: Prentsmiðja Landsins, 1857.

Fell, Michael. *And Some Fell into Good Soil: A History of Christianity in Iceland.* New York: Peter Lang Inc., 1999.

Ferlir. "Bolaöldur—Bolavellir—Bolasteinn—Nautastígur." *Ferlir. is Áhugafólk um Reykjanesskagann,* 2007. https://ferlir.is/bolaoldur-bolavellir-bolasteinn-nautastigur/.

Finnur Jónsson. *Þjóðhættir og ævisögur frá 19.öld. Minnisblöð Finns á Kjörseyri.* Akureyri: Bókaútgáfa Pálma H. Jónssonar, 1945.

Finnur Magnússon, "Work and the Identity of the Poor: Word Load, Work Discipline, and Self-Respect." In *The Anthropology of Iceland,* edited by E. Paul Durrenbergur and Gísli Pálsson. Iowa City: University of Iowa Press, 1989, 140–156.

"Fitjaannáll." In *Annálar 1400–1800,* 2:112–13. Reykjavík: Félagsprentsmiðjan, 1922.

Gils Guðmundsson. *Almannatryggingar á Íslandi. 50 ára saga Tryggingarstofnunar ríkisins.* Reykjavík: Tryggingastofnun ríkisins, 1992.

Gísli Gunnarsson. "Hvers virði var gamli ríkisdalurinn í íslenskum krónum?—Var munur á íslenskum og dönskum ríkisdal?" *Vísindavefurinn,* 2000. https://www.visindavefur.is/svar.php?id=736.

—. "The Structure of the Icelandic Society." In *Monopoly Trade and Economic Stagnation: Studies in the Foreign Trade of Iceland, 1602–1787,* 13–29. Lund: Ekonomisk-historiska institutionen, 1983.

—. *Upp er boðið ísaland: einokunarverslun og íslenskt samfélag 1602–1787.* Reykjavík: Örn og Örlygur, 1987. https://rafhladan.is/handle/10802/9071.

Gísli Á. Gunnlaugsson. "'Everyone's Been Good to Me, Especially the

Dogs': Foster-children and Young Paupers in Nineteenth Century Southern Iceland." *Journal of Social History* 27, no. 2 (1993): 341–358.

—. "Fostering and Kinship in Nineteenth-Century Iceland." In *Orphans and Foster-Children: A Historical and Crosscultural Perspective*, edited by Lars-Göran Tedebrand, 11–33. Umeå: Umeå universitet, 1996.

Gísli Á. Gunnlaugsson and Loftur Guttormsson. "Transition into Old Age: Poverty and Retirement Possibilities in Eighteenth- and Nineteenth-Century Iceland." In *Poor Women and Children in the European Past*, edited by John Henderson and Richard Wall, 251–68. London: Routhledge, 1994.

Gísli Viggósson, Jónas Elíasson, and Sigurður Sigurðarson. "Ákvörðun á flóðhæð í Básendaflóði: Áfangaskýrsla." Reykjavík: Vegagerðin, 2016.

Gjerset, Knut. *The History of Iceland*. New York: The Macmillan Company, 1924.

Guðjón Ólafsson. *Vökulok*, edited by Ólafur Halldórsson and Gunnar Marel Hinriksson. Ritröð Sögufélags Árnesinga. Selfoss: Sögufélag Árnesinga, 2009.

Guðni Jónsson. *Bólstaðir og búendur í Stokkseyrarhreppi*. Reykjavík: Stokkseyringafélagið í Reykjavík, 1952.

—. *Íslenskir sagnaþættir og þjóðsögur*. Vol. I. Reykjavík: Ísafoldarprentsmiðja H.F., 1940A.

—. *Íslenskir sagnaþættir og þjóðsögur*. Vol III. Reykjavík: Ísafoldarprentsmiðja H.F., 1942.

—. *Íslenskir sagnaþættir og þjóðsögur*. Vol. VII. Reykjavík: Ísafoldarprentsmiðja H.F., 1948.

—. *Íslenskir sagnaþættir og þjóðsögur*. Vol. XI. Reykjavík: Ísafoldarprentsmiðja H.F., 1957.

—. "Kæra Þuríðar formanns um heystuld." In *Blanda*, VII:257–260. Reykjavík: Sögufélag, 1940.

—. *Skyggnir*. Vol. II. Reykjavík: Ísafoldarprentsmiðja H.F., 1962.

—. *Stokkseyringa saga*. Vol. I. Reykjavík: Stokkseyringafélagið í Reykjavík, 1960.

—. *Stokkseyringa saga*. Vol. II. Reykjavík: Stokkseyringafélagið í Reykjavík, 1961.

—. "Þuríður formaður." *Sjómannadagsblaðið* 83, no. 1 (1994): 70–71.

Guðný Hallgrímsdóttir. *A Tale of a Fool? A Microhistory of an 18th-Century Peasant Woman*. 1st ed. London: Routledge, 2019.

Guðrún Kvaran. "Hver er merkingin í orðatiltækinu 'að tefla við páfann'?" Vísindavefurinn, 2008. http://www.visindavefur.is/svar.php?id=6998.

—. "Hver er uppruni orðanna í mælieiningunni vika sjávar." Vísindavefurinn, 2007. http://www.visindavefur.is/svar.php?id=6615.

Gunnar Hall. "Fyrsti íslenski óperusöngvarinn Ari Jónsson." *Lögberg*. Oct. 9, 1958.

Gunnar Karlsson. *The History of Iceland*. Minneapolis: University of Minnesota Press, 2000.

—. "Hvenær var síðasta aftakan á Íslandi." Vísindavefurinn, 2004. https://www.visindavefur.is/svar.php?id=4649.

Gunnar Sveinsson. "Rökræður Íslendinga fyrr á öldum um hrossakjötsát." *Skírnir* 136, no. 1 (Jan. 1, 1962): 14–44.

Halldóra Jónsdóttir and Þórdís Úlfarsdóttir, eds. "Tómthús." In *Íslensk nútímamálsorðabók*. Reykjavík: Stofnun Árna Magnússonar í íslenskum fræðum, 2020. https://islenskordabok.arnastofnun.is/ord/42149.

Hannes Davíðsson. Á labbitúr með Guðjóni. *Þjóðviljinn* (31 mars—1 apríl). 1984:4.

Helgi Þorláksson. "Kirkjan í gagnsókn 1570–1630." In *Saga Íslands*,

VI:167–211. Saga Íslands. Reykjavík: Hið íslenska bókmenntafélag, 2003.

"Heyrði talað um þennan frænda minn frá því er ég man fyrst eftir mér.", *Helgar-Tíminn.* Feb. 19, 1984.

Hildur Hákonardóttir. *Blálandsdrottningin og fólkið sem ræktaði kartöflurnar.* Reykjavík: Salka, 2008.

Hjalti Hugason. "Seigfljótandi siðaskipti: Viðhorf og staðalmyndir í siðaskiptarannsóknum." *Ritið* 18 (June 13, 2018): 165–197.

Húsið, sem flestir skoða, og konan, sem það er kennt við. Apr. 30, 1972. *Tíminn Sunnudagsblað 11* (15), 339–341.

Icelandic General Penal Code, no. 221/1940. https://www.government.is/lisalib/getfile.aspx?itemid=dd8240cc-c8d5-11e9-9449-005056bc530c.

Icelandic Online Dictionary (n.d.). https://snara.is/.

Icelandic Roots. "Icelandic Roots | Genealogy Ancestry," 2021. https://www.icelandicroots.com.

Íslendingbók (Iceland Genealogy Database), deCODE and Friðrik Skúlason. https://www.islendingabok.is.

Íslensk nútímamálsorðabók. Stofnun Árna Magnússonar í íslenskum fræðum. Accessed June 12, 2021. https://islenskordabok.arnastofnun.is/ord/42149.

Jackson, E. L. "The Laki Eruption of 1783: Impacts on Population and Settlement in Iceland." *Geography* 67, no. 1 (1982): 42–50.

Jakob Benediktsson. "Landnám og upphaf allsherjarríkis." In *Saga Íslands,* edited by Sigurður Líndal, I:155–195. Reykjavík: Hið íslenzka bókmenntafélag, 1974.

Jón Árnason, ed. *Íslenskar þjóðsögur og ævintýri.* Vol. I. Leipzig: J.C. Hinrichs's bókaverzlun, 1862.

Jón Árnason, Árni Böðvarsson, and Bjarni Vilhjálmsson, eds. *Íslenskar*

þjóðsögur og ævintýri. Nýtt safn. Vol. 3. Reykjavík: Bókaútgáfan
Þjóðsaga, 1955.

Jón Espólín. *Íslands árbækur í söguformi.* Vol. 13. Copenhagen: Hið
íslenska bókmenntafélag, 1821: 3.

Jón Gíslason. "Viðaukar og athugasemdir við söguna af Þuríði formanni." In *Sagan af Þuríði formanni og Kambránsmönnum*, edited
by Guðni Jónsson, 217–230. Reykjavík: Menningar-og fræðslusamband Alþýðu, 1954.

Jón Gunnlaugsson. "Bjarni Pálsson landlæknir." *Læknablaðið* 68, no. 3
(1982): 92–95.

Jón Halldórsson. "Hítardalsannáll 1724–1734." In *Annálar 1400–
1800*, 2:592–670. Reykjavík: Félagsprentsmiðjan, 1922: 592–670.

Jón Pálsson. *Austantórur.* Reykjavík: Víkingsútgáfan, 1945.

Jón Steingrímsson. "Frá Þuríði formanni" in Brynjúlfur Jónsson. *Sagan
af Þuríði formanni og Kambránsmönnum*, edited by Guðni Jónsson.
Reykjavík: Menningar-og fræðslusamband Alþýðu, 1954.

—. *Fires of the Earth: The Laki Eruption 1783–1784*, translated by
Keneva Knutz. Reykjavík: University of Iceland Press, 1998.

—. *A Very Present Help in Trouble: The Autobiography of the Fire-Priest*,
translated by Michael Fell. New York: Peter Lang Inc., 2002.

Jónas Jónasson. *Íslenzkir þjóðhættir.* 4th ed. Reykjavík: Opna, 2010 (1834).

Jónas Kristjánsson, ed. "Skriftaboð Þorláks Biskups." In *Gripla*, V:79–
85. Reykjavík: Stofnun Árna Magnússonar, 1982.

King James Bible. Oxford: Oxford University Press, 2008 (1969).

Kristleifur Þorsteinsson. *Úr byggðum Borgarfjarðar.* Vol. 2. Reykjavík:
Prentsmiðjan Leiftur H.F., 1971.

Kristleifur Þorsteinsson. *Úr byggðum Borgarfjarðar*, Þórður Kristleifsson.
Vol. 2. Reykjavík: Prentsmiðjan Leiftur H.F., 1971.

Lúðvík Geirsson. *Höfuðstaður verslunar: Saga verslunar og kaupmennsku í Hafnarfirði í sex hundruð ár.* Hafnarfjörður: Verslunarmannafélag Hafnarfjarðar, 1994.

Lúðvík Kristjánsson. *Íslenzkir sjávarhættir.* Vol. 2. Reykjavík: Bókaútgáfa Menningarsjóðs, 1982.

—. *Íslenzkir sjávarhættir.* Vol. 3. Reykjavík: Bókaútgáfa Menningarsjóðs, 1983.

—. *Íslenskir Sjávarhættir.* Vol. 4. Reykjavík: Bókaútgáfa Menningarsjóðs, 1985.

Lýður Björnsson. "18. öldin." In *Saga Íslands,* edited by Sigurður Líndal, VIII:5–277. Reykjavík: Hið íslenzka bókmenntafélag, 2006.

—. "Básendaflóðið 1799." *Vefnir* 6, no. 1 (2006): 1–12.

Lýður Pálsson. *Húsið á Eyrarbakka.* Eyrarbakki: Byggðasafn Árnesinga, 2014.

Marta Valgerður Jónsdóttir. "Niðjar síðasta bóndans í Keflavík." *Faxi,* Nov. 1, 1947.

Már Jónsson. "Skagfirskir hórkarlar og barnsmæður þeirra." In *Skagfirðingabók,* 19:106–114. Reykjavík: Sögufélag Skagfirðinga, 1990.

Már Jónsson, ed. *Galdur og Guðlast á 17. Öld* Vol. 1. Reykjavík: Sögufélag, 2021.

—. *Galdur og Guðlast á 17. Öld* Vol. 2. Reykjavík: Sögufélag, 2021.

Mörður Árnason, cd. "Útgerðarmaður." In *Íslensk Orðabók M–Ö.* Reykjavík: Edda útgáfa, 2002.

Matthías Johannessen and Páll Ísólfsson. *Hundaþúfan og hafið.* Reykjavík: Bókfells útgáfan, 1961.

Níels Einarsson. *Culture, Conflict and Crisis in the Icelandic Fisheries: An Anthropological Study of People, Policy and Marine Resources.* Uppsala: University of Uppsala Press, 2011.

Ólöf Garðarsdóttir. "Saving the Child: Regional, Cultural and Social Aspects of the Infant Mortality Decline in Iceland, 1770–1920."

Doctoral thesis, monograph, Umeå universitet, 2002. http://urn. kb.se/resolve?urn=urn:nbn:se:umu:diva-56811.

—. "Residence Patterns of the Elderly in Early Eighteenth-Century Iceland." *The History of the Family* 21, no. 1 (2016): 5–20.

Ólöf Garðarsdóttir and Brynja Björnsdóttir. "The Implications of Divorce in Late Nineteenth and Early Twentieth Century Iceland." In *Journal of Scandinavian History. Special Volume: Historical Perspectives on Divorce and Union Dissolutions in the Nordic Countries.* Vol. 43(1): 91–111, 2018.

Óskar Guðlaugsson. "Í kvaðar nafni." Magister Scientiarum, University of Iceland, 2017.

Páll Eggert Ólason, Ólafur Þ. Kristjánsson, Jón Guðnason, and Sigurður Líndal. *Íslenzkar Æviskrár Frá Landnámstímum Til Ársloka 1940.* Vol. 5. Reykjavík: Hið íslenzka bókmenntafélag, 1952.

—. *Íslenzkar Æviskrár Frá Landnámstímum Til Ársloka 1940.* Vol. 6. Reykjavík: Hið íslenzka bókmenntafélag, 1948.

Páll Eggert Ólason. *Íslenzkar æviskrár frá landnámstímum til ársloka 1940. 3. bindi. J–N.* Vol. 3. Reykjavík: Hið íslenzka bókmenntafélag, 1950.

—. *Íslenzkar æviskrár frá landnámstímum til Ársloka 1940. 5. bindi T–Ö.* Vol. 5. Reykjavík: Hið íslenzka bókmenntafélag, 1952.

Páll Sigurðsson. *Brot úr réttarsögu.* Reykjavík: Hlaðbúð, 1971.

—. "Þróun og þýðing eiðs og heitvinningar í réttarfari." Doctoral thesis, University of Iceland, 1978.

Pétur Hrafn Árnason and Sigurður Líndal, eds. "Árdagar sjálfstæðis." In *Saga Íslands,* XI:83–84. Reykjavík: Hið íslenska bókmenntafélag, 2016.

Pfeiffer, Ida. *A Lady's Second Journey Round the World: From London to the Cape of Good Hope, Borneo, Java, Sumatra, Celebes, Ceram, the Moluccas, Etc., California, Panama, ...Equador and the United States.* Los Angeles: HardPress, 2018 (1855).

—. *Visit to Iceland and the Scandinavia North.* London: Ingram, Cooke, 2007 (1853).

Pfeiffer, Ida, and H. W. Dulcken. *Visit to the Holy Land, Egypt, and Italy.* London: Ingram, Cooke, 2012 (1852).

Sandra Gunnarsdóttir. "Mislingar á Íslandi—Faraldrar 19. aldar." B.Sc., University of Iceland, 2013.

Sandra Gunnarsdóttir, Haraldur Briem, and Magnús Gottfreðsson. "Umfang og áhrif mislingafaraldranna 1846 og 1882 á Íslandi." *The Icelandic Medical Journal* 100, no. 4 (2014).

Senner, W. M. "Magnús Stephensen: Precursor of the 'Fjolnismenn' and Icelandic Romanticism." *Scandinavian Studies* 72, no. 4 (2000): 411-430.

Sigríður Ingibjörg Ingadóttir. "Óegta börn." *Sagnir* 14, no. 1 (June 1, 1993): 54–62.

Sigurður Gylfi Magnússon. "Kynjasögur á 19. og 20. öld." *Saga* 35 (1997): 137–177.

—. *Wasteland with Words: A Social History of Iceland.* London: Reaktion Press, 2010.

Sigurður Líndal. "Upphaf kristni og kirkju." In *Saga Íslands*, edited by Sigurður Líndal, I:227–247. Reykjavík: Hið íslenzka bókmenntafélag, 1974.

Sigurður Líndal, ed. *Saga Íslands VIII.* Reykjavík: Hið íslenzka bókmenntafélag, 2006.

Sigurður Nordal, ed. *Völuspá.* Translated by B. S. Benedikz and John McKinnel. England: Durham and St. Andrews Medieval Texts, 1980.

Sigurður Nordal and Þorbergur Þórðarson. *Gráskinna hin meiri.* 3rd ed. Vol. I. Reykjavík: Bókaútgáfan Þjóðsaga, 1983.

Sigurður Skúlason. *Saga Hafnarfjarðar.* Hafnarfjörður: Bæjarsjóður Hafnarfjarðar. 1933.

Sigurður Þorsteinsson. "Endurminningar Jóns frá Hlíðarenda. Gamalt og nýtt frá Þorlákshöfn." In *Þorlákshöfn I–II.* Reykjavík: Ísafoldarprentsmiðja, 1938.

Skúli Helgason. *Saga Þorlákshafnar til loka áraskipaútgerðar: Veiðistöð og verslun.* Vol. 2. Reykjavík: Örn og Örlygur, 1988.

Smiley, Jane, ed. *The Sagas of the Icelanders.* New York: Penguin Books, 2001.

Snara. Íslensk orðabók. 2021. https://snara.is.

Soffía Laufey Guðmundsdóttir and Laufey Guðnadóttir. "Handritin heima- The Icelandic Manuscripts," 2001. http://www.handritin-heima.is/index.html.

Stone, Ian R. "The Text of Joseph Shackleton's Account of His Visit to Iceland, 1861." *The Polar Record* 41, no. 3 (2005): 223–234.

Sumarliði R. Ísleifsson. "Innan eða utan Evrópu? Ímyndir Íslands og Grænlands á ofanverðri 18. öld og fram eftir 19. öld." *Ritið: Tímarit Hugvísindastofnunar* 15, no. 2 (2015): 65–88.

Unnar Stefánsson. "Báðum megin borðsins." *Sveitastjórnarmál* 48, no. 2 (Apr. 1, 1988): 104.

Valdimar Briem. "Æfisaga Brynjúlfs Jónssonar." *Árbók hins íslenzka fornleifafélags* 30, no. 1 (1915): 1–9.

van Wyhe, John. *Wanderlust: The Amazing Ida Pfeiffer, the First Female Tourist.* Singapore: National University of Singapore Press, 2019.

Vasey, Daniel E. "Population, Agriculture, and Famine: Iceland, 1784–1785." *Human Ecology* 19, no. 3 (1991): 323–350.

Vefsafn.is. "Skaftáreldar 1783." Landsbókasafn Íslands. Accessed July 7, 2021. http://wayback.vefsafn.is/wayback/20041023041810/www.islandia.is/hamfarir/jardfraedilegt/eldgos/skaftareldar.html.

Vigfús Guðmundsson. *Saga Eyrarbakka*. Vol. 1. Reykjavík: Víkingsútgáfan, 1945.

—. *Saga Eyrarbakka*. Vol. 2. Reykjavík: Víkingsútgáfan, 1945.

Vilhjálmur Finsen, trans. *Grágás: Islænders lovbog i fristatens tid*. Vol. 2. 4 vols. Copenhagen: Det Nordiske Literatur-Samfund, 1852.

Willson, Margaret. *Seawomen of Iceland: Survival on the Edge*. Seattle: University of Washington Press, 2016.

Þórður Jónsson. "Viðbúnaður fyrir Kambsrán" in Brynúlfur Jónsson. *Sagan af Þuríði formanni og Kambránsmönnum*. Reykjavík: Menningar-og fræðslusamband Alþýðu, 1954: 232–233.

Þórður Sveinbjarnarson. *Æfisaga Þórðar Sveinbjarnarsonar, háyfirdómara í landsyfirrjettinum: Samin af honum sjálfum*. Reykjavík: Sögufjelag, 1916.

Þorsteinn M. Jónsson, ed. *Gríma hin nýja*. Vol. 3. Reykjavík: Þjóðsaga, 1978.

Þorsteinn Einarsson. "Að renna sér á ís." *Dagur—Íslendingaþættir*, Mar. 18, 2000.

Þórunn Magnúsdóttir. "Sjókonur á átjándu- og nítjándu öld." Unpublished undergraduate thesis, University of Iceland, 1979.

—. *Sjósókn sunnlenskra kvenna frá verstöðvum í Árnessýslu 1697–1980*. Vestmannaeyjar: Prentsmiðjan Eyrún h.f., 1984.

Þórunn Valdimarsdóttir and Pétur Pétursson. *Kristni á Íslandi: til móts við nútímann*. Edited by Hjalti Hugason. Vol. 4. Reykjavík: Alþingi, 2000.

Þorvaldur Þórðarson and Stephen Self. "Atmospheric and Environmental Effects of the 1783–1784 Laki Eruption: A Review and Reassessment." *Journal of Geophysical Research: Atmospheres* 108, no. D1 (Jan. 16, 2003): 159–171.

UNPUBLISHED MATERIALS

Bjarni Guðmundsson. "Æfisögu ágrip prófastsins sáluga séra Jakobs

Árnasonar á Gaulverjabæ," 1879. Lbs 2590 8vo. Iceland National and University Library, Manuscript division.

Gísli Sigurðsson. *Hús og bæir í Hafnarfirði / líf og þjóðhættir í Hafnarfirði frá 14. öld.* box nr 949.121. (A summary of an unpublished manuscript owned by Íris Kristjánsdóttir.) Hafnarfjörður library.

Lýður Pálsson, Private Collection, Húsið, The House Museum, Eyrarbakki, n.d.

Páll Lýðsson. *Þáttur um Sels-Móra.* Unpublished manuscript held at Húsið, The House Museum, Eyrarbakki, n.d.

Þormóður Torfason. "'Útdráttur úr bréfabókum Þormóðar Torfasonar, AM 282–285 b IV fol., það er tekur til Íslands og Íslendinga. Þar með bréfaskipti Þormóðar og síra Torfa Jónssonar í Gaulverjabæ.'" Reykjavík, e.d. Manuscript division. National and University Library of Iceland.

ARCHIVAL MATERIALS

Bréfabók Árnessýslu (sýslumaður diary), Þjóðskjalasafn Íslands (National Archives of Iceland), Reykjavík.

Bækur sáttanefnda. Árnessýsla VI Gaulverjabær, I. Sáttabók 1807–1856 (Mediation court documents), Þjóðskjalasafn Íslands (National Archives of Iceland), Reykjavík.

Dómabók Árnessýslu (Árnessýsla book of convictions) 1840–1851, Þjóðskjalasafn Íslands (National Archives of Iceland), Reykjavík.

Manntal á Íslandi (Iceland Census). Árnessýsla, Manntalsvefur Þjóðminjasafnsins. http://manntal.is.

Manntal á Íslandi (Iceland Census), Gullbringusýsla, Manntalsvefur Þjóðminjasafnsins, http://manntal.is.

Rentukammer 1928-B20/0011 B20—Bréfadagbók 16 1828–1830 (District account records), Þjóðskjalasafn Íslands (National Archives of Iceland), Reykjavík.

Prestþjónustubók Garðaprestakalls 1816–1862. Hafnarfjörður Museum.

Prestþjónustubók Stokkseyrarprestakalls (Stokkseyri parish death records) 1857–1882. Héraðsskjalasafn Árnesinga, Selfoss.

Sýslumaðurinn í Árnessýslu Innsend bréf (District municipal documents), Þjóðskjalasafn Íslands (National Archives of Iceland), Reykjavík.

INDEX

Note: Icelandic names are listed by first name first and patronymic second in keeping with the traditional Icelandic naming system.

ABOUT THE AUTHOR

·»«·*

Anthropologist and writer, Margaret Willson has traveled extensively, in Brazil, Papua New Guinea, Mongolia, Australia, Europe, and Iceland. Her eclectic nonacademic jobs have included abalone diving and being a deckhand on fishing boats off the south coast of Tasmania.

She received her Ph.D. in Anthropology from the London

School of Economics and is currently an Affiliate Associate Professor with the Departments of Anthropology and Scandinavian Studies at the University of Washington, and a Senior Associate Scientist at the Stefánsson Arctic Institute in Iceland.

Her previous books include *Seawomen of Iceland: Survival on the Edge* and *Dance Lest We All Fall Down: Breaking Cycles of Poverty in Brazil and Beyond*. She lives in Seattle with her partner and their cat Mister.